THEN & NOW®

BAY CITY

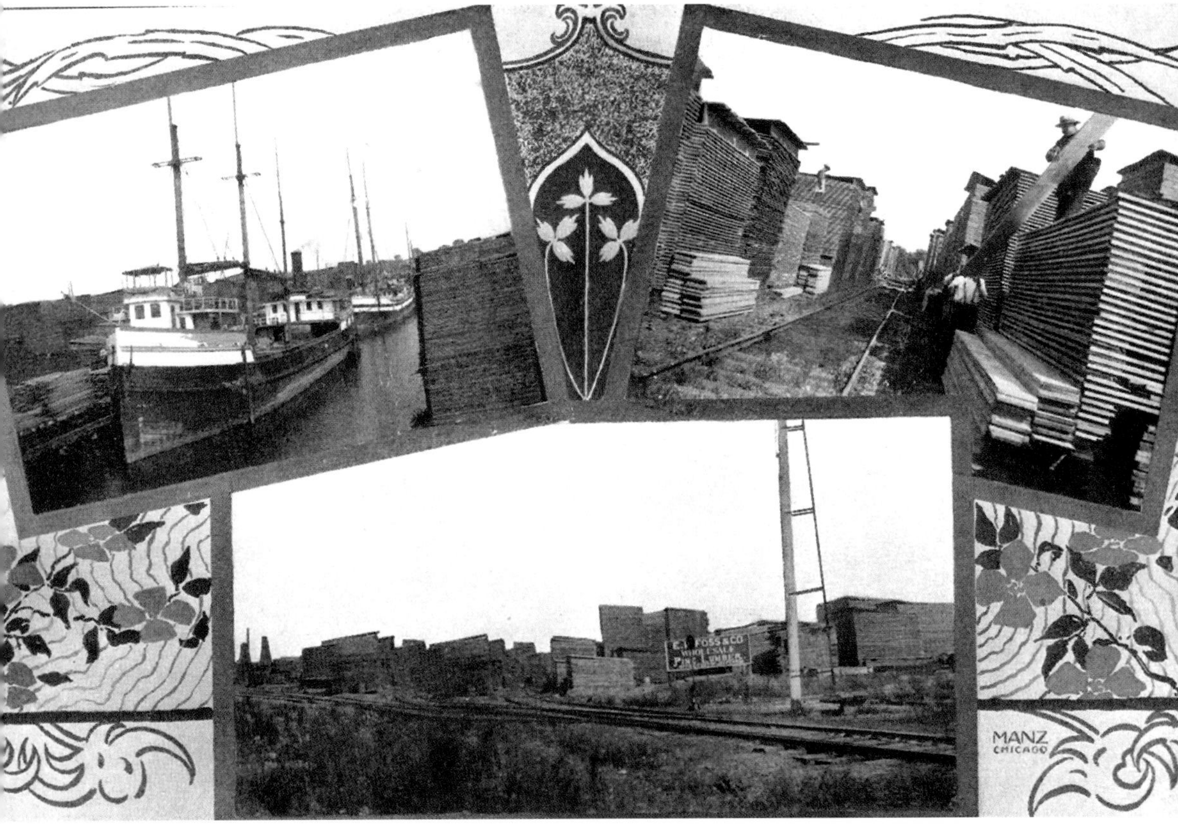

E.B. Foss & Company. Lumbering and shipping were the two twins of the history of Bay City 125 years ago. We had an original growth forest and the Saginaw River for getting logs to the Bay City sawmills as well as taking cut lumber to customers. Edgar Foss came to Bay City at the age of 17 and learned the lumber business from the bottom up. He and his brother purchased their first mill in 1879 in Kawkawlin. They then moved to the west side of Bay City and finally established their business at 1705 North Water Street on the east side. E.B. Foss manufactured dressed lumber at one of the largest mills in the country.

THEN & NOW®

BAY CITY

Leon Katzinger

ARCADIA
PUBLISHING

ISBN 978-0-7385-3331-5

Published by Arcadia Publishing
Charleston, South Carolina

Printed in the United States of America

Then and Now is a registered trademark and is used under license from
Salamander Books Limited

Library of Congress Catalog Card Number: 2004109843

For all general information contact Arcadia Publishing at:
Telephone 843-853-2070
Fax 843-853-0044
E-mail sales@arcadiapublishing.com
For customer service and orders:
Toll-Free 1-888-313-2665

Visit us on the Internet at www.arcadiapublishing.com

This book is dedicated to Jerry, my wife of 36 years and best friend. She makes everything possible.

Contents

Acknowledgments

There are many people I wish to thank. Thanks to my son Joe for getting me through my medical crisis. Thanks to my son Josh for all of his technical assistance. Thanks to both sons for all of your love.

Thanks to Ron Bloomfield and A.J. Flood for their advice on historical accuracy. Thanks to Dr. Oesterling and his staff for getting me through my cancer.

Thanks to all who helped and shared in your special ways. That includes Lois Niemann, Rich Niemann, June Soehnel, Cal Lehman, John Walthers, Keith Shore, Leo Borrello, and, especially, everyone at Monitor Pharmacy.

Thanks to my editor, Maura Brown, for her patience and kind support.

Finally, thanks to Don and Jean Bouckaert for our long friendship and their strength during adversity.

INTRODUCTION

In 1970, Joni Mitchell wrote a song called "Big Yellow Taxi." In it, she uses the line, "They paved paradise and put up a parking lot." All too often, that has been the story in Bay City. In the 1960s, the Washington Theater, an elegant building that included a full orchestra pit and a balcony, was torn down and a parking lot was constructed. In the 1980s, the charming Grand Trunk Depot, just east of Sage Library, was torn down for a parking lot.

Fortunately, that is not always the case. It appears that the former train depot downtown may be saved (although it is surrounded by parking lots). Our beautiful City Hall was restored to its glory, as was the Sage Library. Individual homeowners, especially along Center Avenue, have done much to preserve their homes as they might once have looked. One Shearer Building is gone, but the remaining one is being converted to condominiums. And, much of the community supports the idea of preserving the Bijou (State) Theater. So, there is hope.

The majority of the "Then" pictures in this book come from three sources. The first is *The Cities of the Bay* published by the International Publishing Company in 1888. In its introduction, Bay City is referred to as the chief city of northern Michigan. It goes on to state that Bay City is "beautifully situated on the right bank of Saginaw River four miles from Saginaw Bay, the most important arm of Lake Huron." It doesn't slight West Bay City. West Bay City is cited as "the chief ship building point in Michigan ranking first on the chain of the Great Lakes for the number of wooden vessels constructed within the past five years." *The Cities of the Bay* describes and shows pictorially how Bay City and West Bay City looked in 1888.

My second source was *The History of Bay County Michigan, Illustrated, 1883*, published by H.R. Page & Co. It does not have photographs, but it uses line drawings and flowery language to tell the story of Bay City and Bay County from the perspective of many early pioneers. The introductory paragraph gives a sense of its scope: "All American history, whether local or general, opens amid similar scenes, and its pictures have a common background." It is my hope to use those pictures to remember buildings no longer here.

My third main source was *History of Bay County, Michigan and Representative Citizens* published by Richmond and Arnold in 1905, often referred to as (Augustus) Gansser, its author. Gansser mixes biographies of pioneer citizens with striking photographs. His book starts with early Michigan history and traces the growth of the area, focusing on government, natural resources, the lumber boom, other industries such as salt and coal, plus a look at schools and churches. In his opening paragraph on the joining of the two Bay Cities in 1905, he waxes: "The year 1905 will ever mark a memorable epoch in the annals of the thriving communities situated on the banks of Michigan's mightiest inland stream, who in this year of grace have joined together that which man should never have kept asunder!"

The "Now" pictures in this book were taken by me with the help of my wife, Jerry, who helped align the present view with the "Then" outlook. After writing *Bay City in Vintage Postcards* and *Bay City and Beyond* I received questions from many people about where a particular building once stood or if it indeed still stood. My hope is that *Bay City: Then and Now* answers some of those questions while preserving the precious memories of our past. You, dear reader, will be the judge of that.

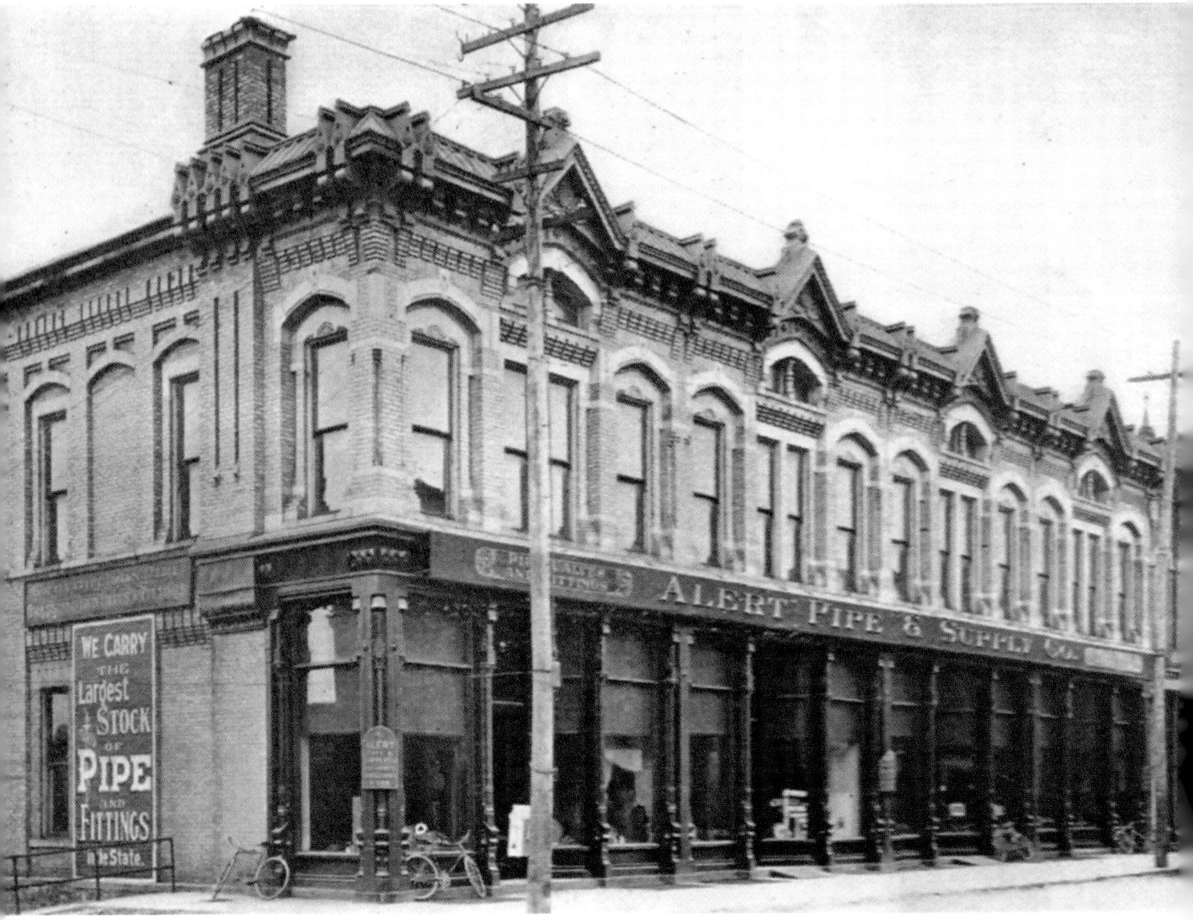

ALERT PIPE AND SUPPLY COMPANY. Many of the pictures in this book are located on North Water Street, which was both an early part of the business community and "Hell's Half Mile" where lumbermen came to spend their hard-earned wages. This 1905 photo of Alert Pipe and Supply Company at 1001–1007 North Water Street is a later version of the photo on page 66 of this book. Alert Pipe was Michigan's largest supplier of mill and salt block supplies in a city known for its many sawmills and salt mines. In later years, it was the warehouse for C.E. Rosenbury & Sons. John H. Walther was the last tenant, selling fireplace equipment, pumps, and seeds from the southern end of the building until 1980, when the building became vacant.

Chapter 1
West Side

Midland Street, East from Henry. West Bay City was formed in 1877 when the three villages of Banks, Wenona, and Salzburg combined, after several years of ongoing discussion. The state legislature passed the bill incorporating the city. Elections were held in May of 1877 and David Arnold was elected as the first mayor. Peter Lind was the last mayor and helped the two Bay Cities merge in 1903.

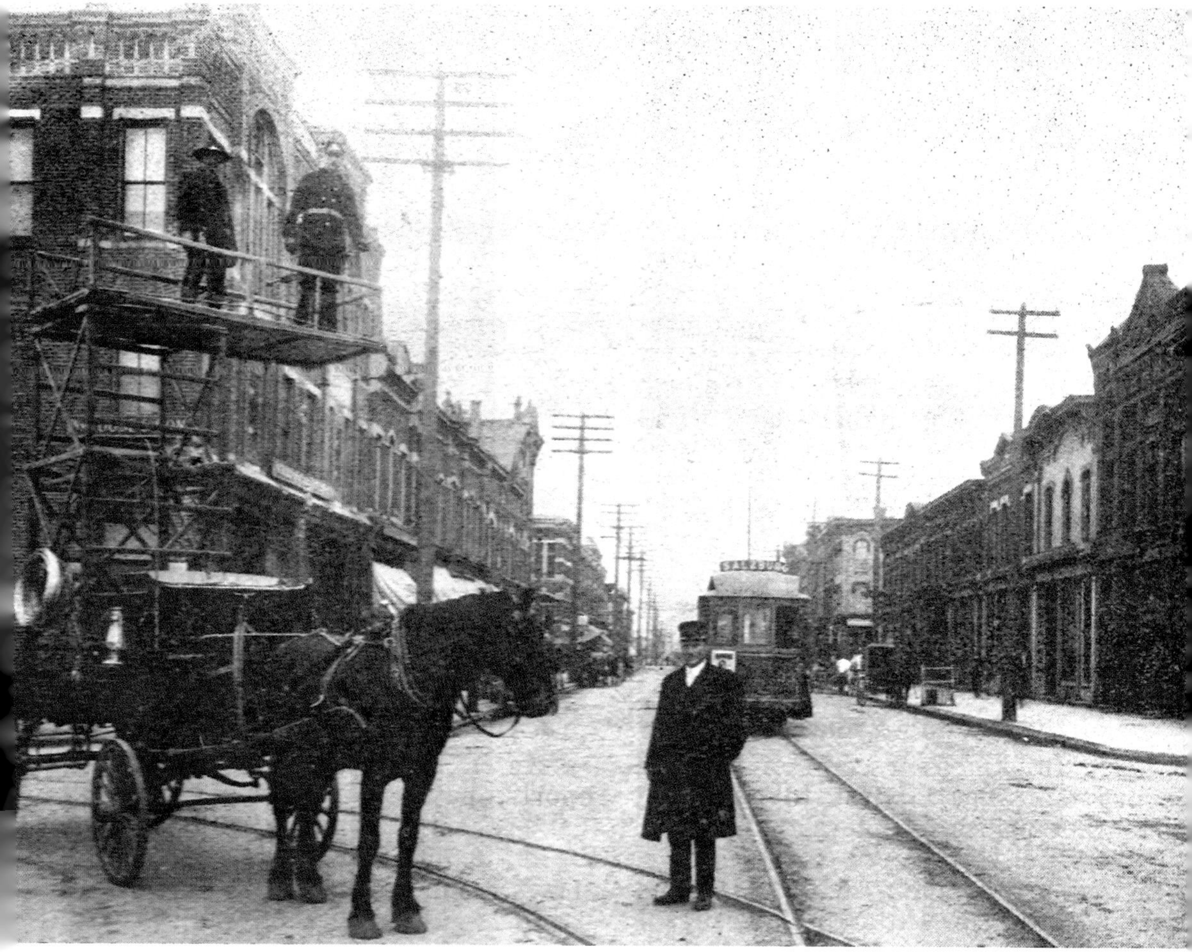

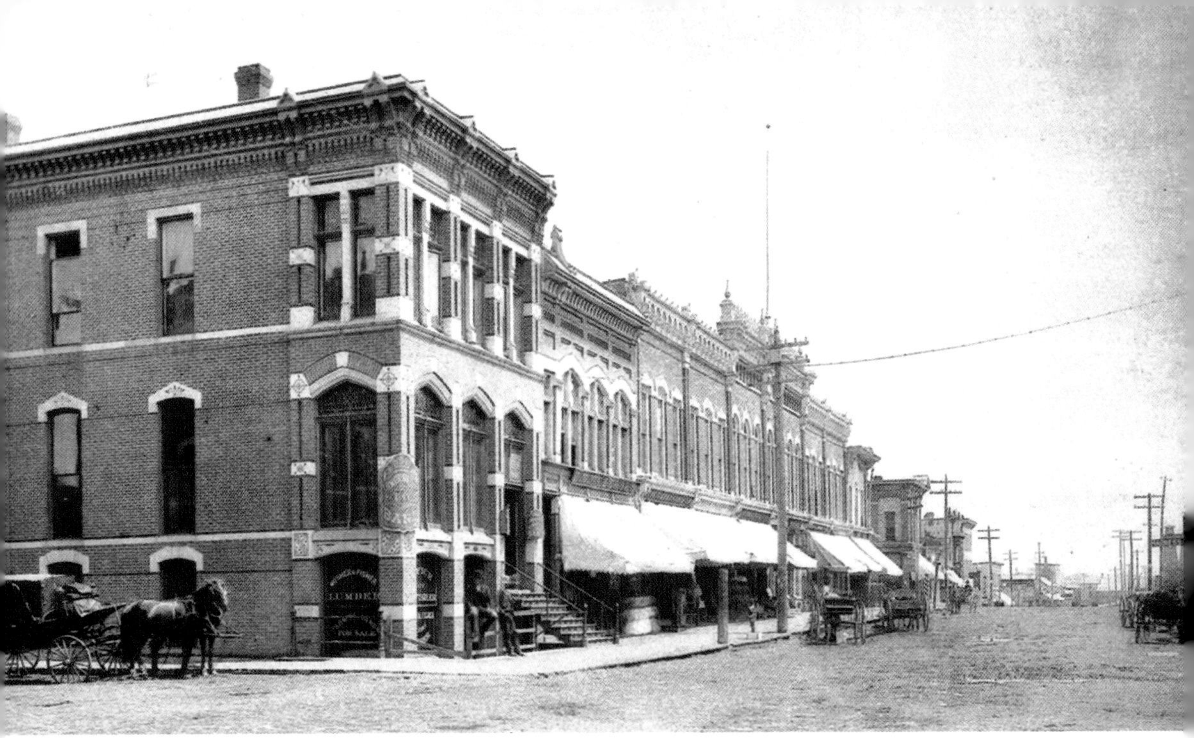

MIDLAND STREET, LOOKING EAST. This was the heart of West Bay City, containing business and city offices. This block looks much as it did 100 years ago. City offices are now on the east side of town. The Lumberman's State Bank building stood on the corner. Today, Owl Antiques, one of many antique shops in the downtown areas on both sides of the Saginaw River, is located in one of the buildings that look much the same.

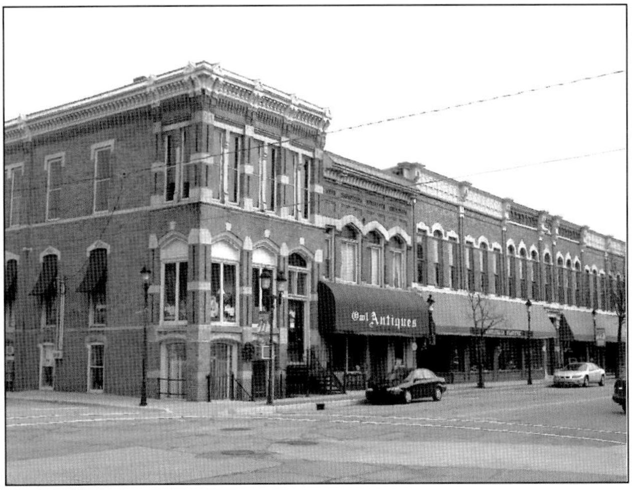

MIDLAND STREET, LOOKING EAST.

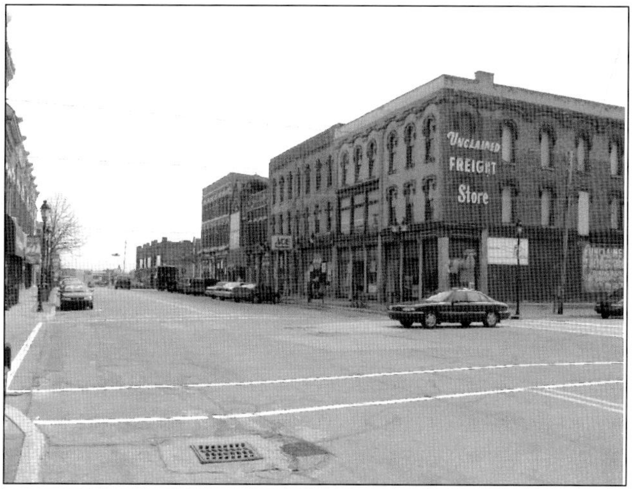

MIDLAND STREET, LOOKING EAST.

MIDLAND STREET, LOOKING EAST. Here is another block that looks much the same; the site where Babo Groceries once stood is now the home of Unclaimed Freight. In fact, Unclaimed Freight takes up 80 percent of the business block with addresses from 700–708 East Midland Street. Between 1910, when Babo Grocery closed, and 1940, when Unclaimed Freight started its business, there were a succession of clothing stores, meat markets, billiard parlors, and various other businesses on the block. The streets aren't cedar anymore—they are paved.

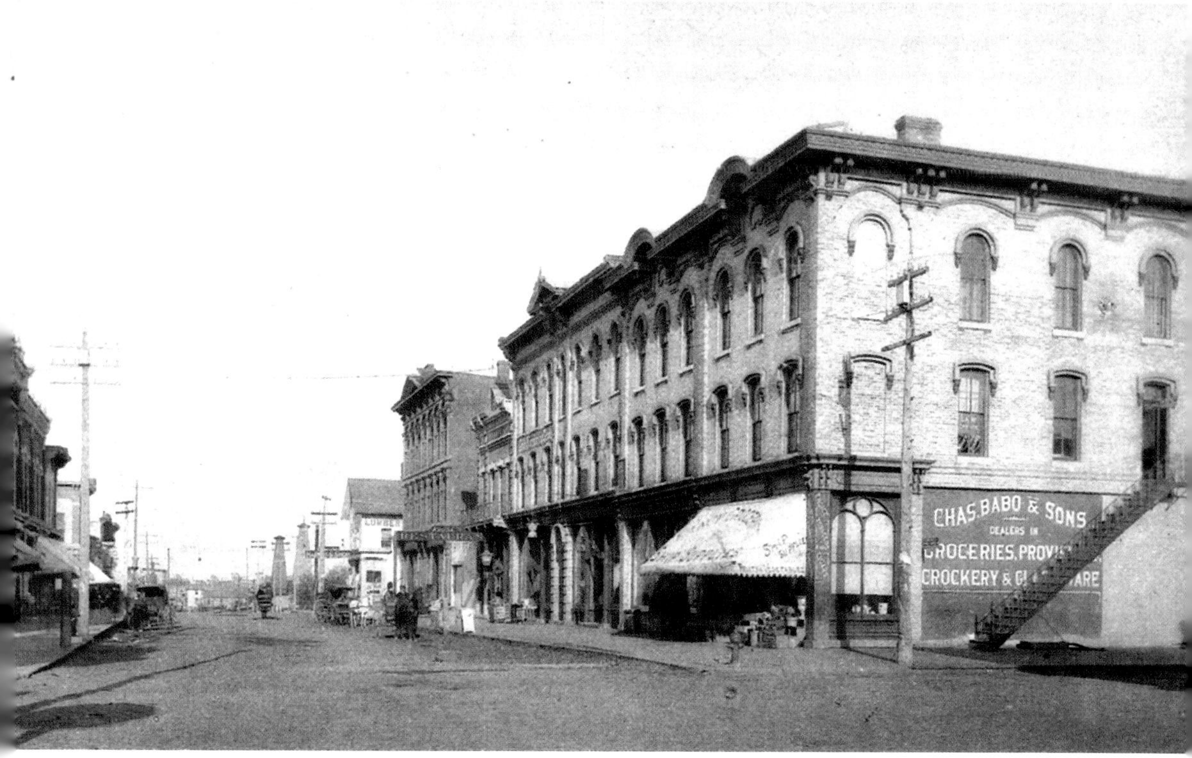

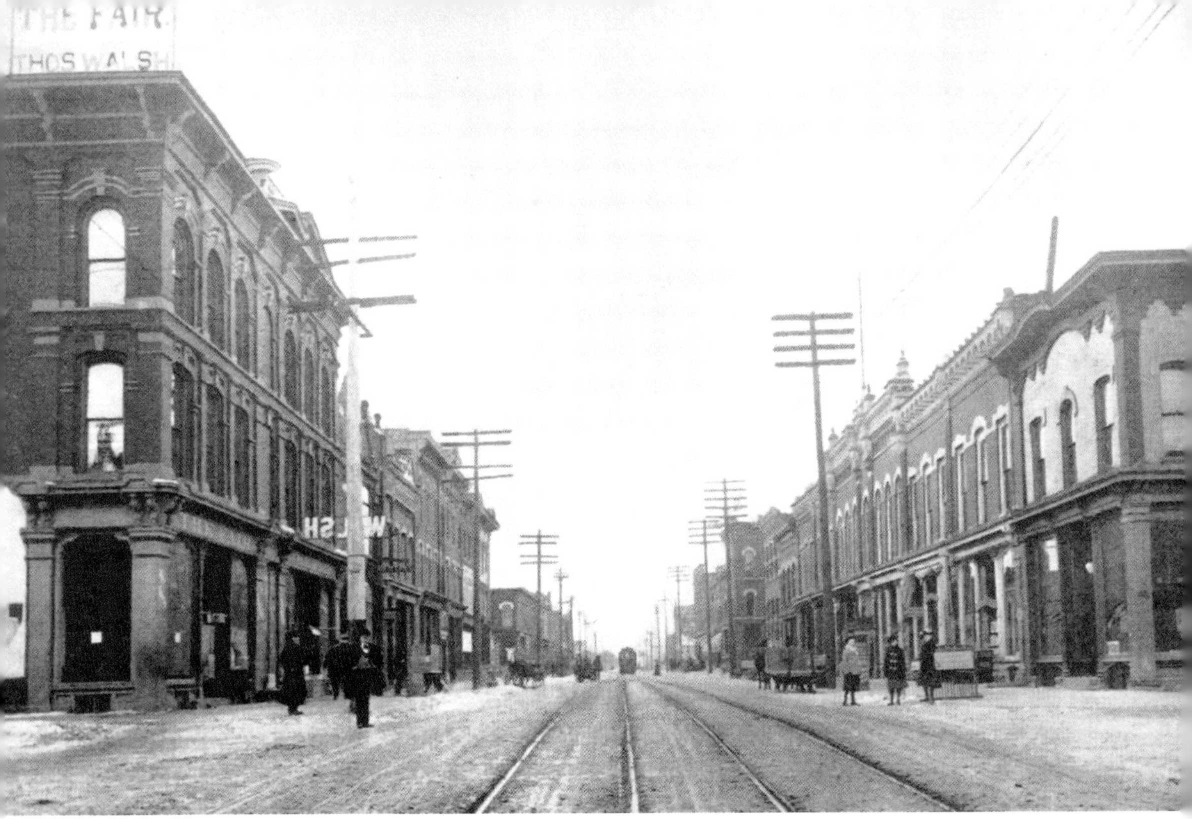

MIDLAND STREET, LOOKING WEST. Viewed from one block further east on Midland Street, it is once again amazing how much the buildings look the same. On the left in earlier years stood the Sage General Store, and until recently, Kirchman Brothers. Lucky's Record Shop was located on the right side of the street. I still have three R.C.A. Nipper dogs that I purchased just before Lucky's closed in the early 1990s. Lucky's Pub is in the old Lucky's Records building.

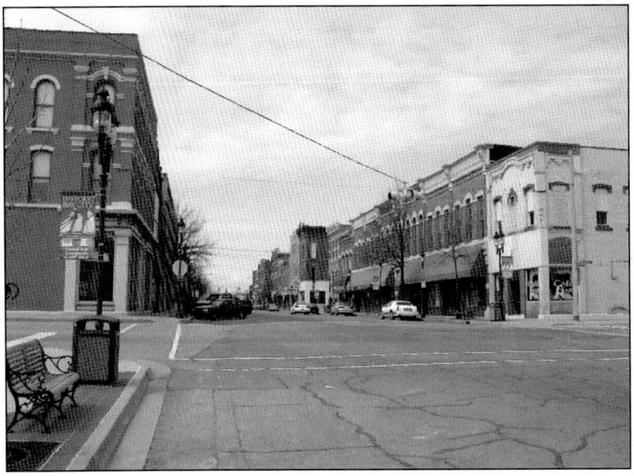

MIDLAND STREET, LOOKING WEST.

FISHER BLOCK. Despite the fact that the fancy ornamentation is gone from the roofline (as it is in most places) the Fisher Block building still has much of its original charm. The West Bay City City Commission met on the second floor to do city business. In addition to their normal city processes, they also dealt with lawsuits from people injured by wooden sidewalks. Wholesale Electric occupies the lower floor today.

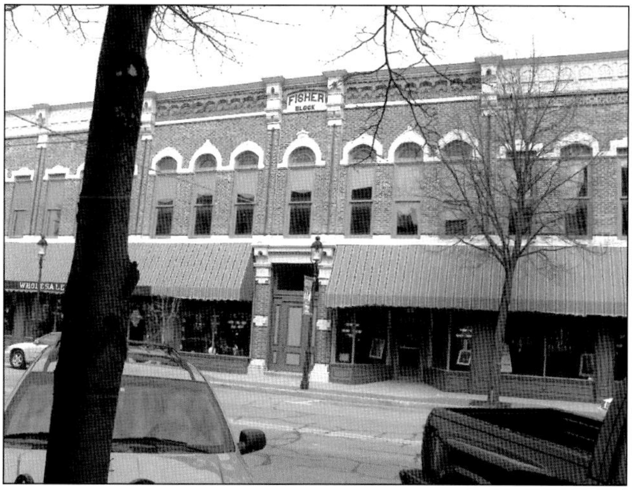

FISHER BLOCK.

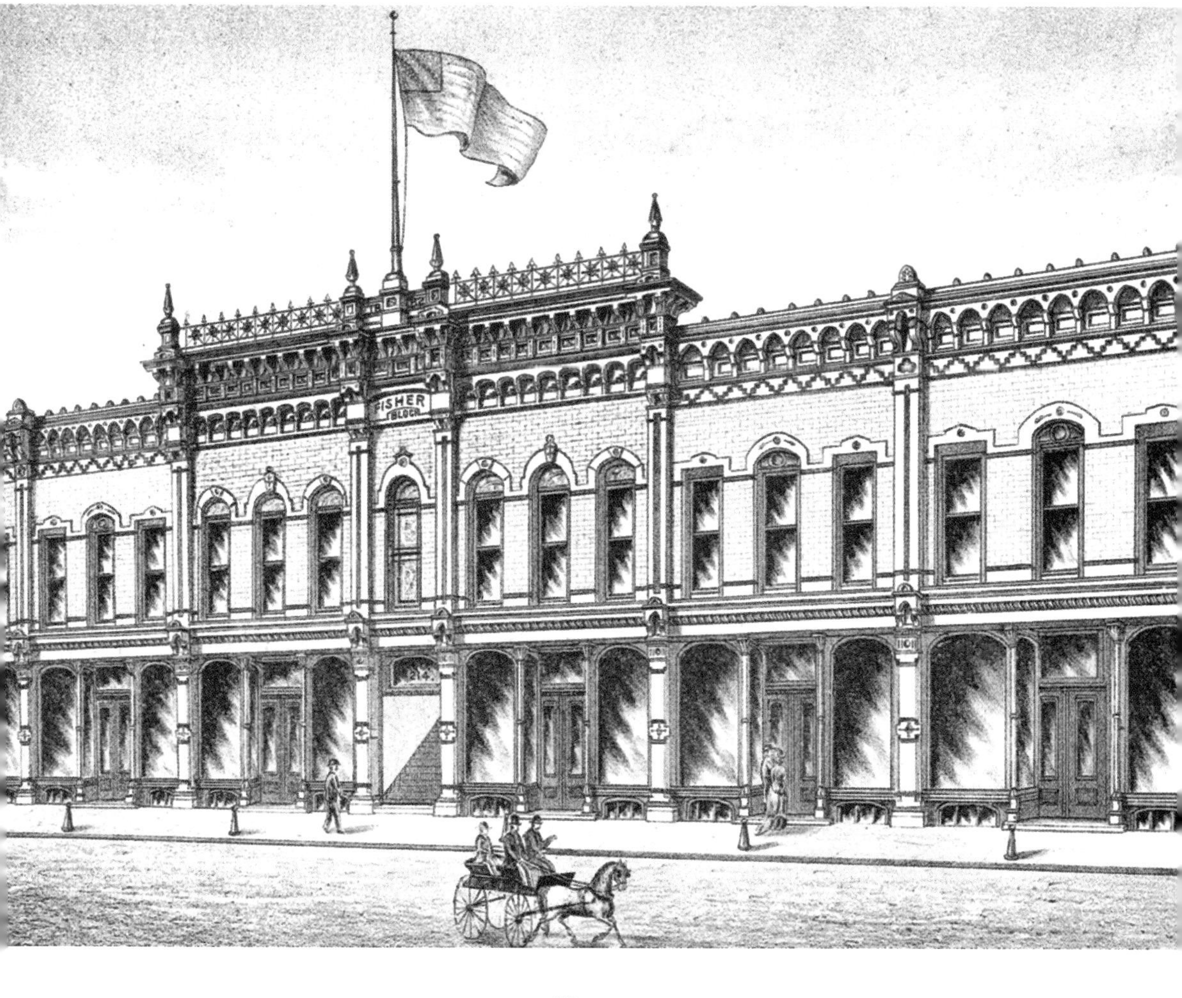

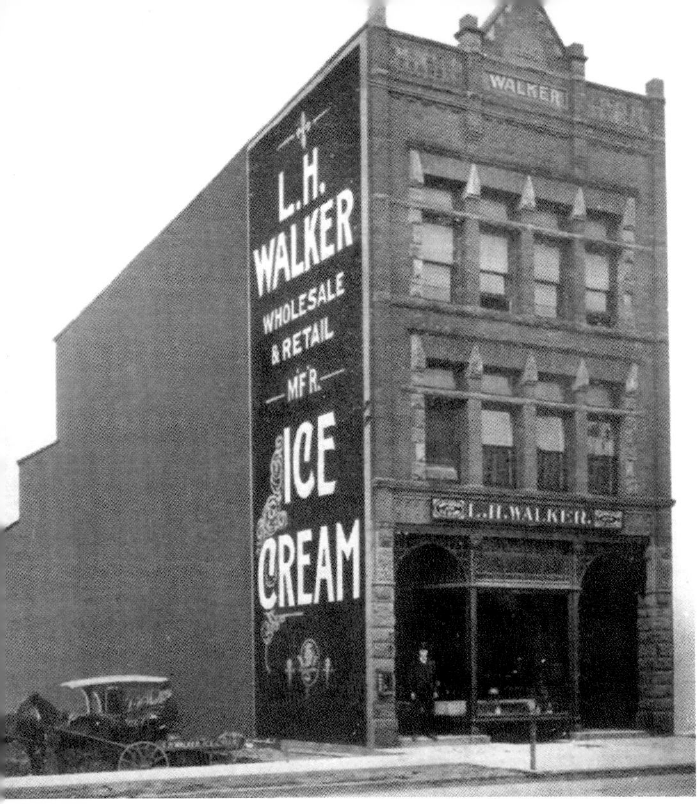

L.H. Walker. At some time in its history, the Walker building had the triangle-shaped brickwork on the top and the Walker name removed from the building. Located at 505 East Midland Street, a building was added directly to the west, covering the Walker Ice Cream sign painted on the brickwork. Over the years, various businesses have occupied the Walker building, with the latest being Touch of Mexico restaurant.

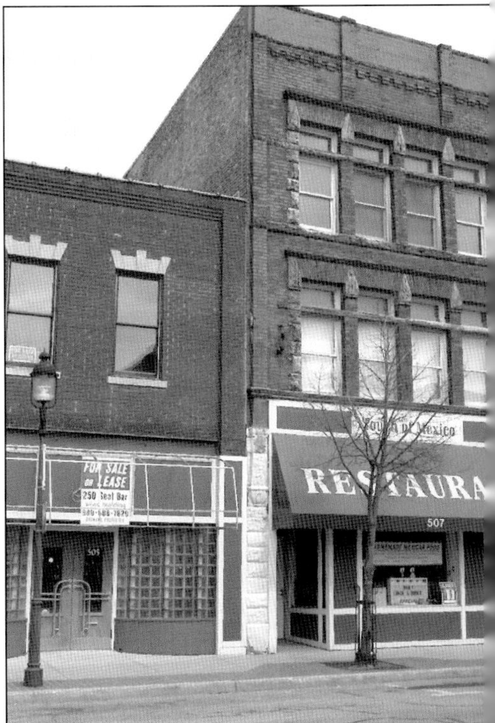

Former L.H. Walker Building.

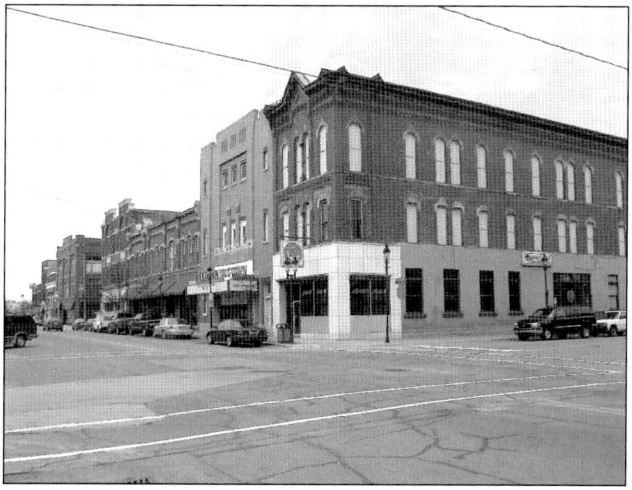

MIDLAND STREET, LOOKING WEST.

MIDLAND STREET, LOOKING WEST. The George L. Mosher Hardware building was built in 1881 on the northwest corner of Midland and Linn Streets. The first floor contained hardware, stoves, and tin items. The second floor was used for offices and the third floor housed the Wenona Lodge of the Masons, No. 256. Besides being a hardware man, Mr. Mosher also served as chief engineer of the Wenona Fire Department. The second and third floors of the Mosher building look much the same today. The first floor is now Fidelity Mortgage.

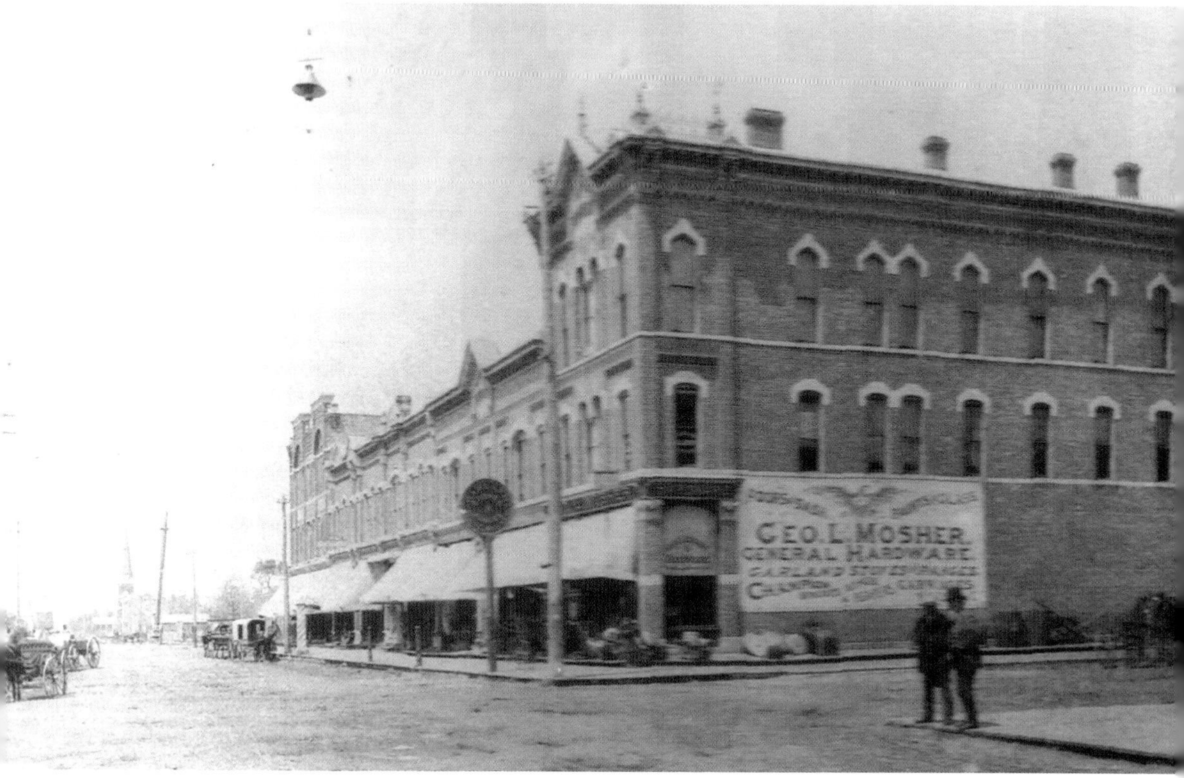

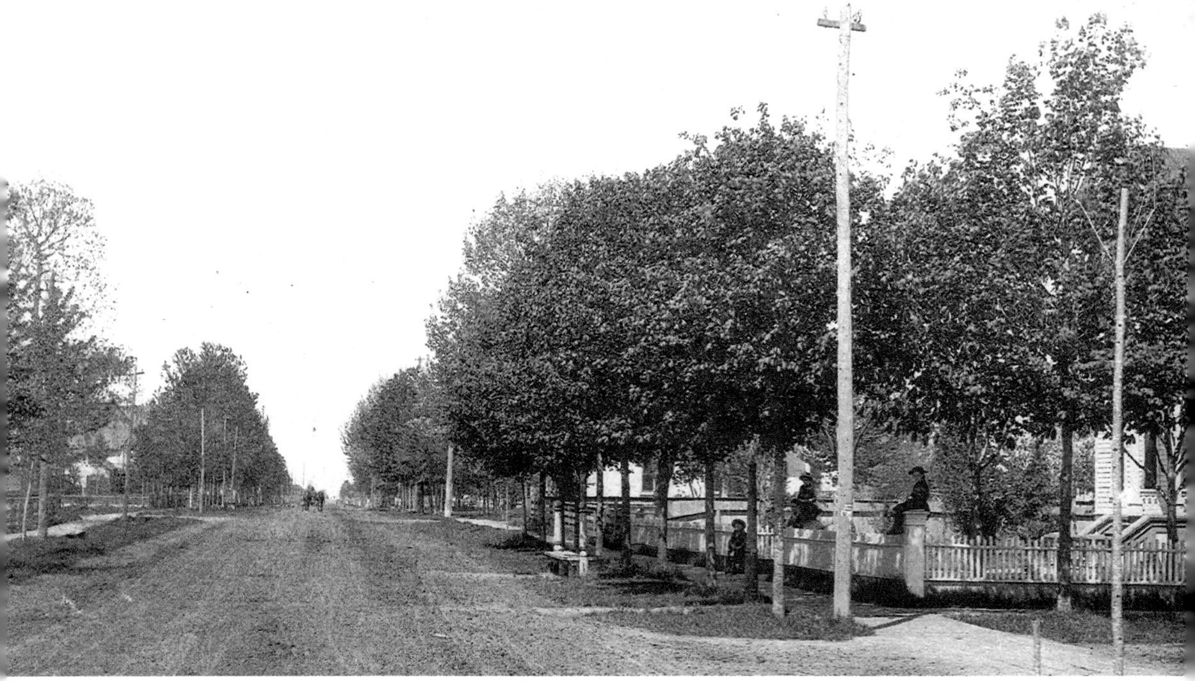

MIDLAND STREET, LOOKING WEST FROM CORNELIA STREET. In 1878, Wenona had streets with the names of Cornelia, Centre, Corbin, Crapo, Faxon, Hamilton, Johnson, Madison, Michigan Park Avenue, and Washington. The years that passed and especially the consolidation with Bay City made many of the names just a footnote in history. This view is actually Midland Street and Erie Street looking west. The third house from the right on Midland and Chilson was the Chilson farmhouse. It is now Eichhorn's Antiques.

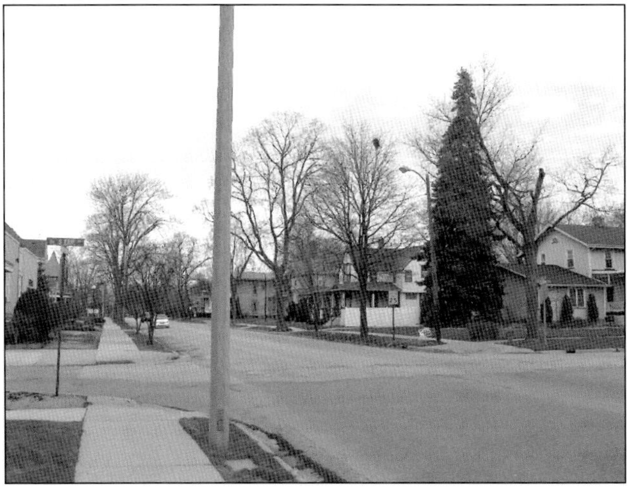

MIDLAND STREET, LOOKING WEST FROM ERIE STREET.

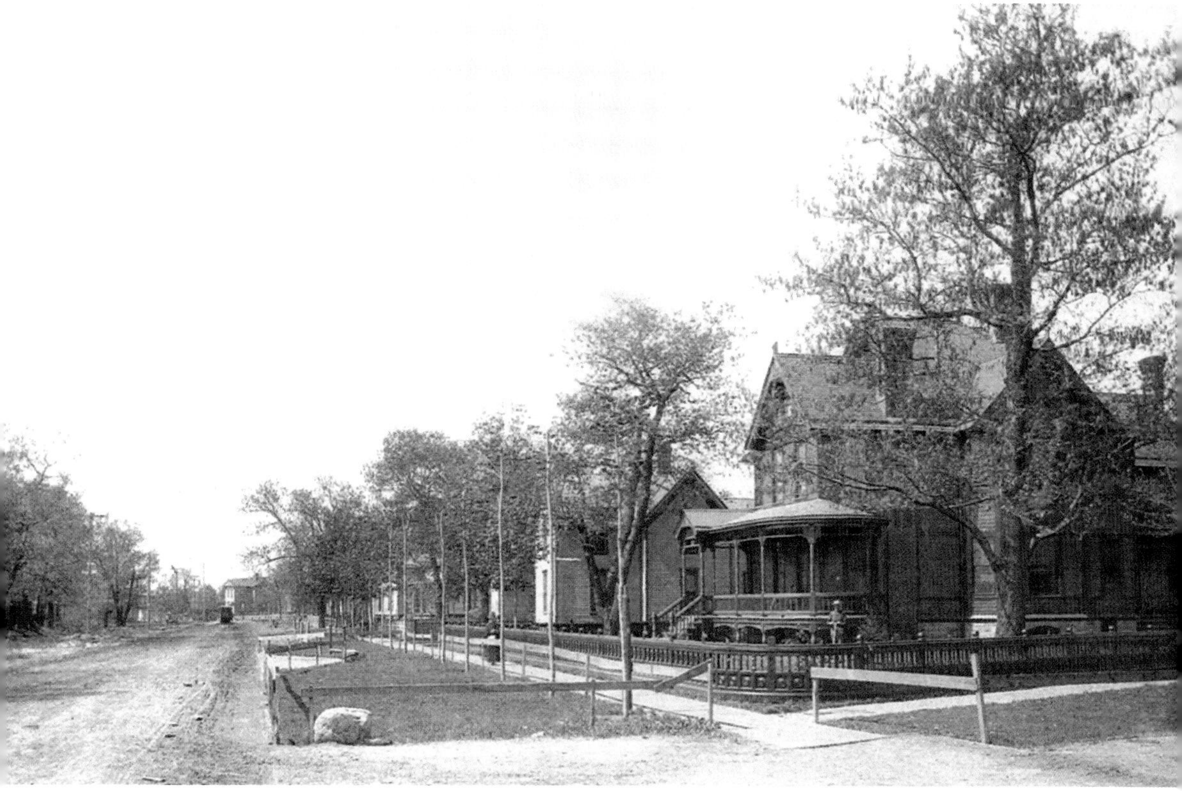

AUSABLE STREET, SOUTH FROM NORTH UNION. Ausable Street was one of the main connectors between the villages of Wenona and Banks. The view has not changed very much in the past 140 years. If you went north or east from here, you were in "Banks," originally part of the area called Bangor. Banks was named for Civil War General Nathaniel Banks and was incorporated in 1871. Banks joined with Wenona and Salzburg to form West Bay City in 1877.

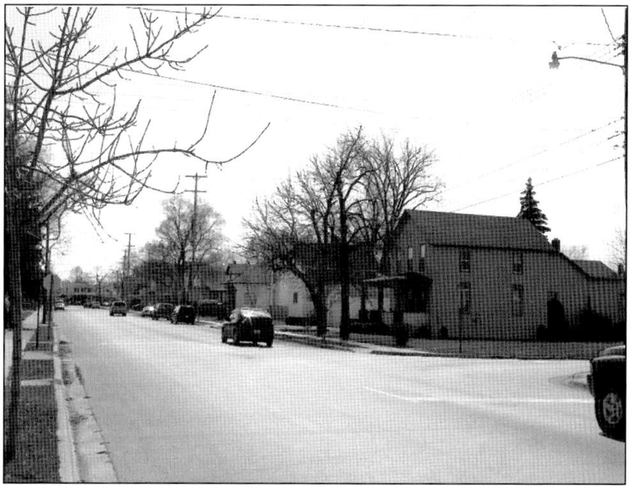

STATE STREET, SOUTH FROM NORTH UNION.

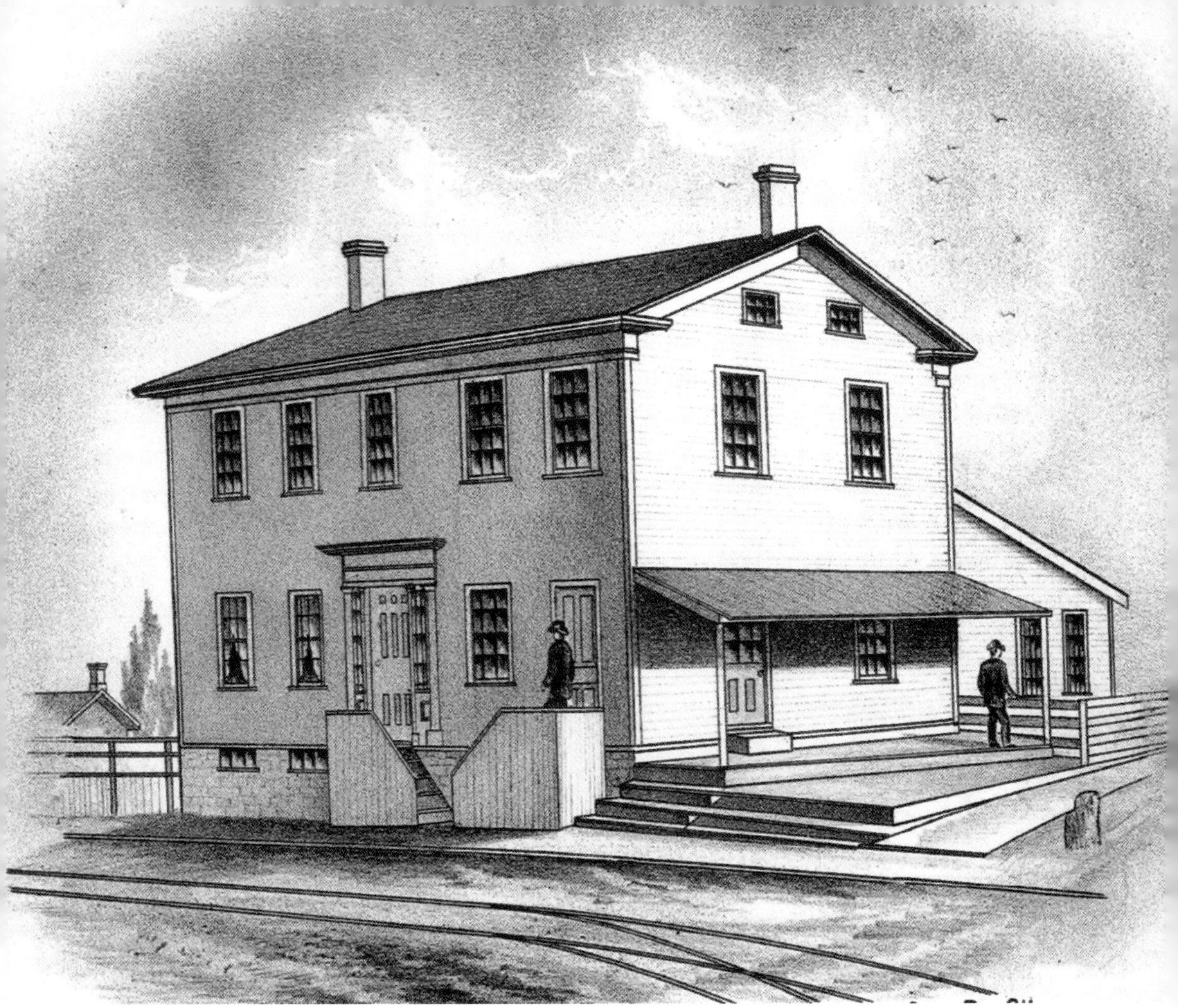

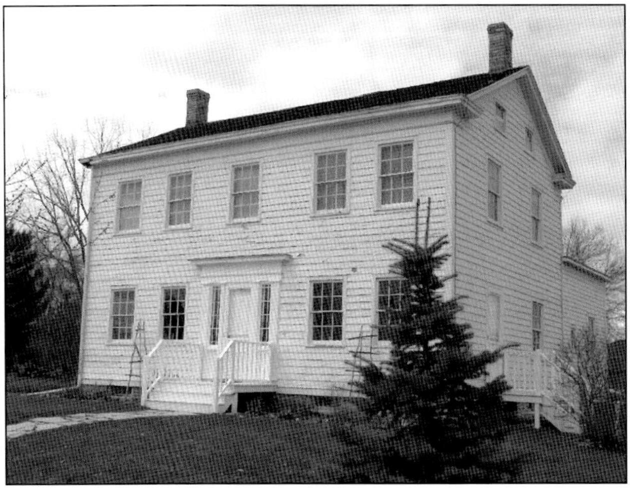

TROMBLEY HOUSE.

TROMBLEY-CENTRE HOUSE. For many years, the Trombley House (also known as the McCormick Home, the River House, and the Centre House) stood just a block south of Lafayette Avenue on Water Street. After an extensive community effort, it was moved by barge across the Saginaw River in 1981 to its present home in Veteran's Memorial Park. Visitors may tour the Trombley House on special occasions such as the Fourth of July Festival.

Chapter 2
SAGINAW RIVER

THIRD STREET BRIDGE. The Saginaw River has always been the dividing line for that which is east of the river and west of the river. A Belinda Street Bridge, a Cass Avenue Bridge, and the Third Street Bridge carried people and vehicles over the Saginaw River. This view of the Third Street Bridge looks from the east side toward the west where the Sage Mill once stood. It is now Veterans' Memorial Park.

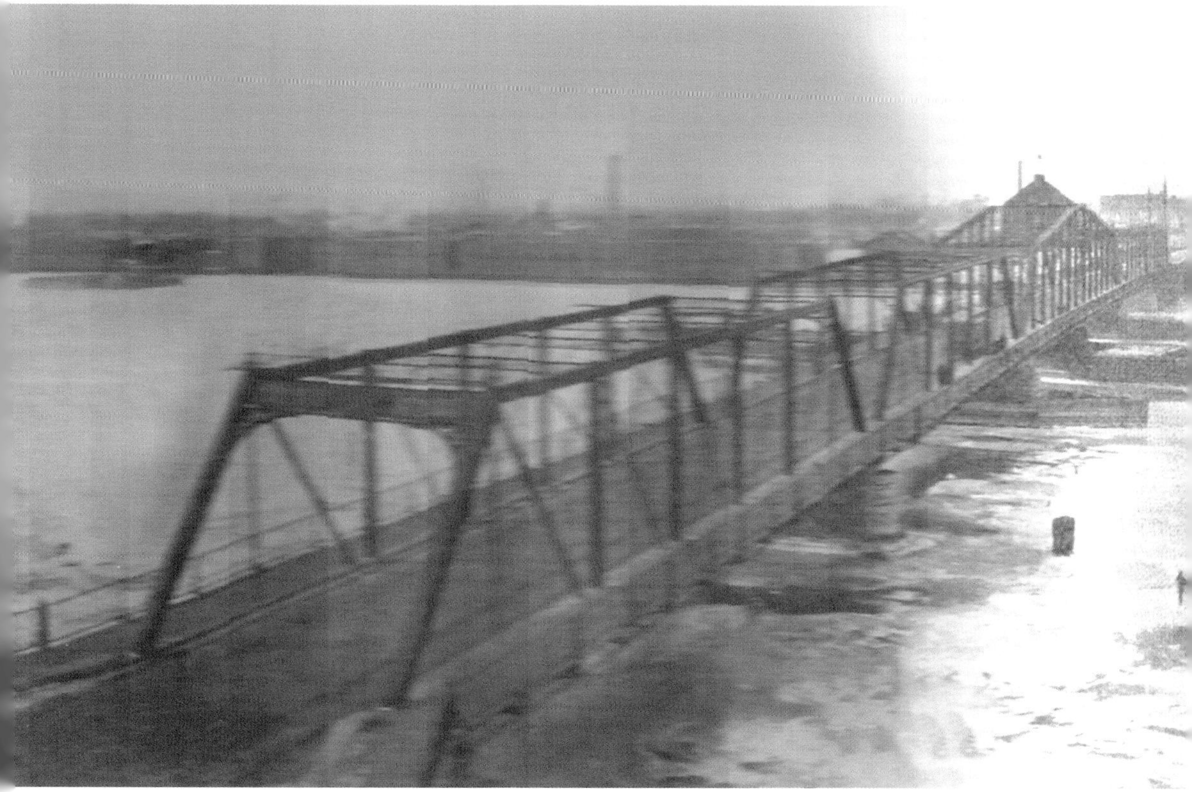

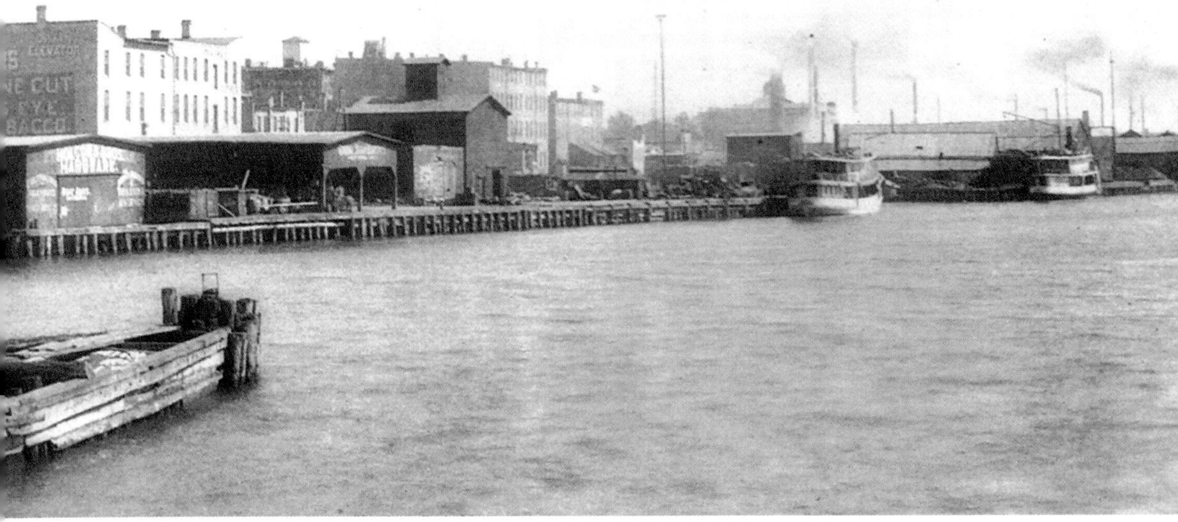

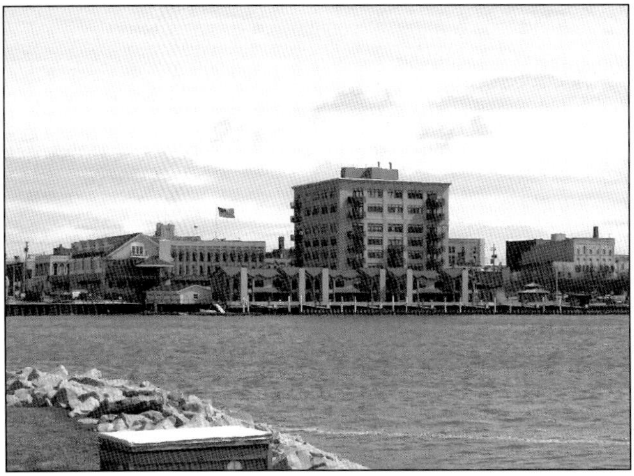

RIVER VIEW, SOUTH FROM NEAR FORMER THIRD STREET BRIDGE SITE.

RIVER VIEW, SOUTH FROM THIRD STREET BRIDGE. The skyline of downtown Bay City has never included really tall buildings. It does show many business enterprises built right along the river to take advantage of the water transportation. In the 1880s when lumber was king, many fortunes were made along the Saginaw River. The modern view shows commercial and residential uses as the way the river's edge is used today.

CAPTAIN DAVIDSON'S SHIPYARD. Captain James Davidson built more than 100 wooden ships in his shipyard on the west side of the river between Crump and Fisher Streets. Captain Davidson lived in New York but moved to 601 Center Avenue when he started his business here. The remains of several of his wooden ships are visible on the west side of the river just east of the shipyard's location. A plaque and slip are now all that remain to remind us of this once-great shipyard.

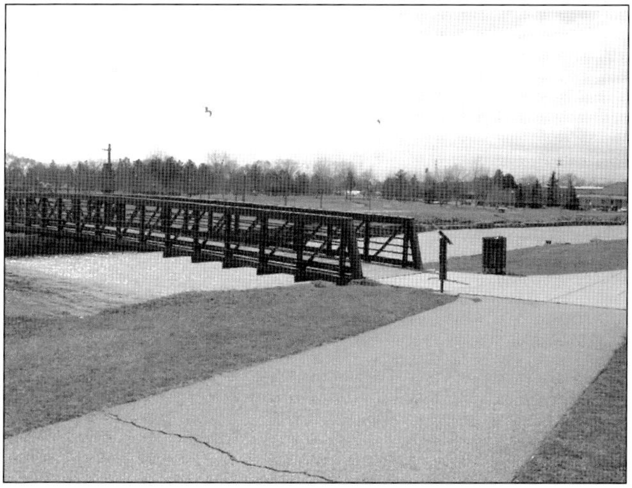

FORMER DAVIDSON'S SHIPYARD SITE.

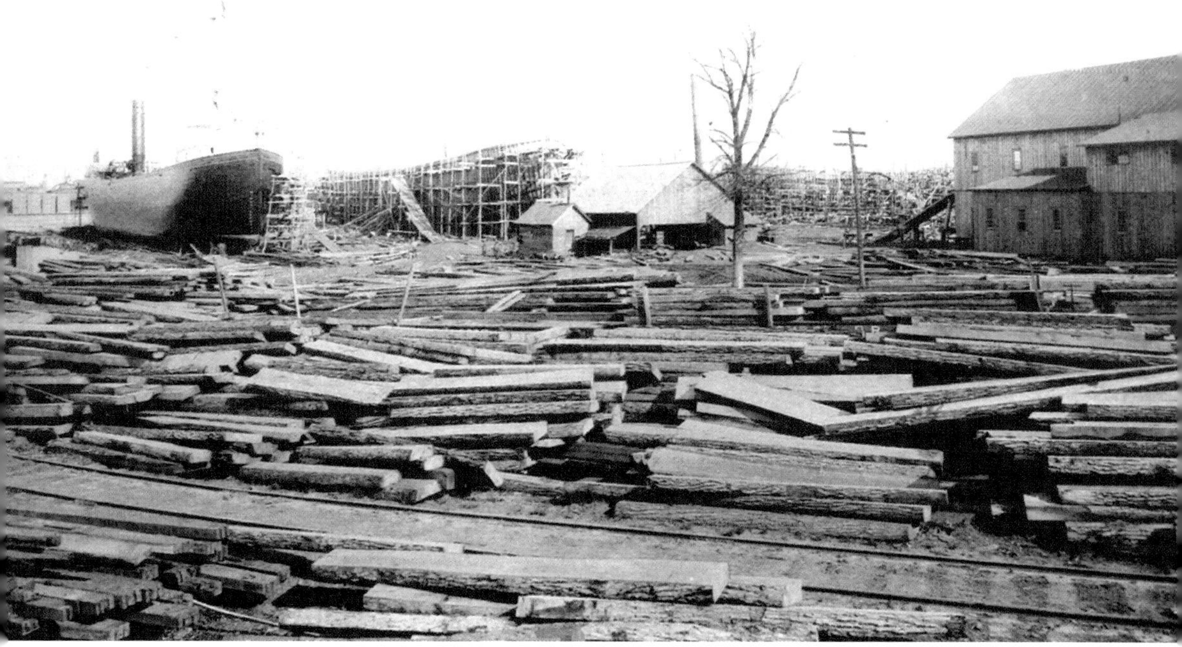

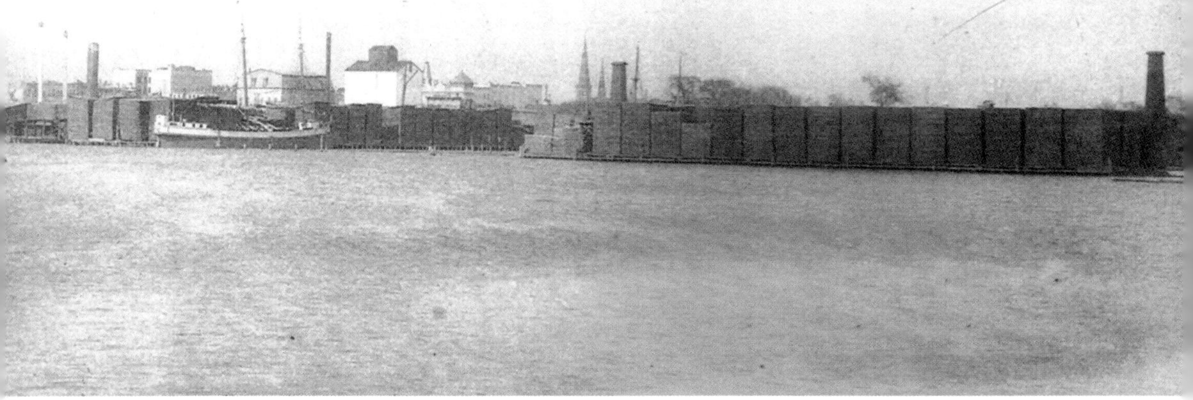

VIEW ACROSS THE RIVER FROM DAVIDSON'S SHIPYARD. Looking east across the Saginaw River in the 1880s, one would have seen nothing but businesses associated with lumbering. Among the businesses were N.B. Bradley, William Peter Sawmill and Salt Block Company, Eddy, Avery, and Eddy at the foot of 11th Street and the F.E. Bradley Sawmill and Salt Block Co. at the foot of 10th Street. In recent years, Bay Aggregates was located here. The community hopes to develop this prime riverfront property.

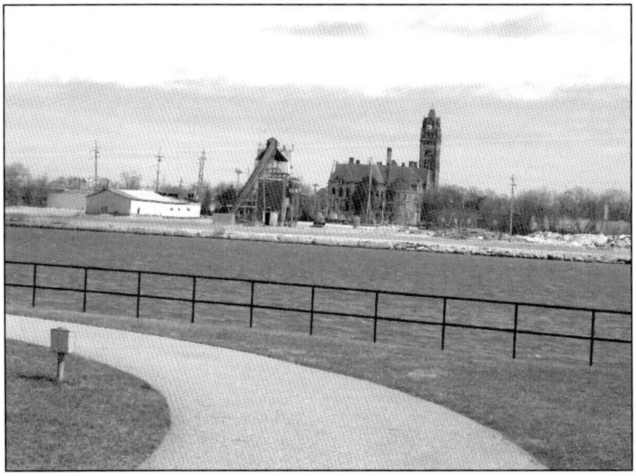

VIEW ACROSS THE RIVER FROM FORMER DAVIDSON SITE.

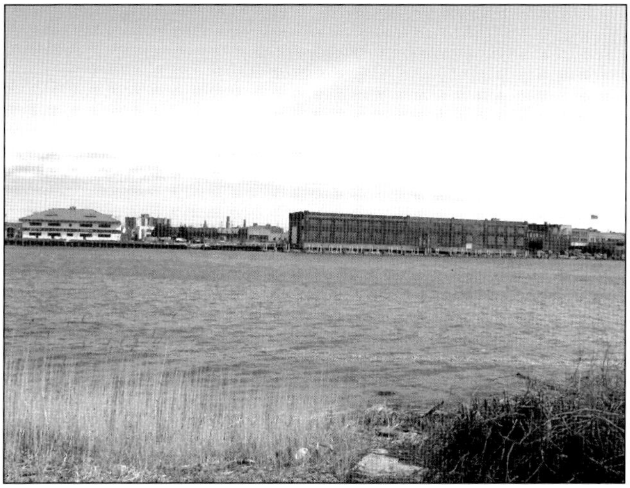

River View from Near Railroad Bridge.

River View from Railroad Bridge. It is hard to imagine the Saginaw River filled with floating logs, each with their own log mark, bound for one of the more than 100 sawmills located along both sides of the Saginaw River. In 1882, 858,344,000 feet of lumber and 176,376,500 shingles were shipped from Bay City mills. Across the river was the Pitts & Co. Sawmill and Salt Block. Defoe Shipbuilding Company was here for many years and, until just recently, H. Hirschfield and Sons Scrap Metal used the property.

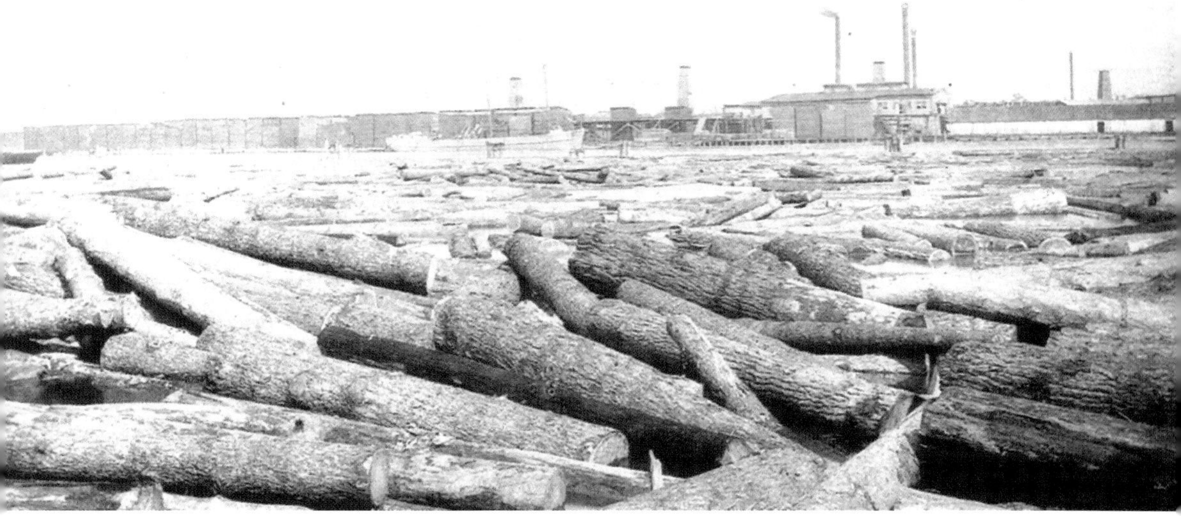

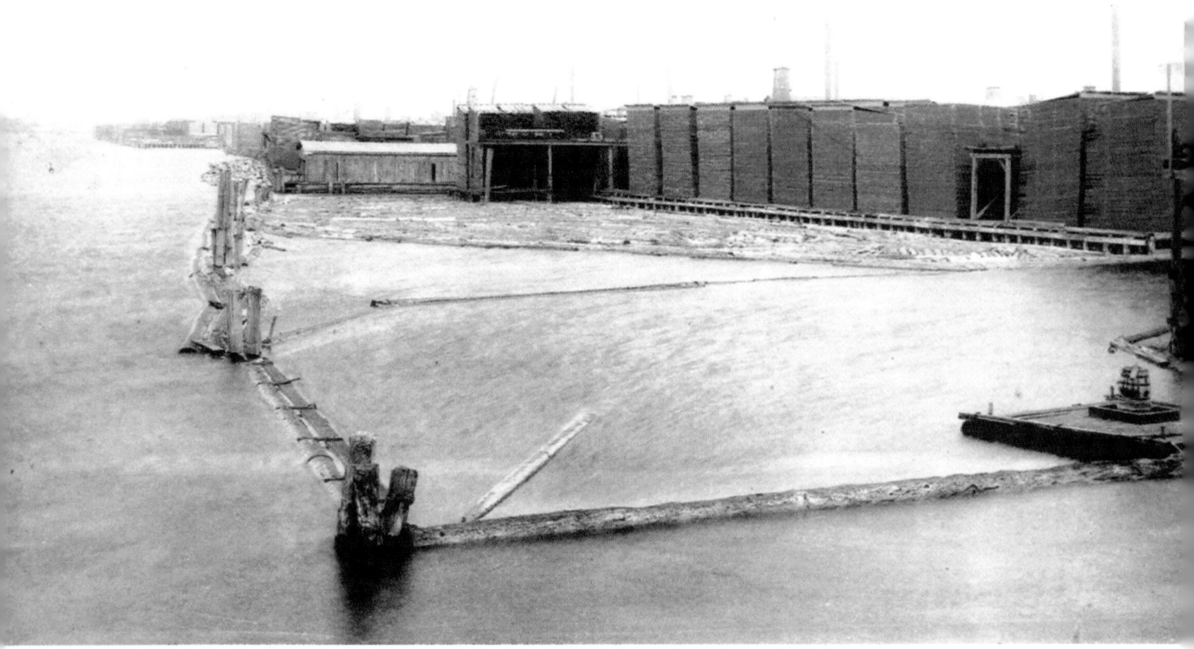

VIEW ON EAST SIDE OF RIVER, LOOKING NORTH. West Bay City Mayor Peter Lind had a company that was skilled at building the log booms required to contain the logs until the sawmills were ready to process them. While the exact location of this picture is not known by the author, it is a view that was repeated many times on both sides of the Saginaw River.

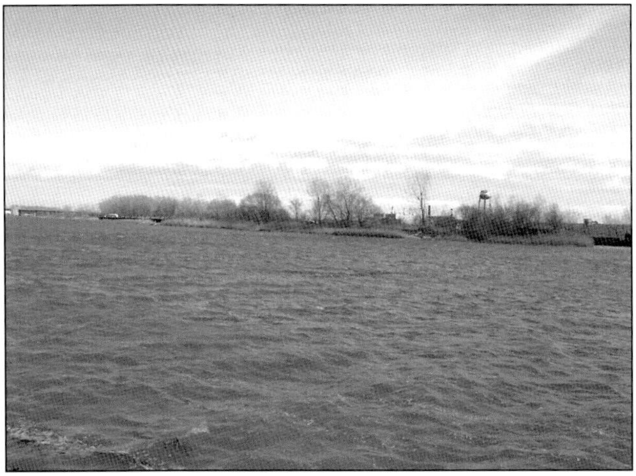

EAST SIDE OF RIVER, LOOKING NORTH.

VIEW ALONG RIVER, EAST FROM MICHIGAN PIPE. In 1881, the Michigan Pipe Company, which was located between what were then Henry and Lord Streets (Van Buren and Grant Streets), began manufacturing wooden water and sewer pipes along with steam pipe casings, gas pipes, chain pumps, and tubing. The former wooden pipe company was located behind what is now General Motors Powertrain.

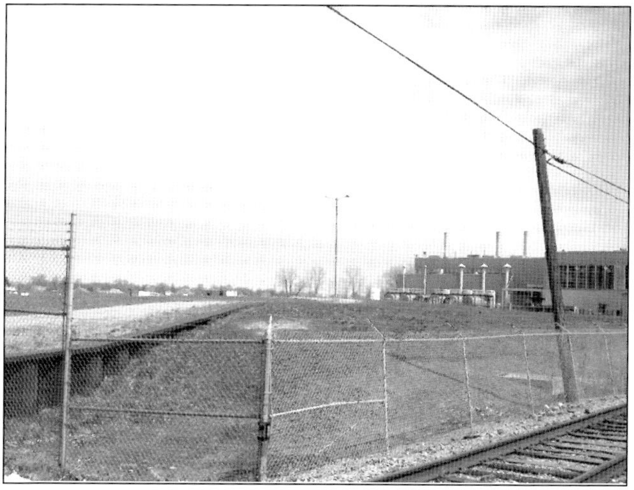

EAST FROM FORMER MICHIGAN PIPE.

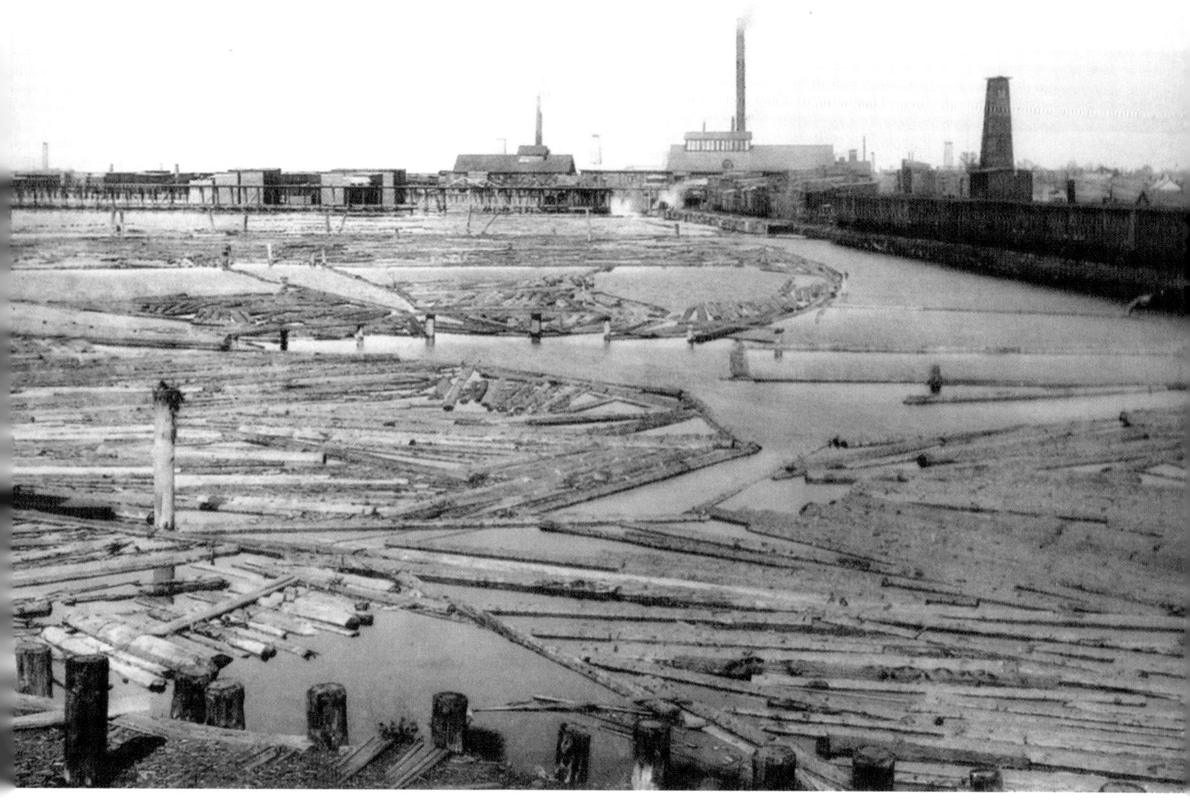

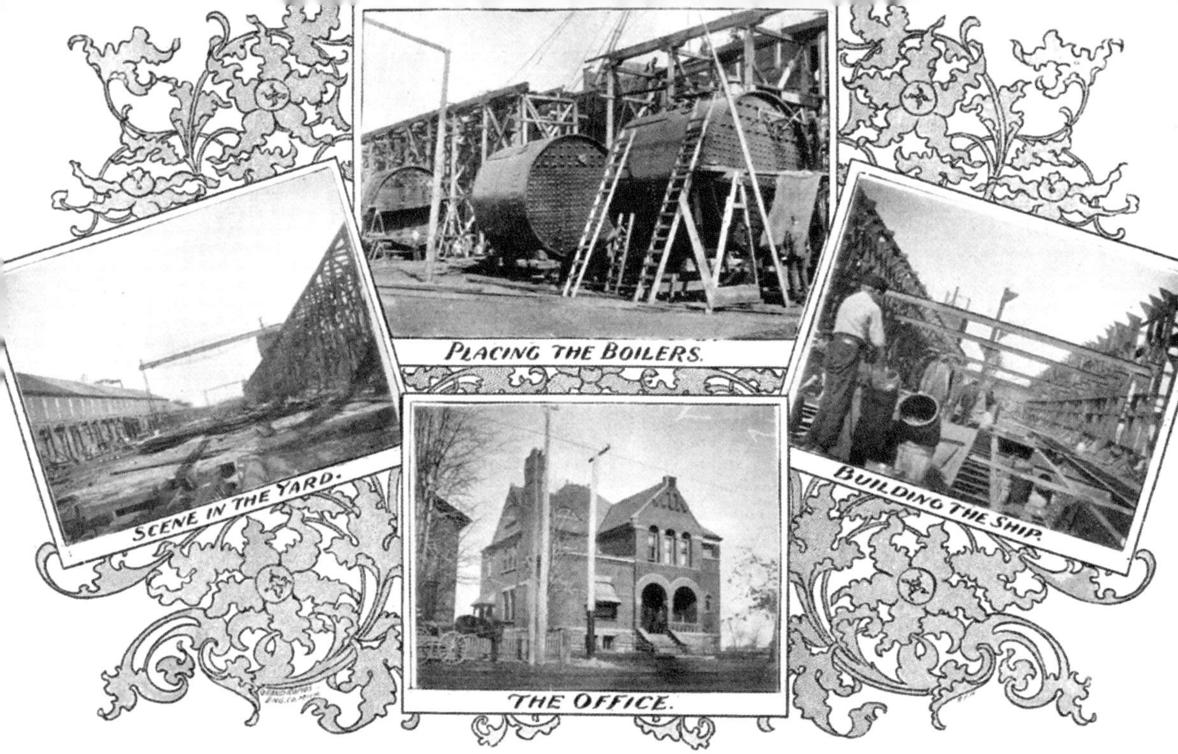

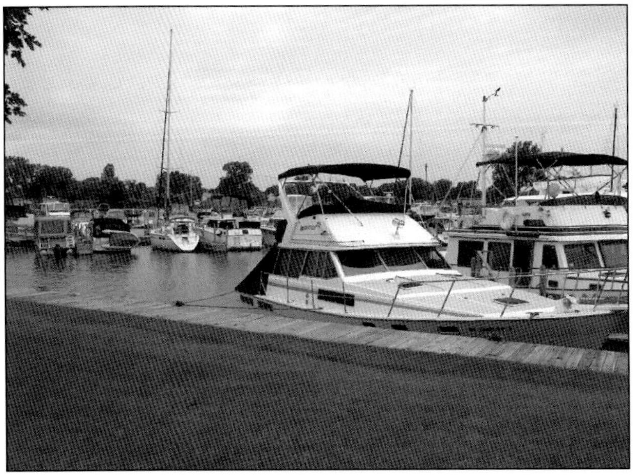

WHEELER'S LANDING.

SCENES AT SHIPYARD OF F. WHEELER. Frank Wheeler's shipyard was on the west side of the river where the aptly named Wheeler's Landing marina is today. Wheeler's shipyard built both steel and wooden vessels that plied the Great Lakes. The last Wheeler ship, the *Henry C. Frick*, was launched in 1905 before the shipyard went bankrupt. The American Shipbuilding Company ran the yard until it closed in 1913. The last Wheeler vessel in service was the *Niagra* sand hauler built in 1897 and it, too, has been scrapped.

F. Wheeler Shipyard. This picture shows the hull of a Wheeler ship under construction. At one point, the Wheeler yard had a payroll of over 700 men. This led to the building of Corbin School on Litchfield to teach children of the Wheeler workers. The lower picture shows a launching and the fine clothing people wore to celebrate the creation of a new ship.

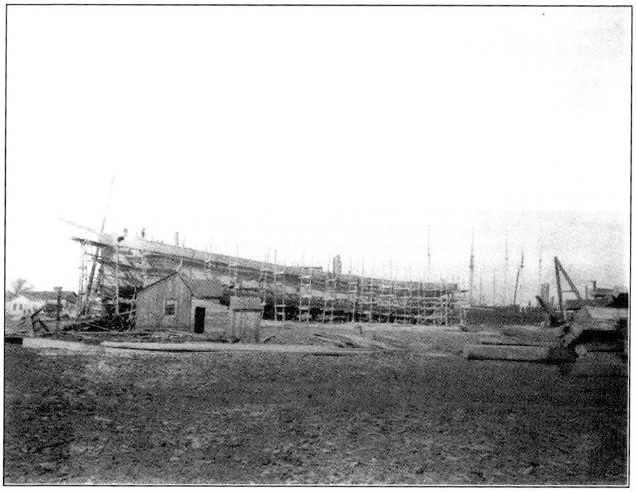

A Launching at Wheeler.

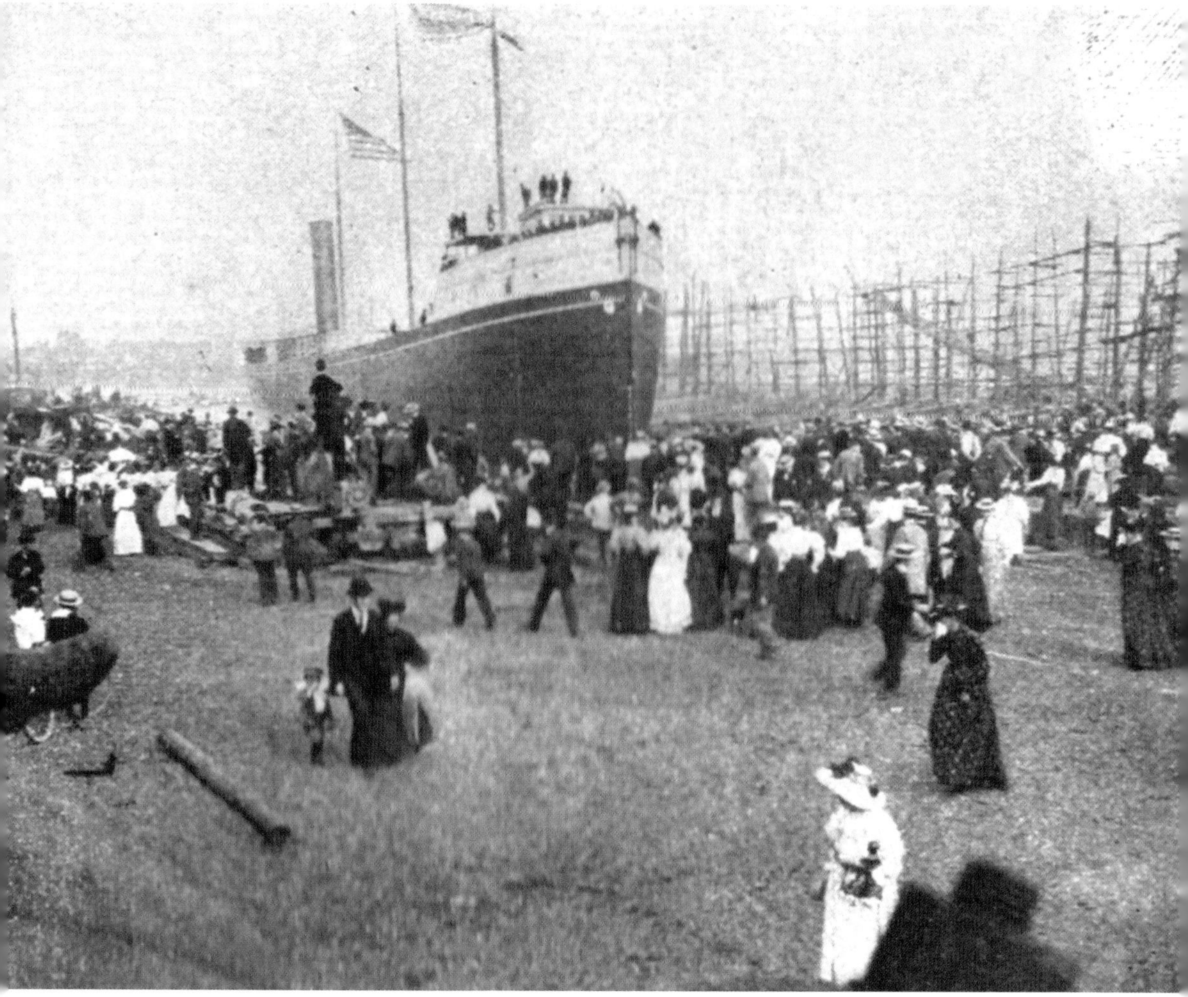

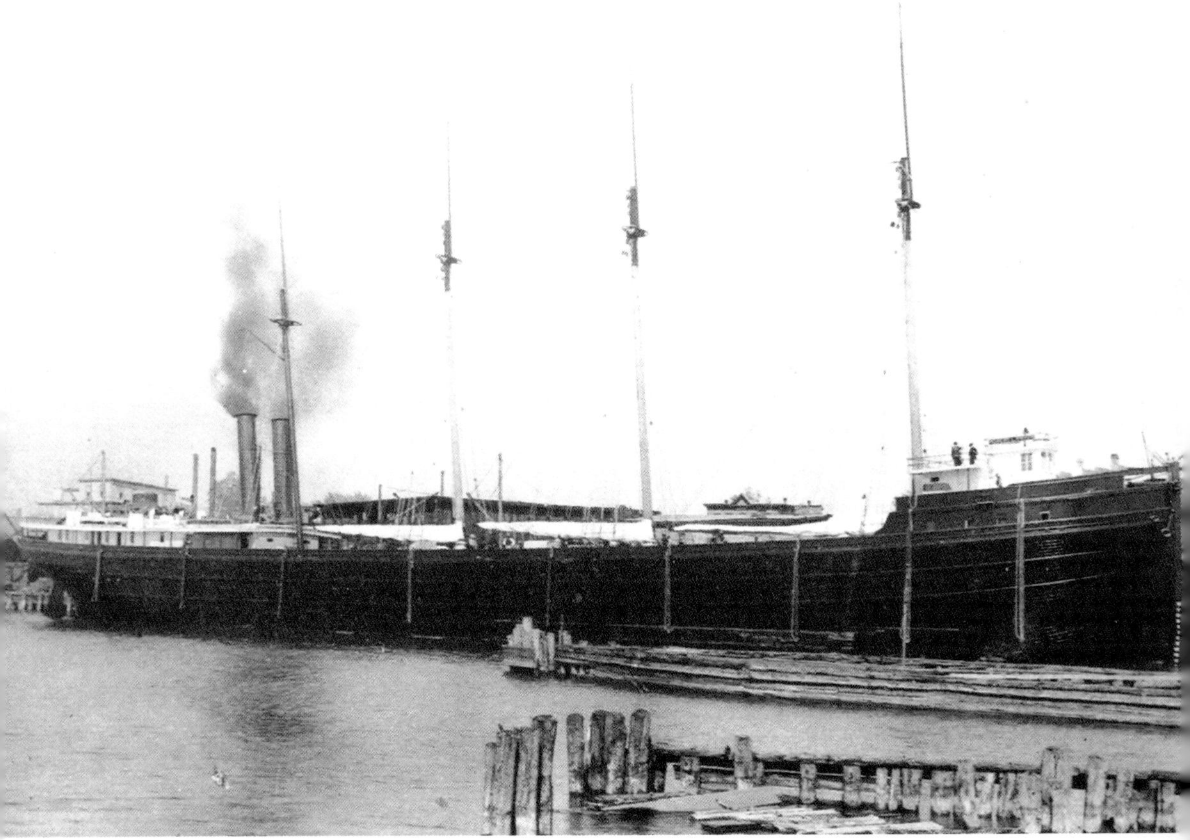

ROBERT F. FRYER. The *Fryer* was built at the Wheeler yard in 1888. According to *Vessels Built on the Saginaw: Volume I*, the *Fryer* was 281 feet and one inch long with a beam of 41 feet four inches and a depth of 20 feet. In 1914, the *Fryer* was converted to a floating grain dryer in Thunder Bay, Canada. It was put to the torch and scuttled on July 29, 1930. Today, Wheeler's Landing has docks for boats and this lighthouse-like building, which together serve as a reminder of the Wheeler Shipyard days.

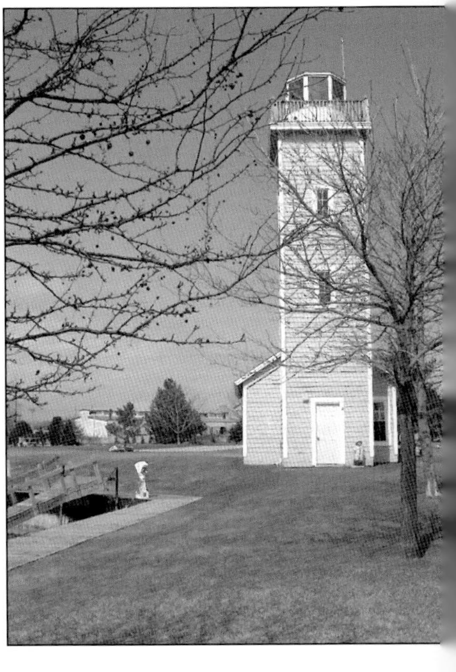

WHEELER LANDING TOWER.

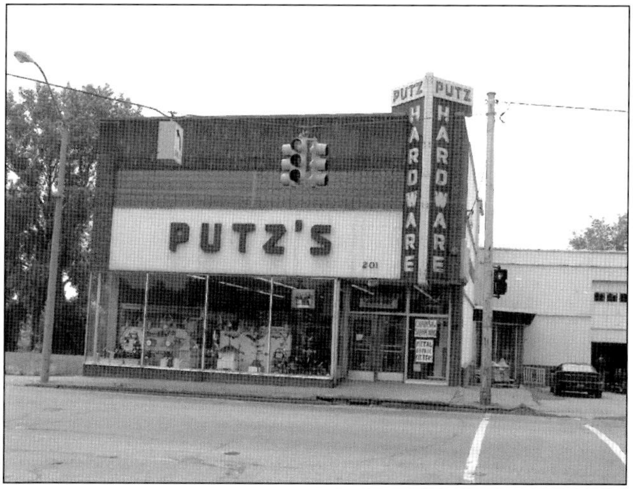

JOHN W. PUTZ HARDWARE.

GEORGE L. FRANK HARDWARE. George Frank and his sons, Adam and Charles, were the people to see in the early decades of the 20th century if you needed hardware. Located at what is now the southern foot of Wenona Street near the Lafayette Bridge, the store offered hardware, paints, plows, pumps, implements, Jewel stoves, mowers, hay loaders, and rakes. John W. Putz began running the business in 1916 and his son, Theodore, took over in 1937. Ted was joined by his son, the late Ronald Putz, and his daughter, Lois. Lois Niemann is still there today.

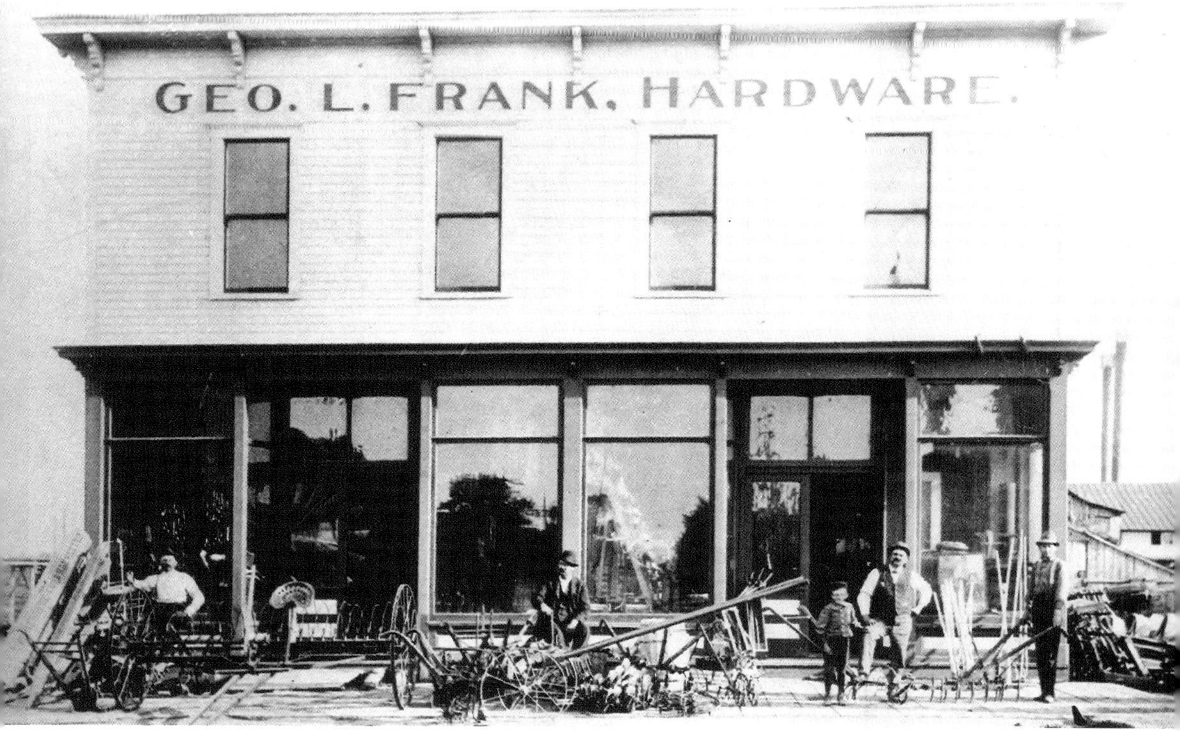

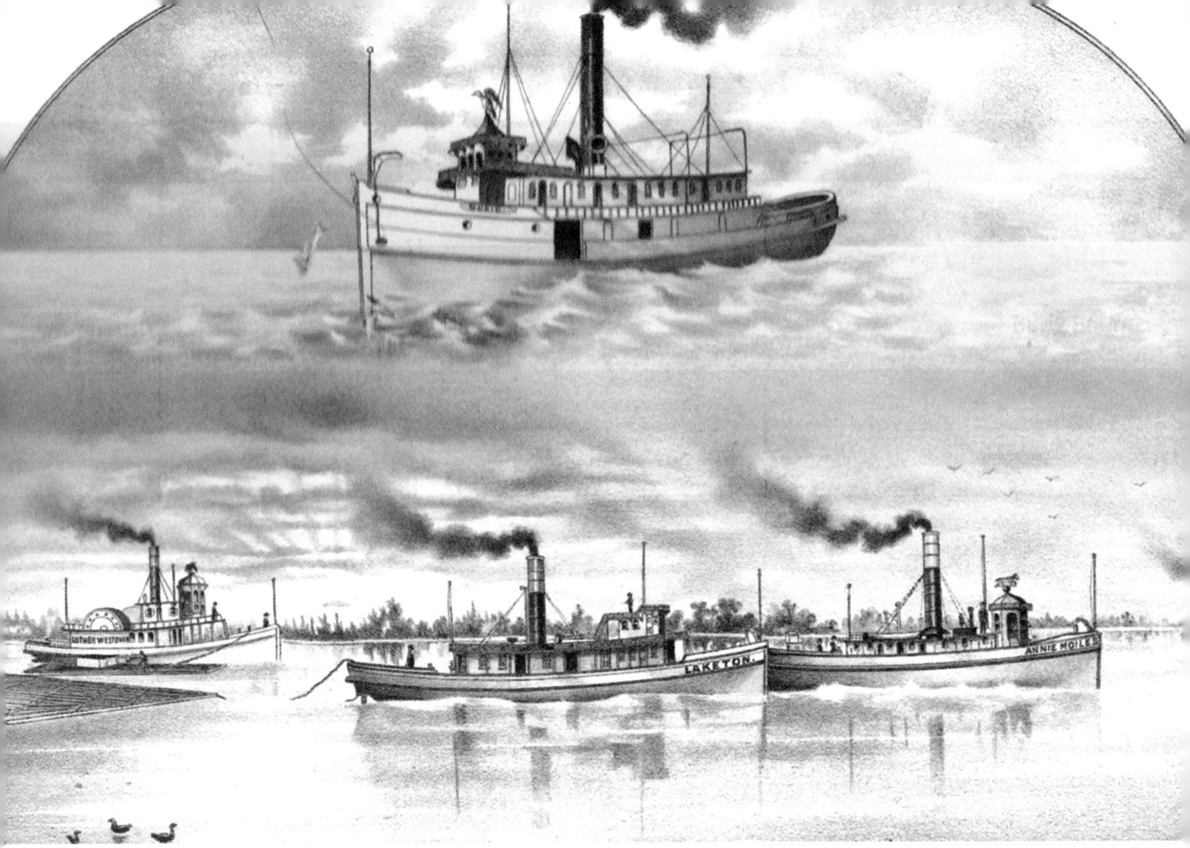

MITCHELL AND BOUTELL TUGS. It was 1867 when Mitchell and Boutell began their tugboat business in an office on the southwest corner of Second and Water Streets. Their principal business was towing and delivering logs to the Saginaw River sawmills and ports along the Lake Huron shore. Of the four vessels shown here, only the *Luther Westover* was built in Bay City (at F.W. Wheeler). Today, the site is a boathouse that may become condominiums in the near future.

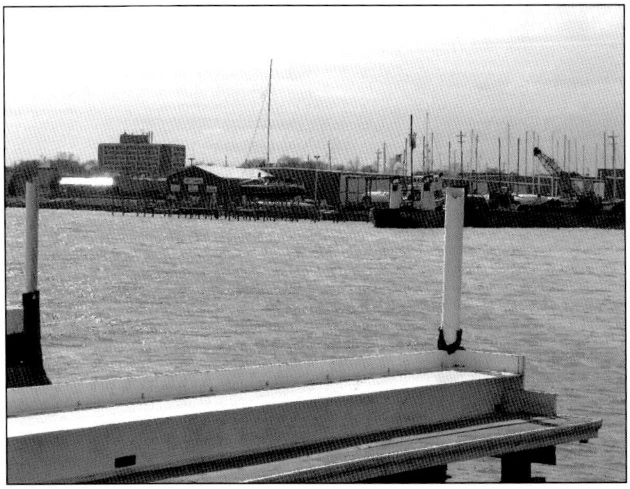

RIVER VIEW.

Chapter 3
Business and Industry

Industrial Works. Bay City is presently trying to develop riverfront property at the foot of Columbus Avenue that once housed one of the largest crane and hoist manufacturing companies in the world. The Industrial Works (later Industrial Brownhoist and American Hoist) manufactured rail traction and crawling tractors, wrecking cranes, pile drivers, and grab buckets that were used around the country and around the world. The machines and equipment were designed, fabricated, and constructed on this site.

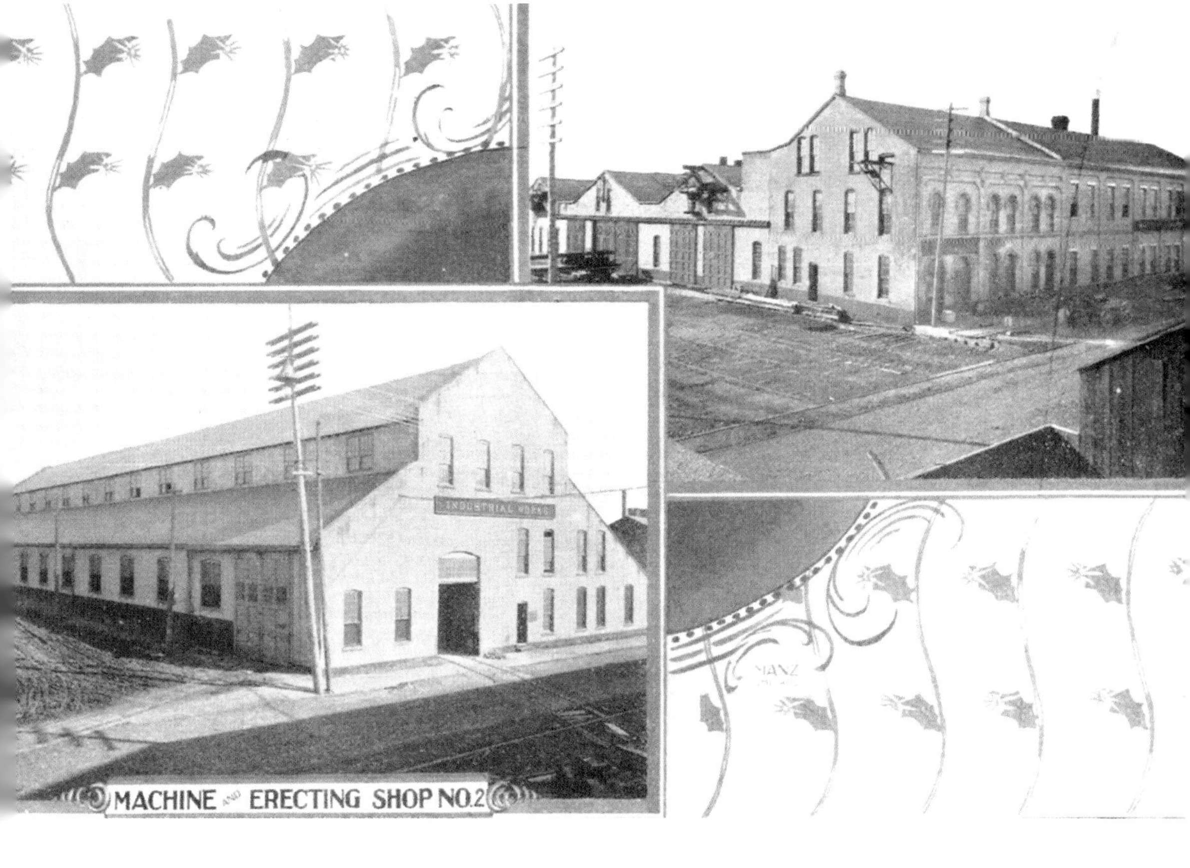

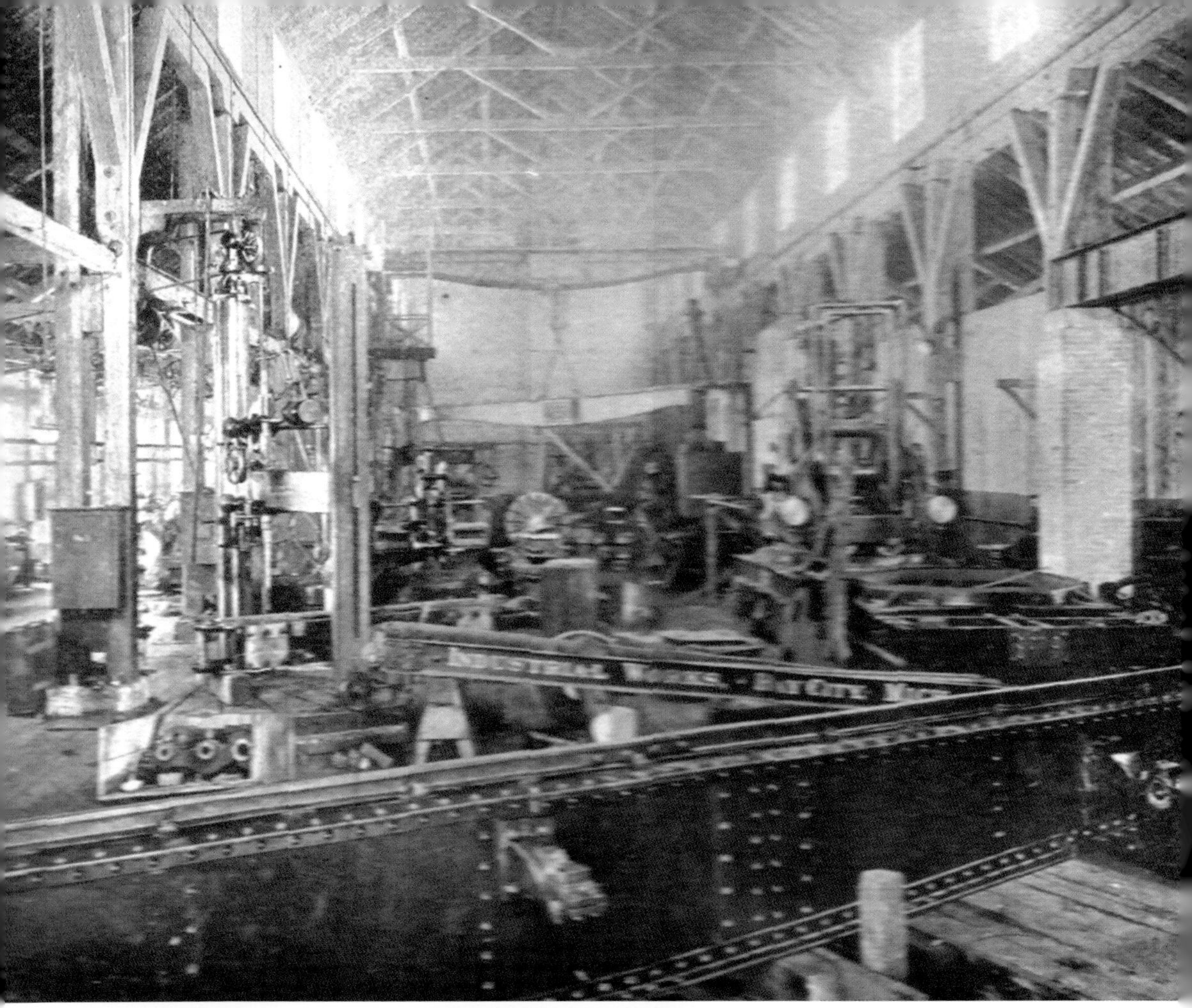

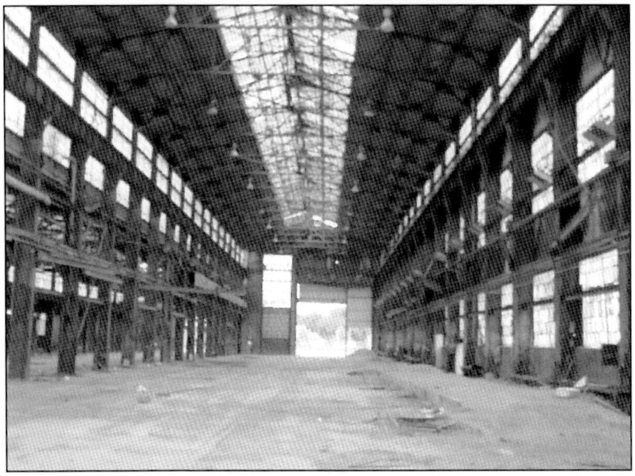

FORMER INDUSTRIAL WORKS SHOP.

INDUSTRIAL WORKS ERECTING SHOPS. The Erecting Shops were the last stop in a construction sequence that included buildings where the Metallurgical Department chose the best metals and materials. In addition, buildings housed the Design Shop, the Foundry to forge the iron, steel, and bronze, the Pattern Shop, the Tool Room, the Machine Shop, the Test Track, the Boiler Shop, the Pipe Shop and a Power House to supply the power to every building. The I.W. truly built all cranes from start to finish. It is hoped that some buildings will survive the eventual use of the property if the Uptown at RiversEdge project comes to fruition. The "now" photo is actually of the interior of the Machine Shop.

NORTH AMERICAN CHEMICAL. Located at the far southeast corner of Bay City's East Side, North American Chemical Company began business in 1898 on land that had been the McGraw Mill with the purchase of 25 salt wells from the McGraw Lumber Company. They were connected to an English company named the United Alkali Company and the ruins I used to explore in the early 1970s were still referred to as the Alkali. Their turbines supplied power to the plant and to Bay City until 1927, when Consumers Power began doing so.

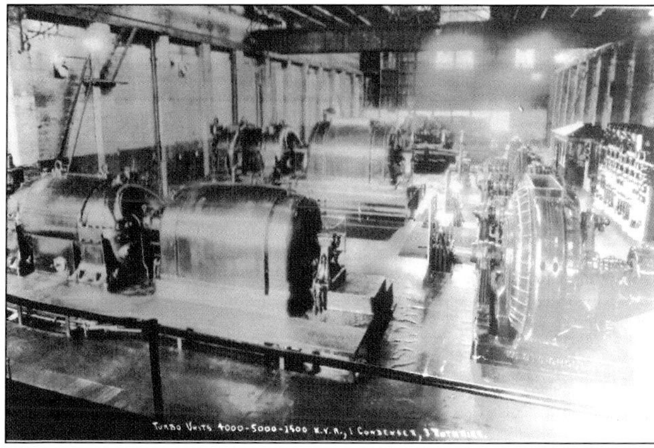

TURBINE OF NORTH AMERICAN CHEMICAL.

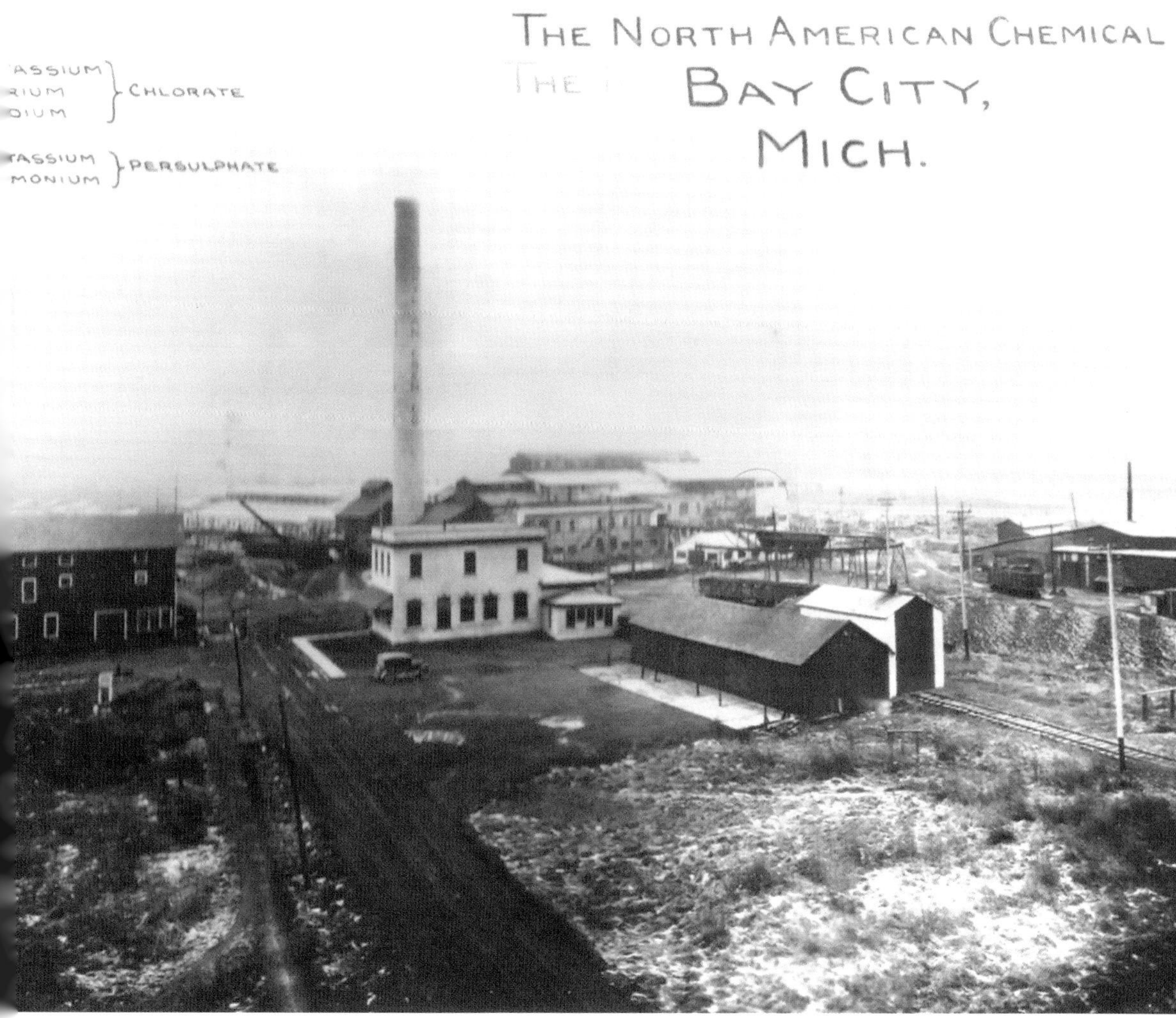

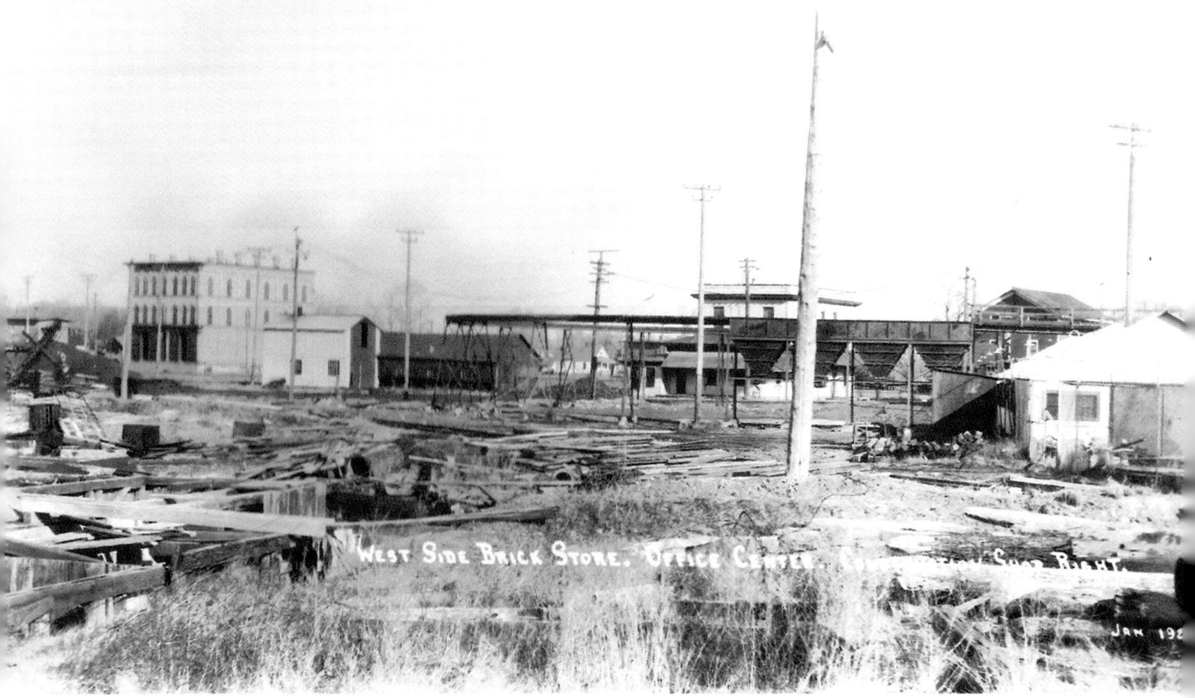

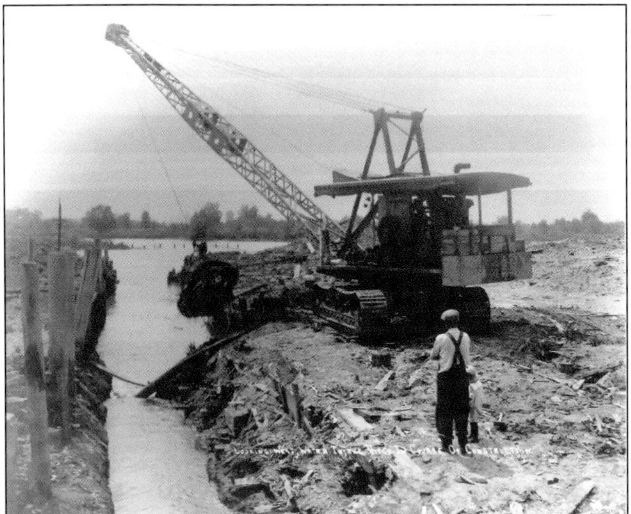

Looking West.

West Side of North American. In addition to North American Chemical, Bay City also had Michigan Chemical Co. and American Chemical Company, because there was so much salt in the ground. North American stayed in business for more than 30 years using both railroad and river to ship their products. The plant's location on the river required it to be built on pilings. It took between 300 and 500 men two years to complete the construction.

Office and Staff, 1898. The office of the North American Chemical Company was at Harrison and 40th Streets when the company opened in 1898. Among the company's products were bleaches, dyes, and specific chemical products. James Clements Airport is on land that was called "the farm" in company photographs. I was fortunate enough to purchase a 30-year pictorial at the Ronald and Ted Putz estate that was the source for the North American pictures.

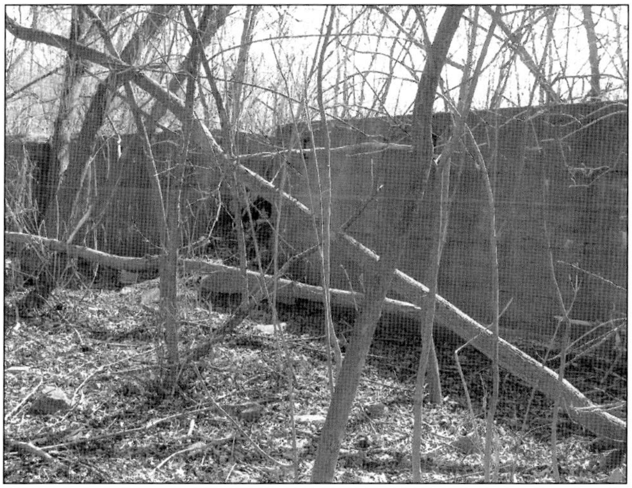

North American Ruins.

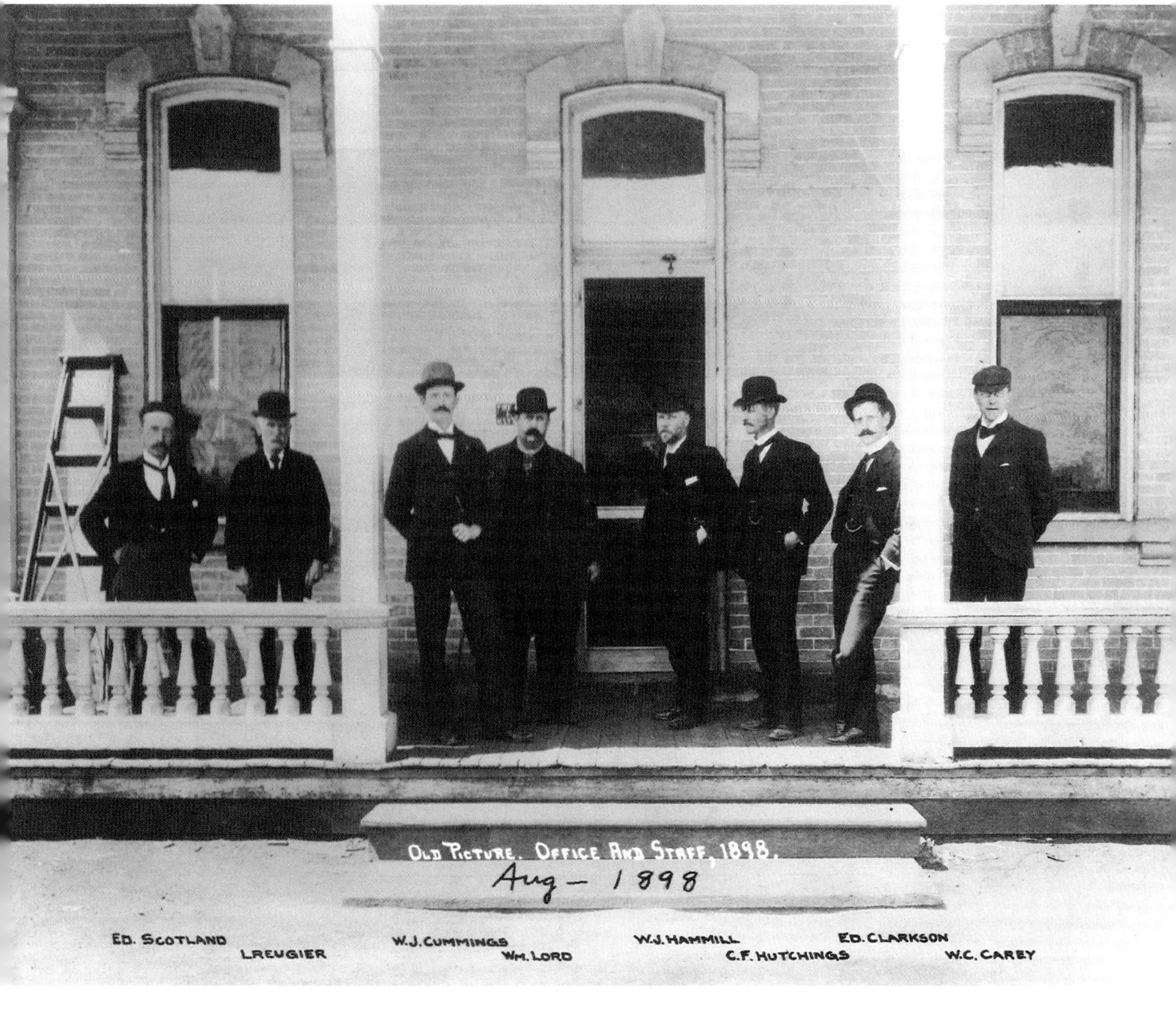

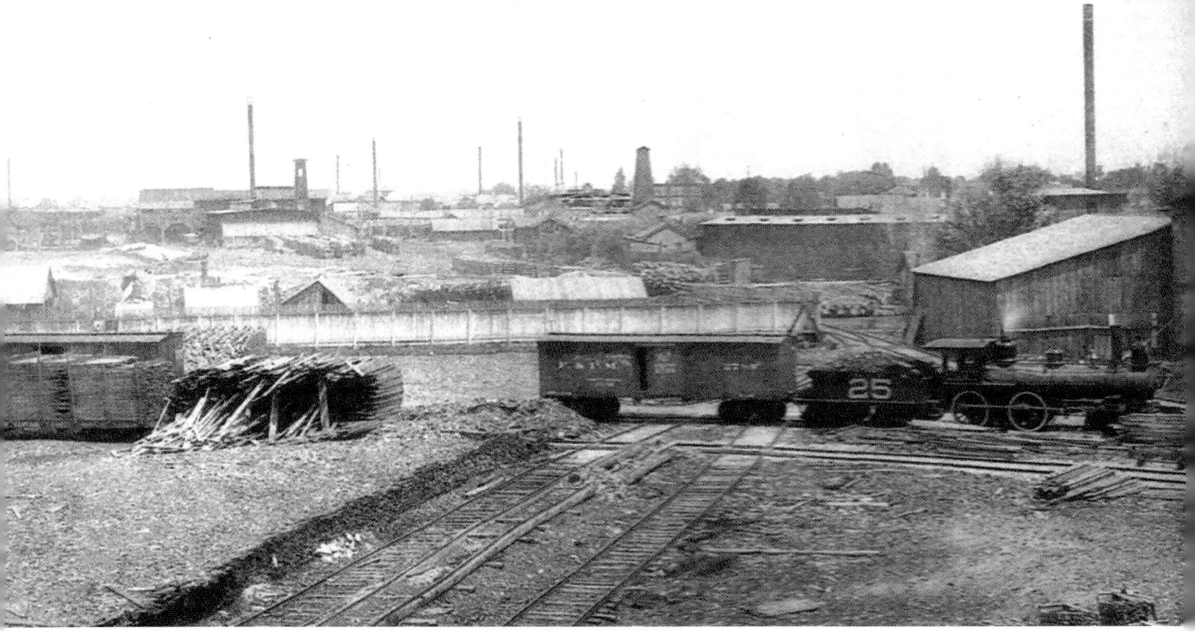

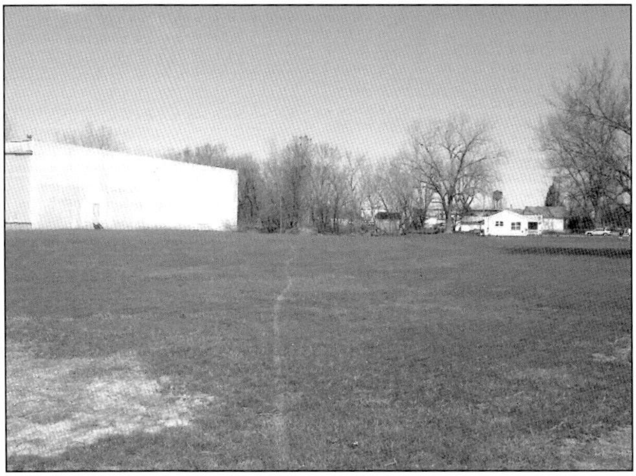

North from Former McGraw Mill.

North, from McGraw Mill. When this 1888 picture was published, the view was from Harrison and 41st Streets looking north. Most likely, we are viewing Bousfield and Company that was at 37th Street, and the Birdsall and Barker Lumber and Salt Mill, which was the property nearest the river. Today, it is a much more tranquil view.

BIRD'S-EYE VIEW FROM WATERWORKS. The Waterworks was located at the foot of North Trumbull just north of the intersection at North Water Street. This picture probably shows the Eddy Sheldon Company lumberyard and Eddy Brothers and Company Yard. The 1886–1887 Polk City Directory gives the address as 2941 North Water Street. Today, it is a pleasant grassy area.

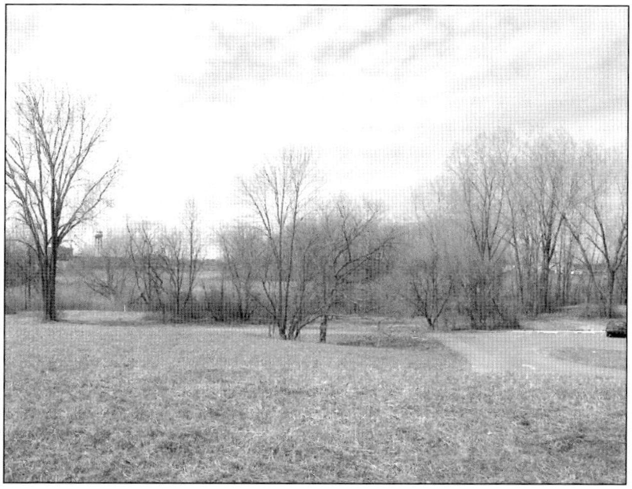

BIRD'S-EYE VIEW FROM FORMER WATERWORKS SITE.

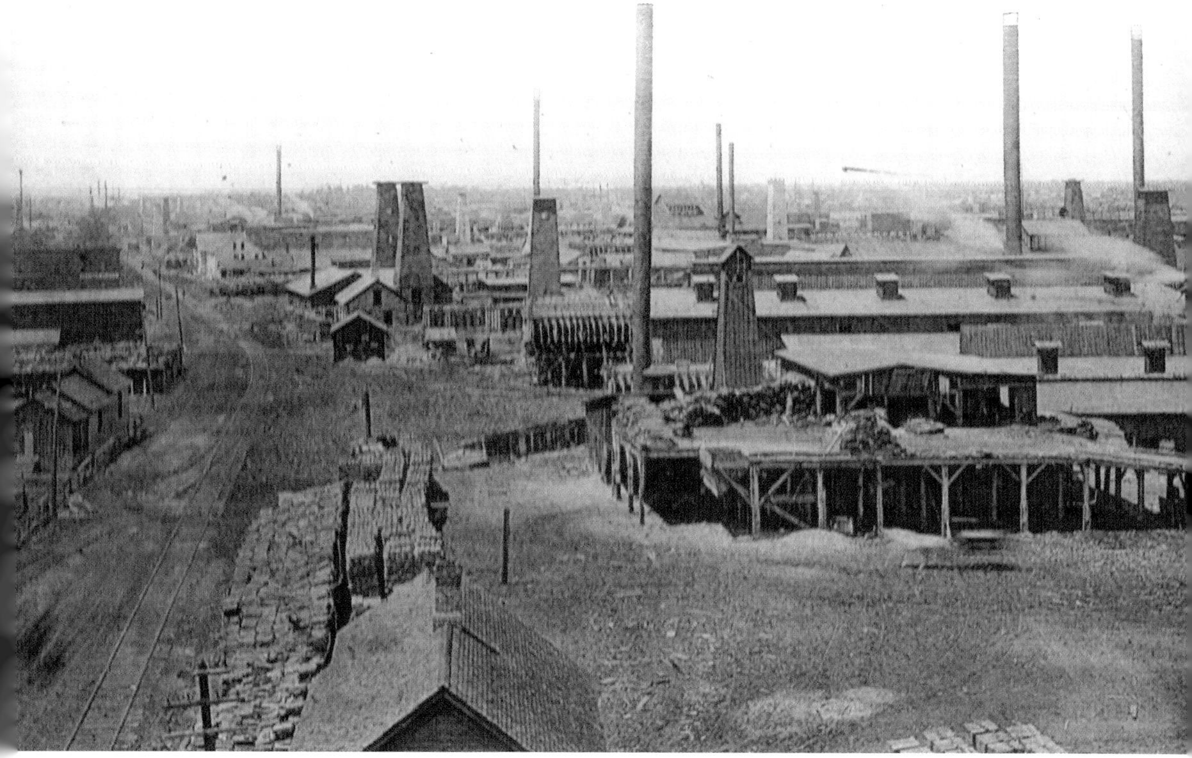

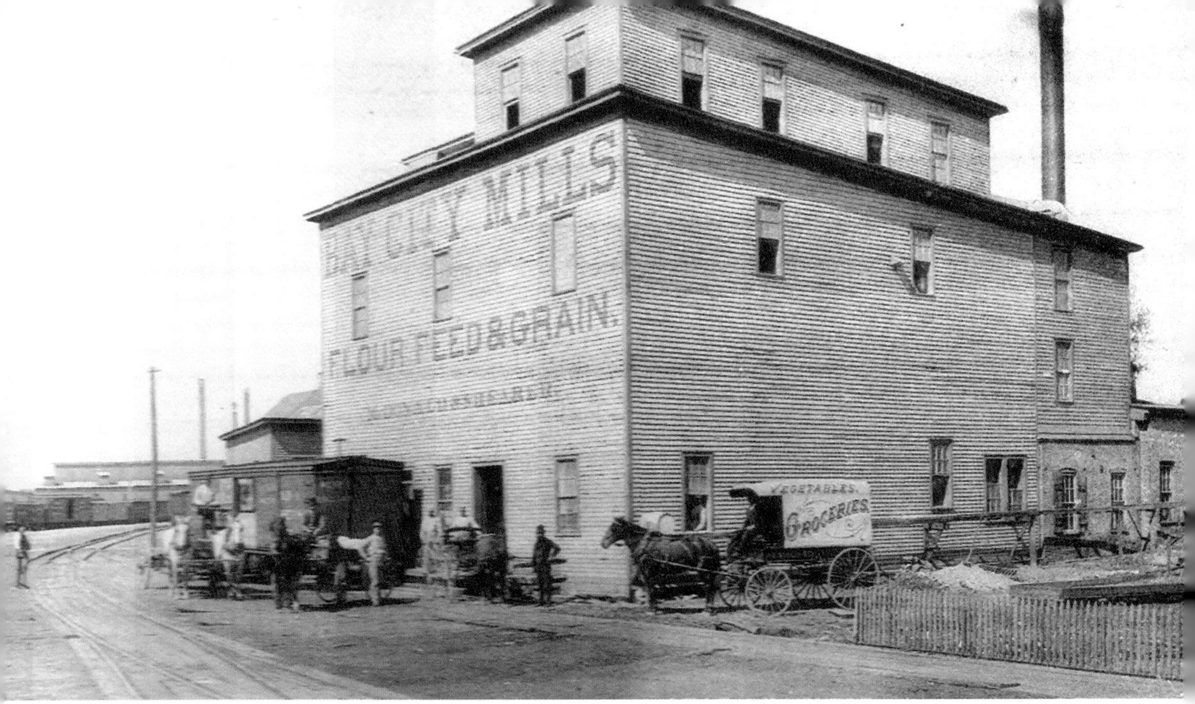

BAY CITY MILLS. The Bay City Mills, also known as the J.N. McDonald & Company Mill, was located on the corner of First and Water Streets according to the 1868 Directory. It was built as a gristmill in late 1867 and could produce 20 barrels of grain a day with its two runs of stones. This equated to 100,000 bushels a year, which was all sold locally. The place where flour, feed, and grain were once sold is now an empty lot.

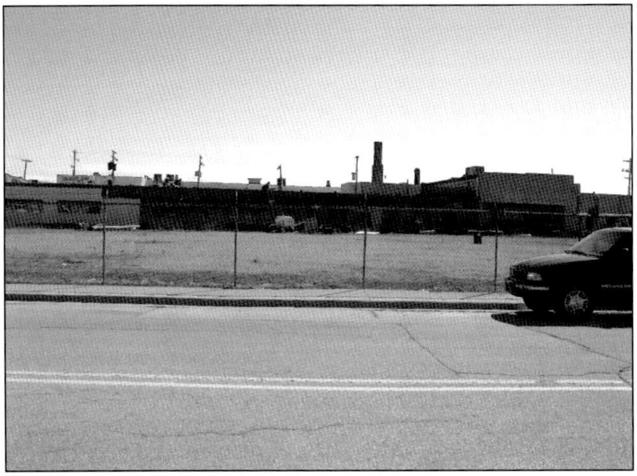

FORMER SITE OF BAY CITY MILLS.

BOUTELL BROS. OFFICE. In 1897, the Boutell Brothers (William and Lorenzo) established their fuel and mason supplies store on the west side of Water Street near Second Street with their office at First and Water. Their kilns provided a product called Kelly Lime. They were touted as handling the highest grade of coal. Their Lehigh Coal "burns to less Clinkers than any other coal" according to an 1898 ad. The "now" picture shows the view near the river at First and Water Streets.

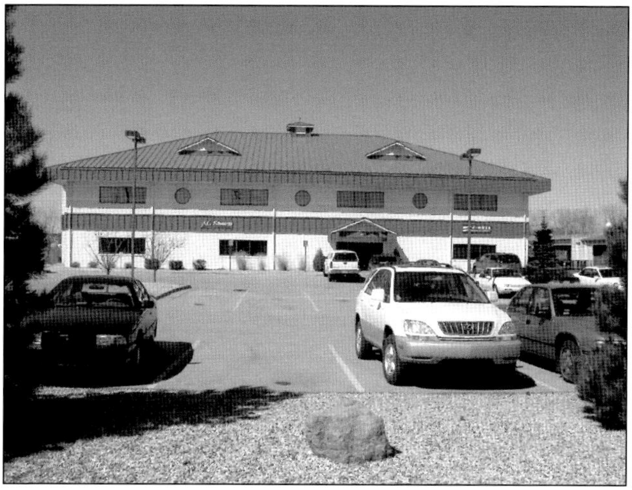

FORMER SITE OF BOUTELL BROTHERS.

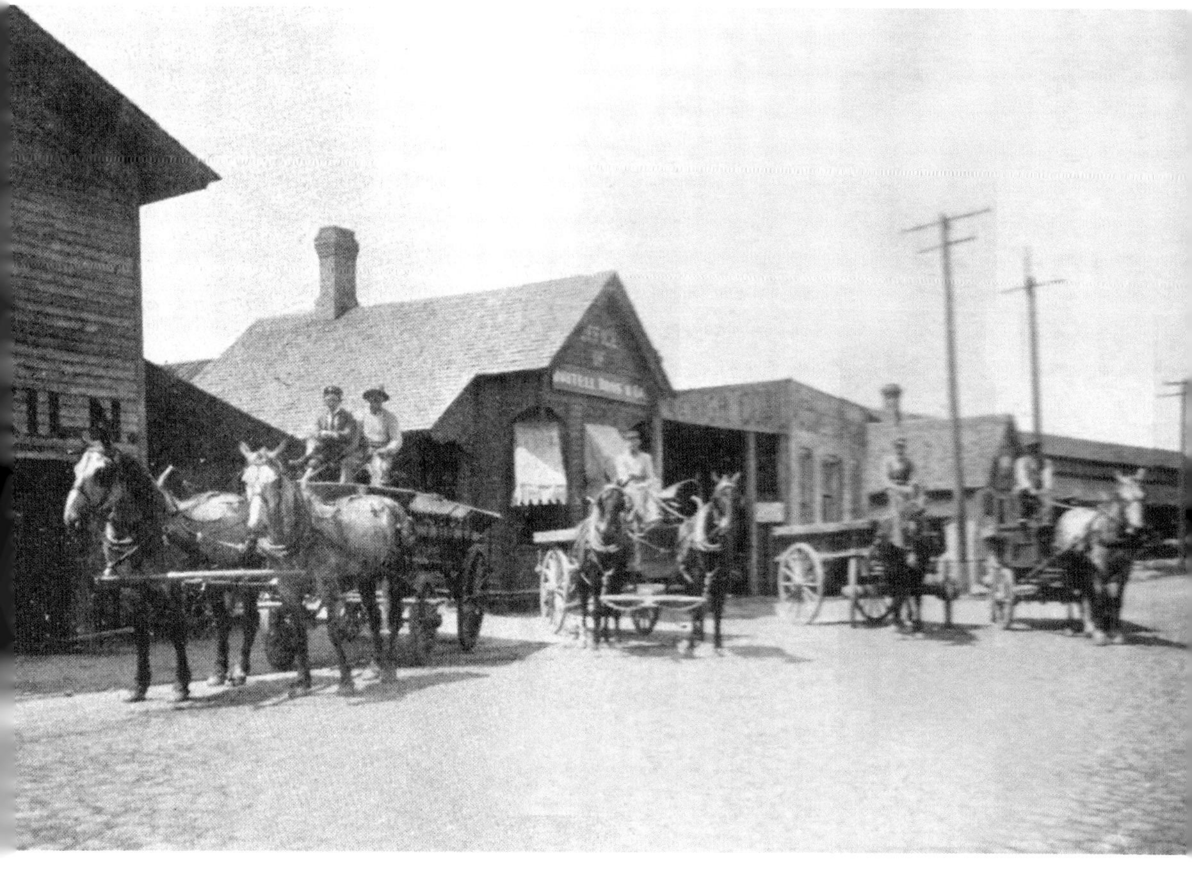

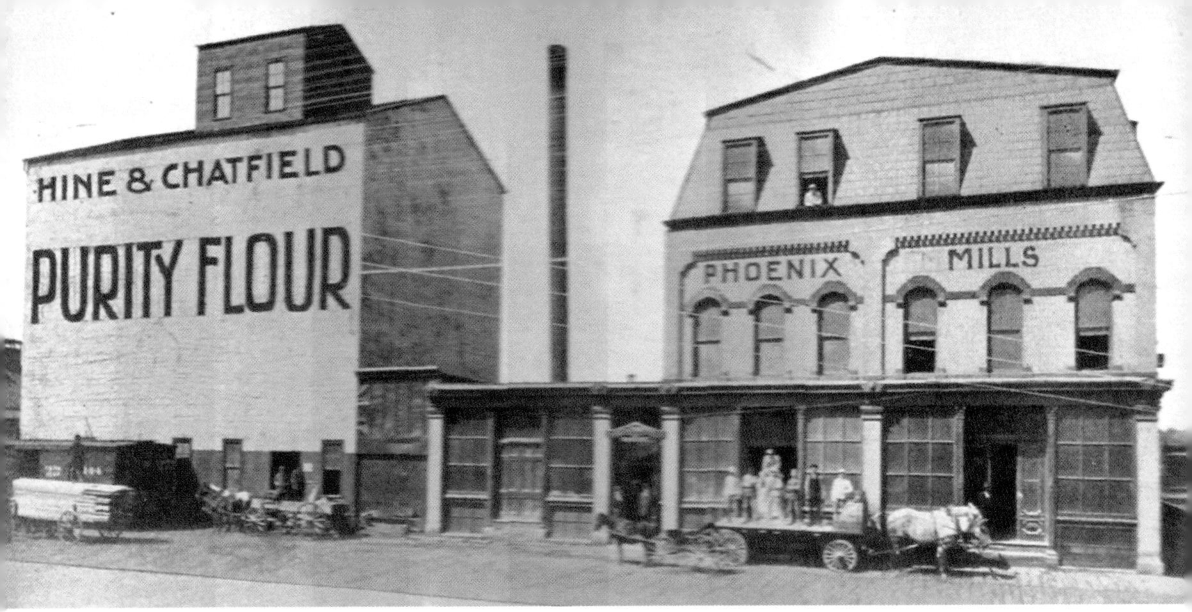

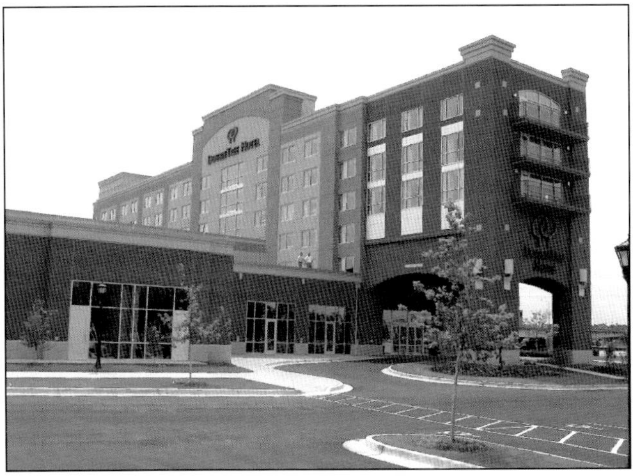

HINE & CHATFIELD. In 1883, Hine & Chatfield purchased the Phoenix Flouring Mills and Elevator at 513 North Water Street. In that year, they had a capacity of 250 barrels of flour and 20 tons of feed. They could also store 60,000 barrels. The claim was made that their Purity brand flour was the best winter-wheat flour made in northern Michigan. Besides flour, they bought and sold grass seeds and seed grains year-round. When a fire completely destroyed the mill in 1886, a new mill was built and named the Phoenix Mill. The beautiful new Doubletree Hotel is just north of the original location.

DOUBLETREE HOTEL.

CRUMP MANUFACTURING. The Crump Manufacturing Co. began doing business in West Bay City in 1881. They employed over 100 men, manufacturing wholesale and retail lumber materials including fancy and dovetail boxes, crating, box shooks, siding, and flooring. This building is the second on the site, the first was destroyed by fire in 1888. Rousseau O. Crump was a three-term congressman with a reputation for integrity. He died in 1902. A plaque marks the Crump factory location in Veteran's Park. The Nate Doan Santa house was moved near the Crump location.

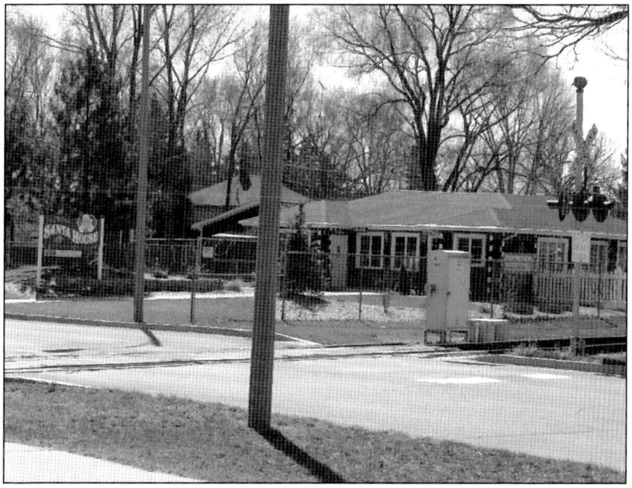

NATE DOAN SANTA HOUSE.

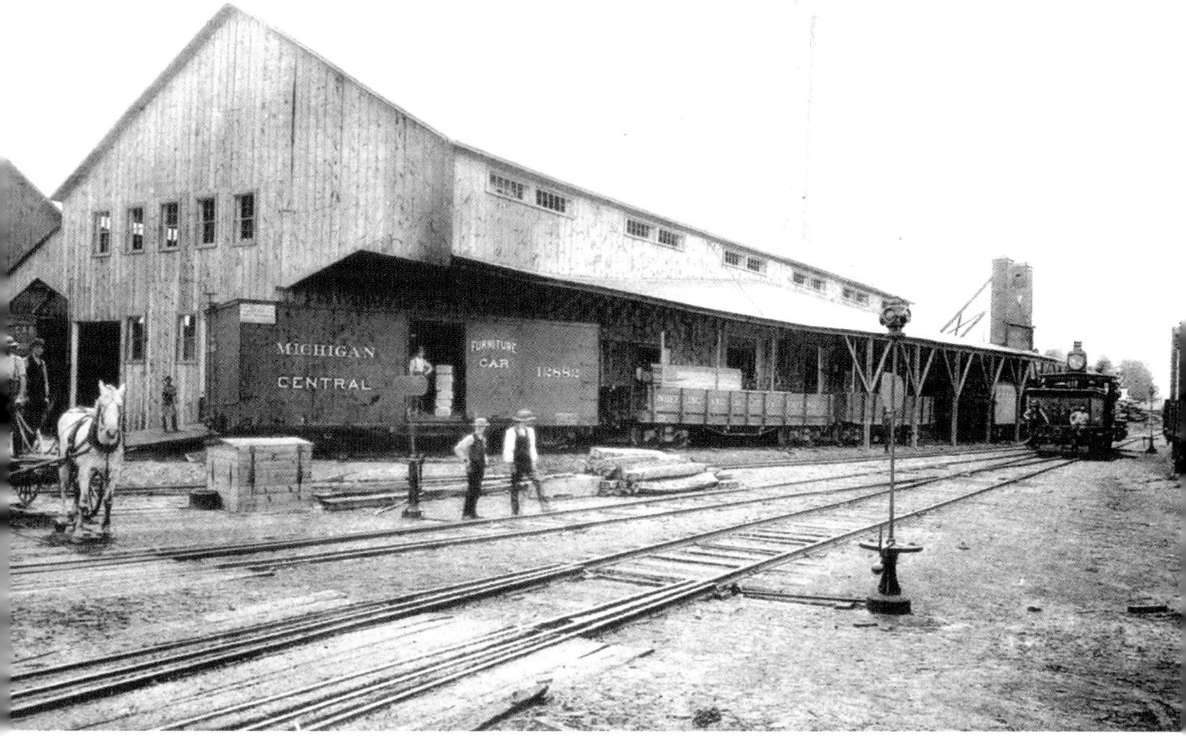

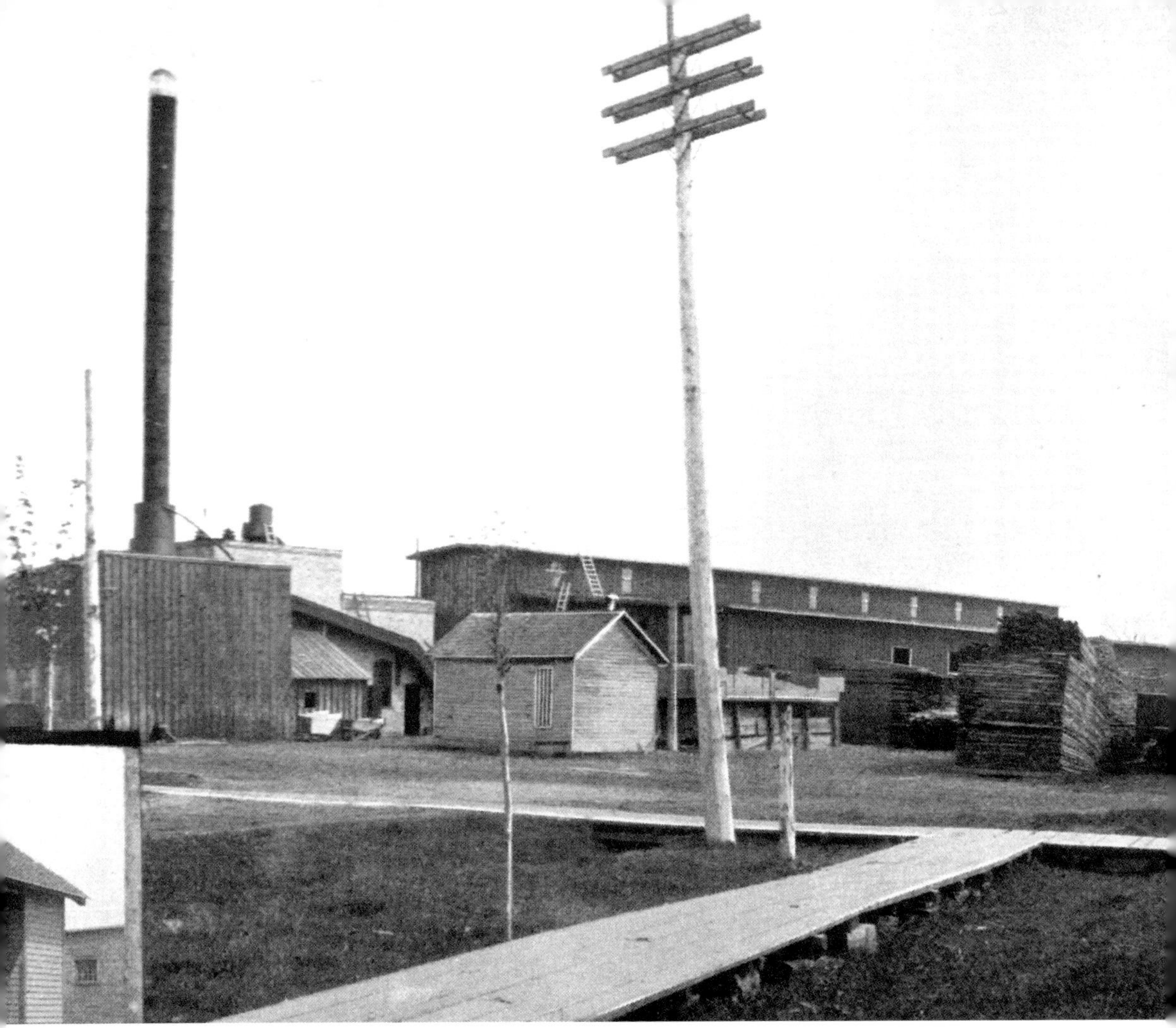

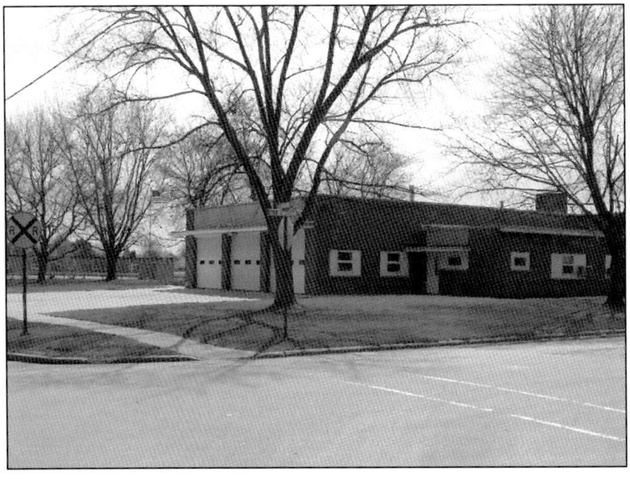

FORMER MICHIGAN BOX.

MICHIGAN BOX. Michigan Box Company was one of seven box-making companies listed in the 1895 Polk City Directory. The business was located on the east side of Jennison Avenue, south of the corner of Fremont near the Flint & Pere Marquette railroad tracks. By 1906, the property was used by the Quaker Shade Roller Company. Today, a fire station stands there, just west of MacGregor School.

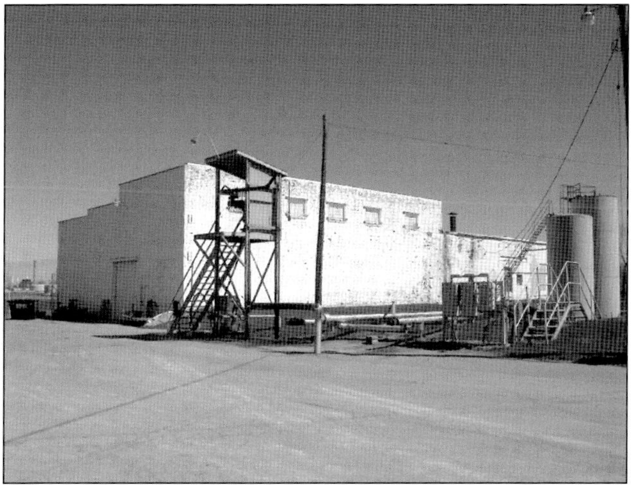

FORMER MICHIGAN CHEMICAL.

MICHIGAN CHEMICAL. Local author Les Arndt wrote that Michigan Chemical developed in relation to the emerging sugar beet industry at the turn of the last century. It was located at 321 Woodside Avenue in Essexville (near Scheurmann Street) and portions of the original building are still standing. Michigan Chemical produced fertilizer from beet waste. Today it is the home of Liquidfuels.

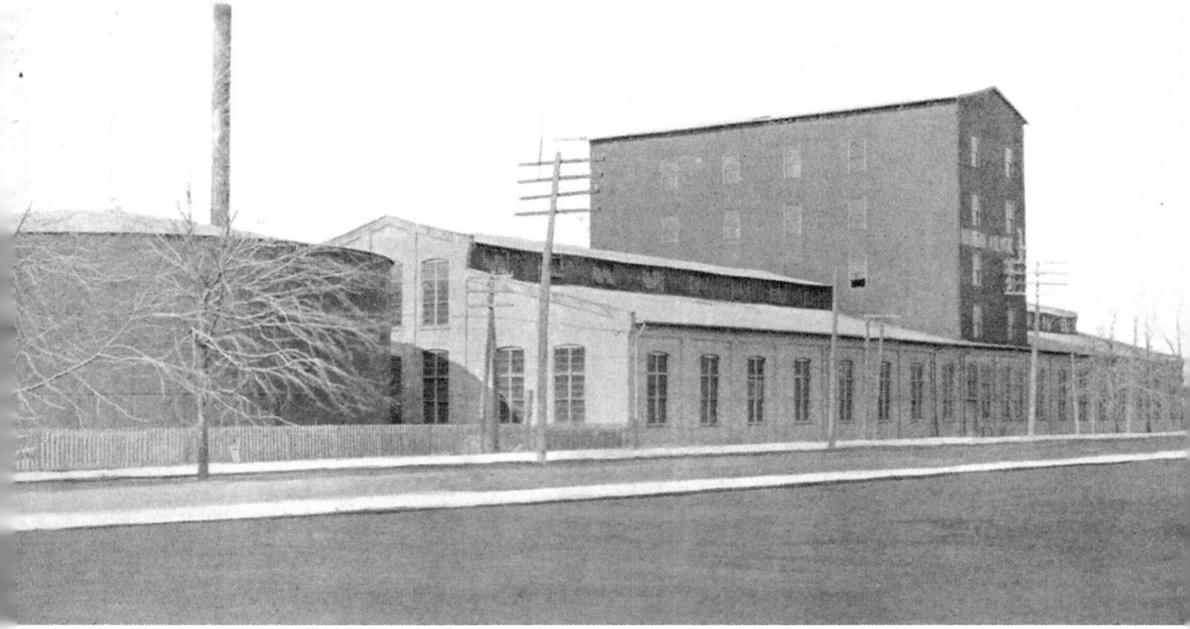

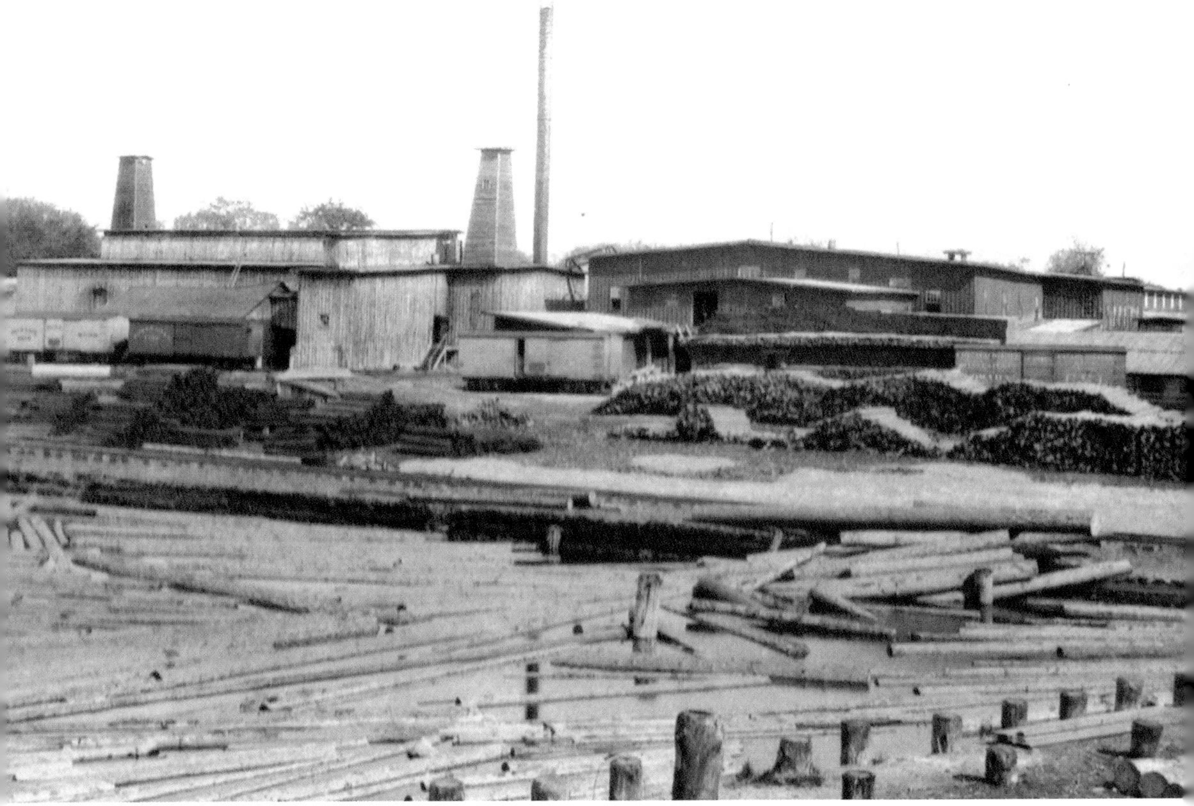

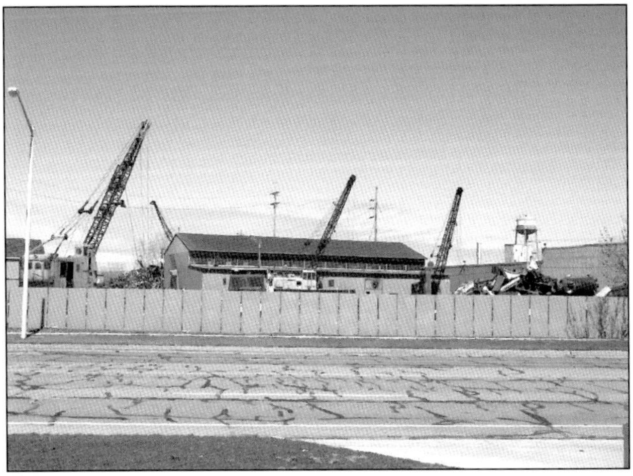

FORMER MICHIGAN PIPEWORKS.

MICHIGAN PIPEWORKS. While it sounds unusual today, with the abundance of lumber 150 years ago, it was natural to find other uses for wood. One of those uses was water pipes. Michigan Pipeworks was located at the foot of Madison Avenue near the western end of what is now the General Motors Powertrain plant. The plant covered 50 acres, employed 50 men in 1882, and produced 500,000 feet of pipe in 1883. For many years, H. Hirschfield & Sons Scrapyard occupied the eastern edge of the site, where OmniSource operates today.

MICHIGAN SUGAR FACTORY. Author Thomas Mahar describes Michigan Sugar, located at Woodside and Scheurmann Streets in Essexville, as the first successful sugar beet processing plant in Michigan. As the supply of trees dwindled at the end of the 1800s, lumberjacks were looking for work and lumber owners were looking for new ways to make money. Many went to work in the sugar factory. The factory ceased operations in the early 1930s. Today the warehouse building houses Hydorn Carpet, Berner Medical Systems, and Lakeshore Diagnostics.

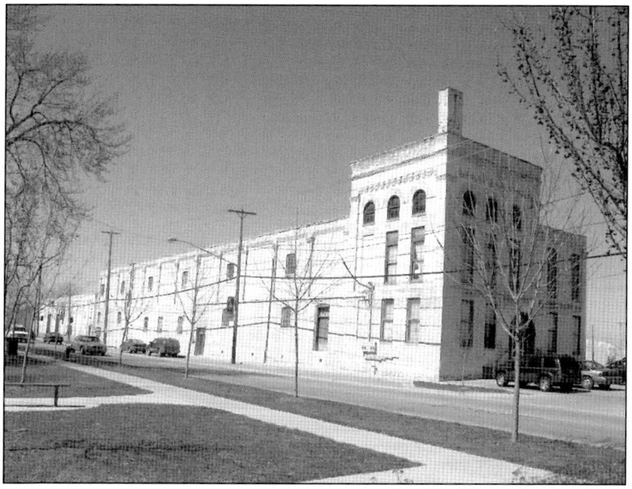

FORMER MICHIGAN SUGAR FACTORY.

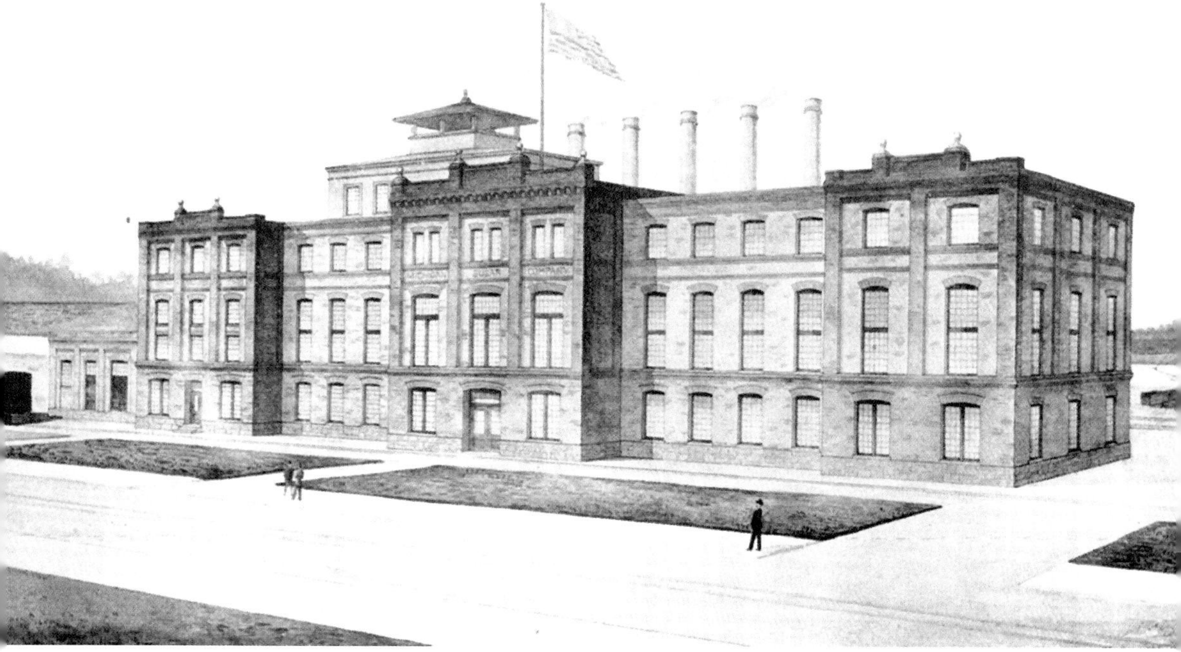

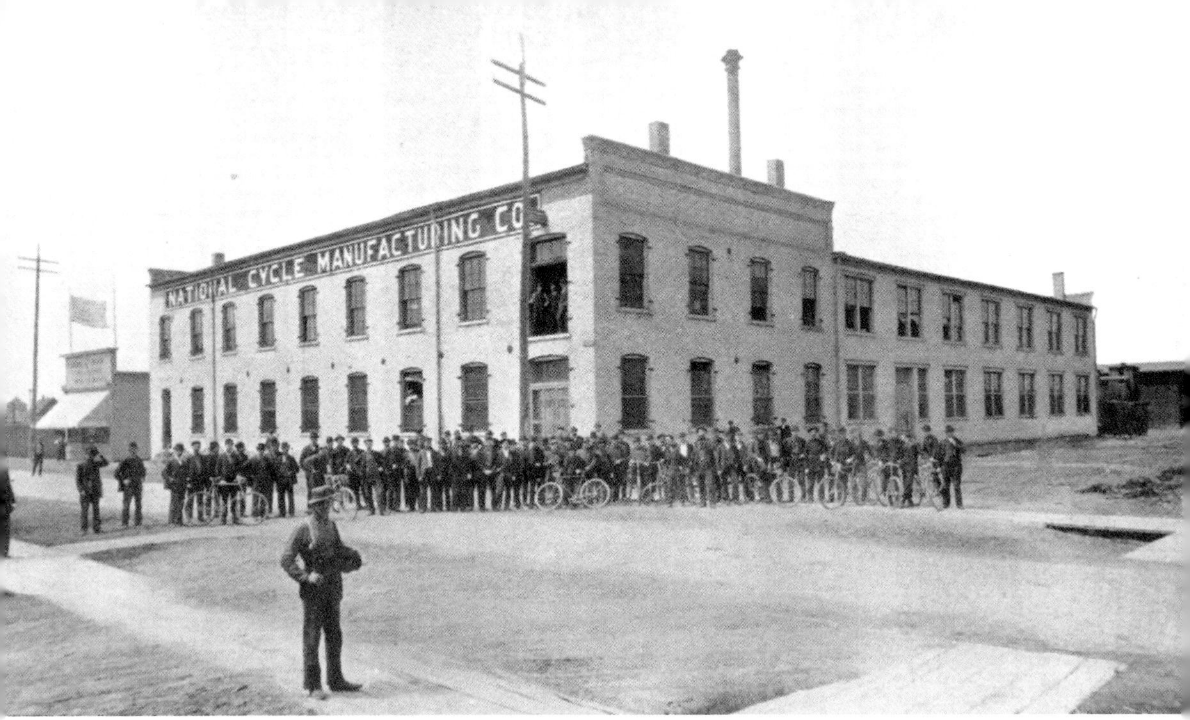

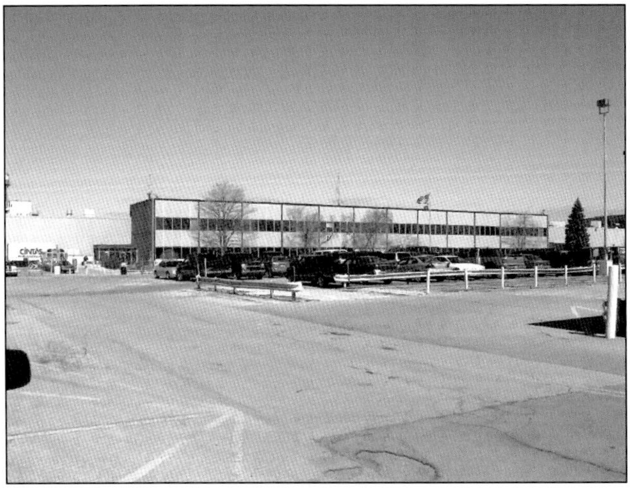

POWERTRAIN.

NATIONAL CYCLE. From 1892 to 1915, National Cycle bicycles were manufactured at this plant at Madison and Crotty Streets with Henry B. Smith as president. As bicycles captured the heart of the nation, the National was recognized as a quality product, priced from $50 to $125. The company also produced a few Natco trucks in its last few years. It was sold to Louis Chevrolet in 1916. A lot of carburetors were made there over the years. It is the GM Powertrain plant today.

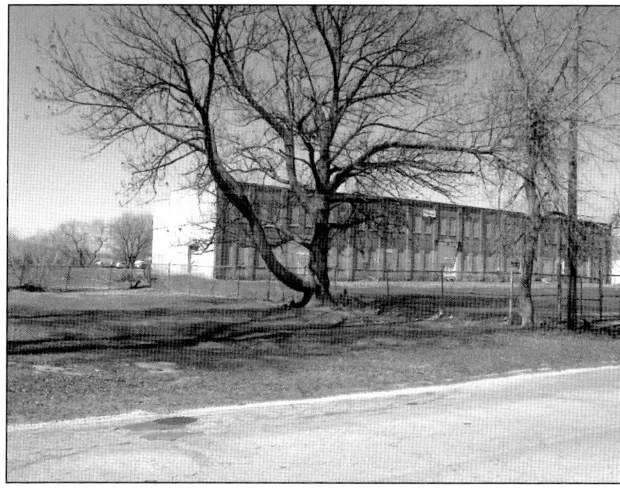

FORMER PARAMOUNT CIGAR SITE.

PARAMOUNT CIGAR FACTORY. The address of the Paramount Cigar Factory in 1883 was 600 Harrison Street. Bay City made cigars for many years. The 1873 Directory lists 18 manufactures of cigars. Strangely enough, by 1879 only two are listed. But, in 1895, 17 were listed and Paramount had been renamed Bateman and Fox. Today, it's just a grassy area.

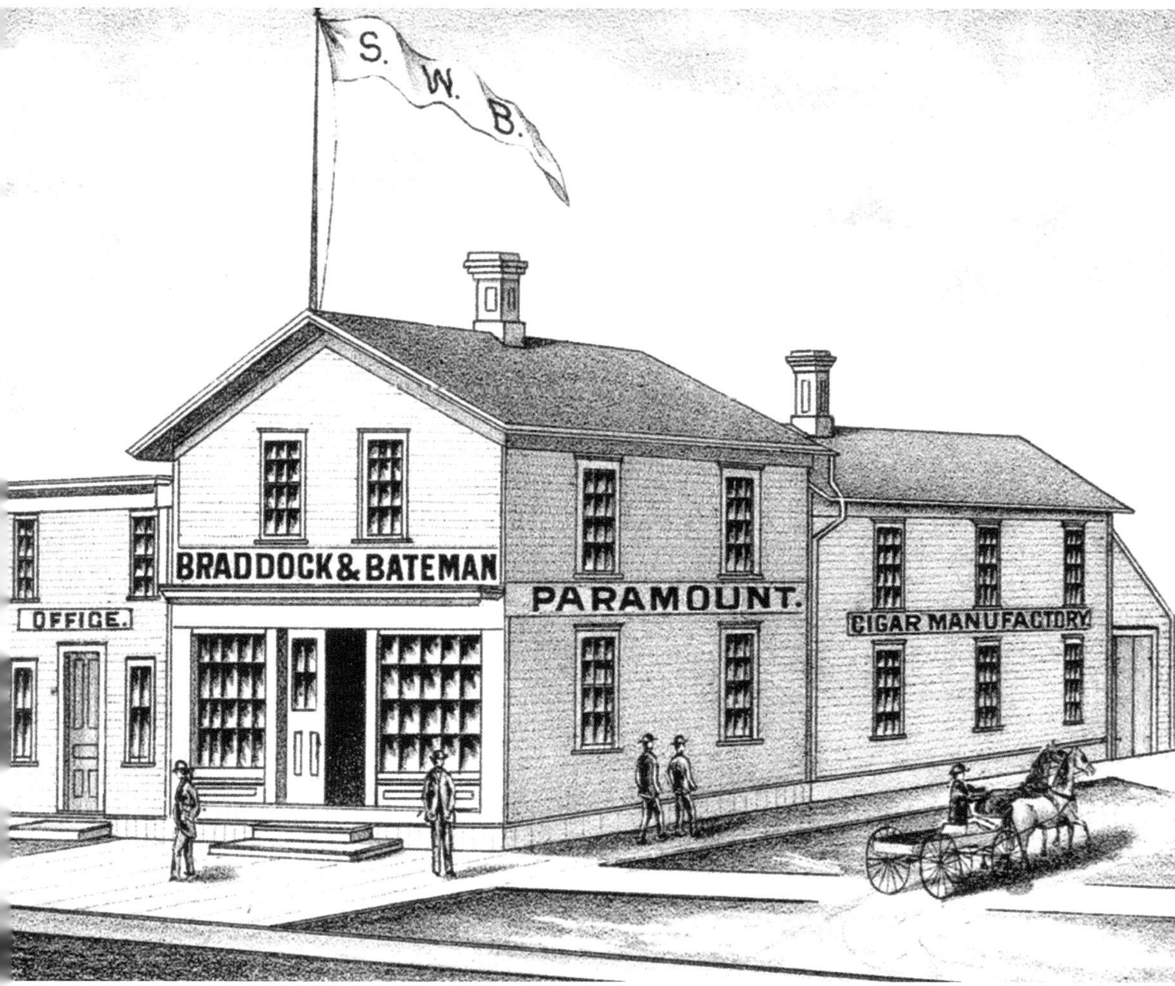

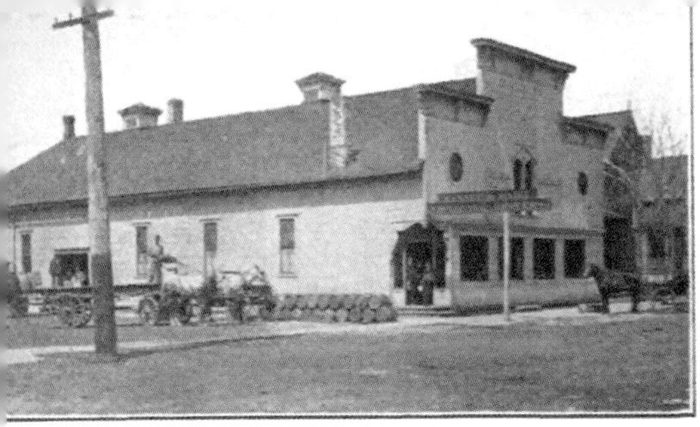

TANNER & DAILY, WHOLESALE GROCERS

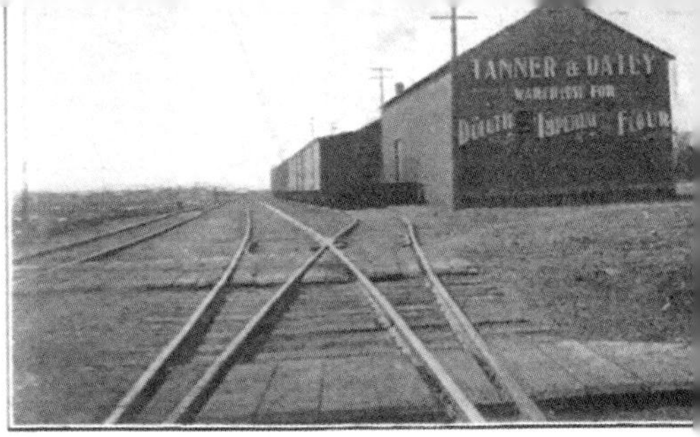

TANNER & DAILY, WAREHOUSE No 1

ANNER & DAILY

Jas. R. Tanner H. J. Daily

WHOLESALE GROCERS

ST BAY CITY, MICH.

Wholesale
Distributers for
Duluth Imperial Fl

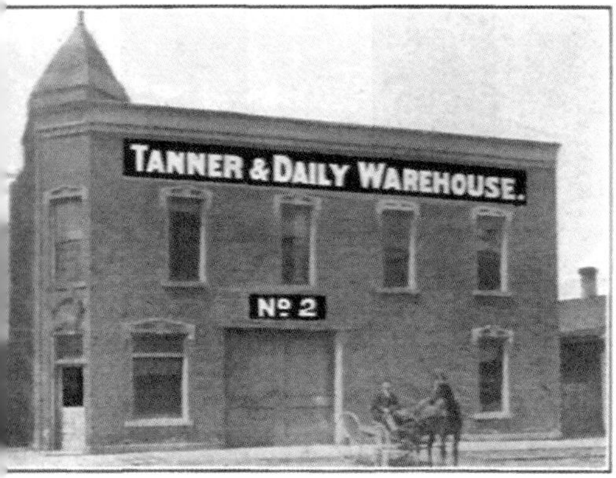

TANNER & DAILY, WAREHOUSE No. 2

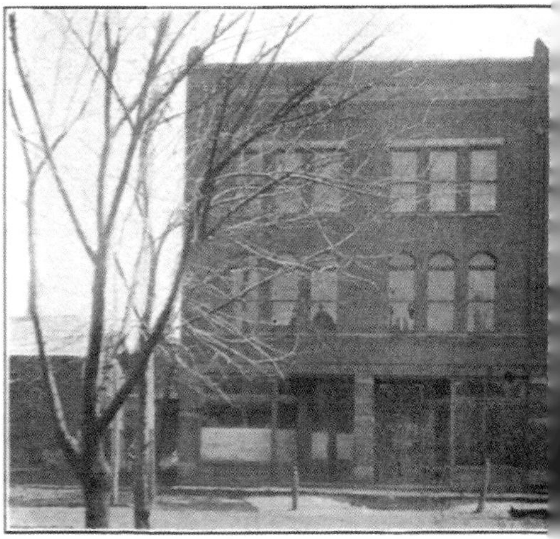

TANNER & DAILY, WAREHOUSE No. 3

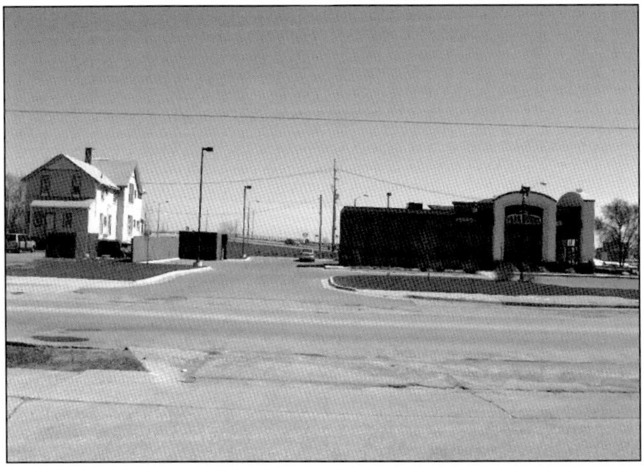

FORMER SITE OF TANNER & DAILY.

TANNER & DAILY. The corner of Linn and Michigan Streets (now Linn and Walnut) was the home of the main office of the wholesale grocer, Tanner & Daily. Originally Walsh & Tanner, it took the Tanner & Daily name in 1901. The firm of James R. Tanner and Harry J. Daily served northern Michigan and required four warehouses for their stock. The West Side Opera House was also part of what became their showroom. Papa John's Pizza is located just east of where their showroom once stood.

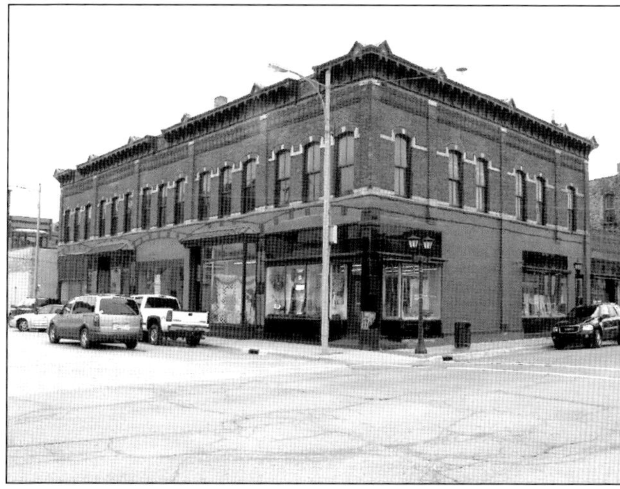

FORMER TIERNEY'S.

TIERNEY'S BIG BICYCLE STORE. Edward and James Tierney had whatever you needed, whether it was a National Cycle, sporting goods, real estate, or a loan. They were located at 200 to 204 Fifth Street. In an 1898 ad, they stated that the store was open until 12 o'clock midnight during the wheeling months. In addition to carrying seven lines of bicycles, they also had 100 bicycles to rent. The driver of the van in front of the present-day store is Mrs. Kim Rodriguez with her triplets, Adam, Becca, and Samantha.

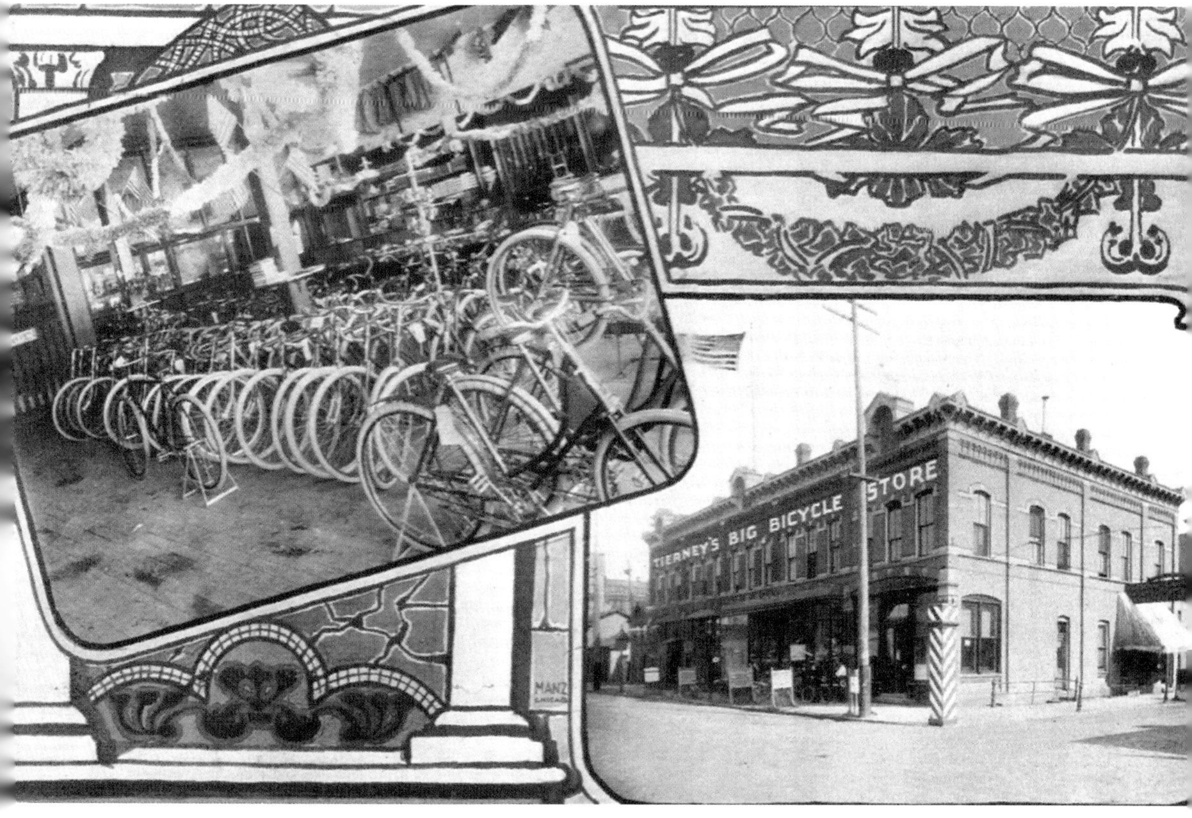

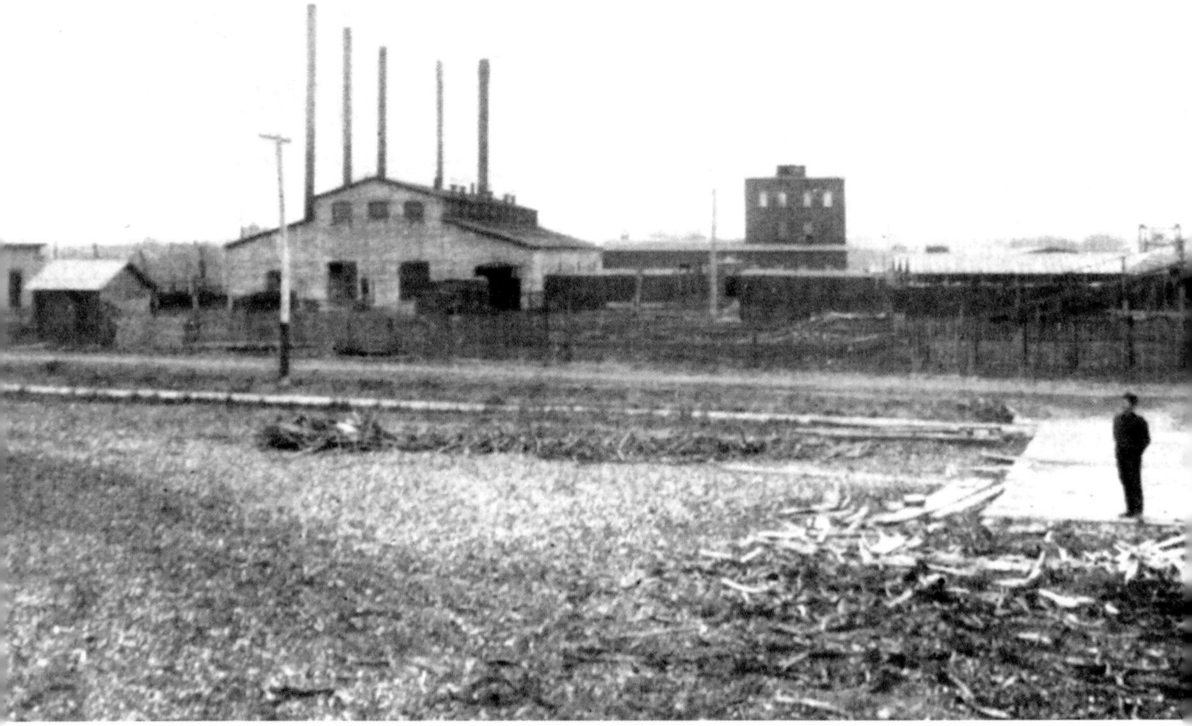

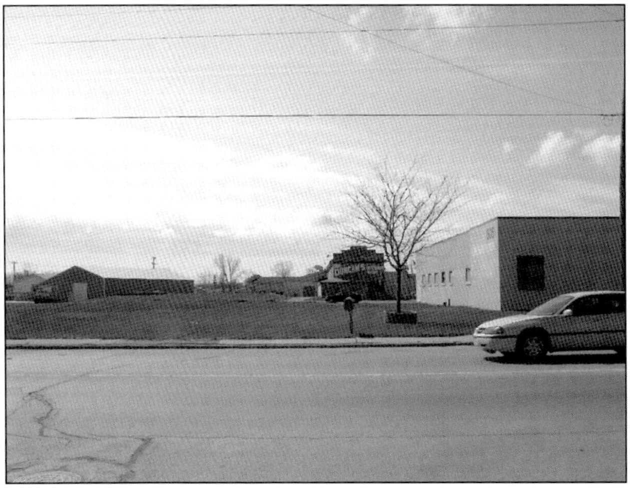

Former W.D. Young.

W.D. Young. The W.D. Young Chemical and Flooring Factories were both located on the southeast corner of Salzburg and Warner Streets with an address of 509–603 Salzburg. Walter D. Young came to Bay City in 1870 and was involved in a log-towing company, the Bay City Brewing Co., the Young Transportation Co., the Young Coal and Wood Co., and his flooring plant which was famed for the quality of its product, the "Finest Maple Flooring." Duncan's Sport's Shop is in the only building that still remains.

Chapter 4
SERVICES

FIRE STATIONS. A city with so much wood naturally had a lot of fire stations. This 1898 picture shows six of them. No. 1 served as headquarters on Washington Avenue, located just north of the State Theater. No. 2 stood at 213 Belinda Street, a street eliminated by the Independence Bridge. No. 3 still stands on the first block of Washington Avenue. No. 4 was at 34th and Taylor Streets. No. 5 was at 413 Lafayette Street, and No. 6 was at Seventh and Johnson.

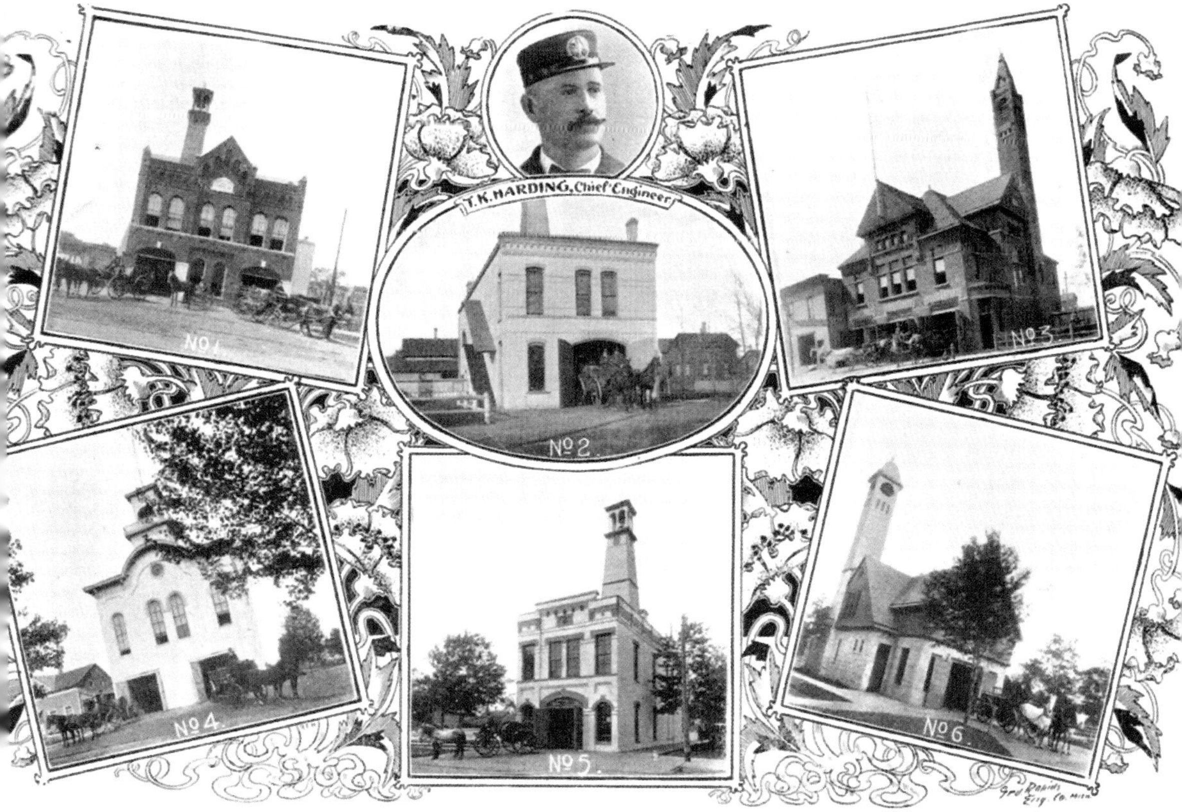

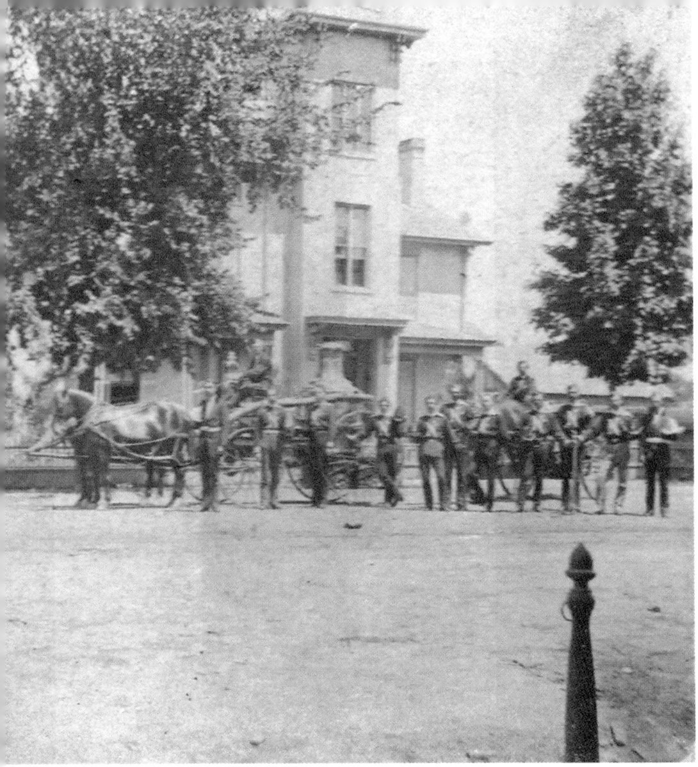

Neptune Fire Company. In 1883, Bay City had four hose companies and one hook and ladder company. They were Co. No. 1 Vigilant Hose Company and steamer "Neptune," No. 2 Neptune Hose Company on the east side of Saginaw Street between Center and Fifth Streets, No. 3 Rescue Company, No. 4 Night Hawk hose company, steam fire engine Alert, and Hook & Ladder. My best guess is that the Neptune Company (taken as a stereoview) was on Saginaw Street near the site of my "now" picture of Old City Hall restaurant which was in the neighborhood.

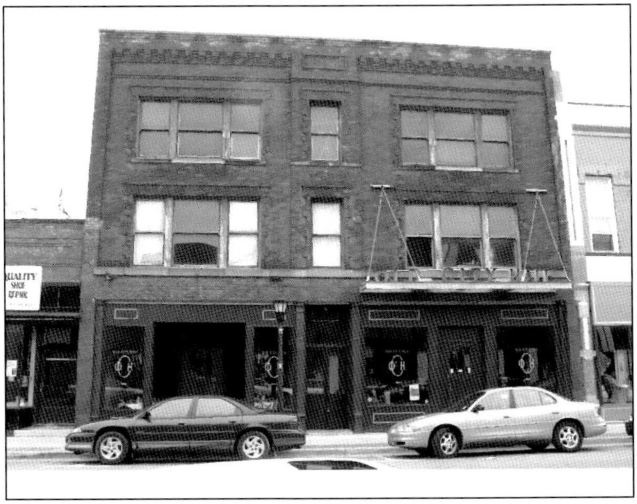

Old City Hall.

FIRE DEPARTMENT HEADQUARTERS. This was the Second Ward fire station and hose house located on Washington between Fourth and Fifth Streets. It was enlarged and altered in 1904 and ultimately replaced by the modern new fire station built on the corner of McKinley and Adams Streets in 1913. It was replaced because the department was becoming motorized and horse-driven fire rigs became a thing of the past. The building still stands minus the hose tower, triangular centered roof, and horse barn doors, and is home to the Bay Arts Council, Man in the Moon, and Dock of the Bay. Not bad for an 1883 building.

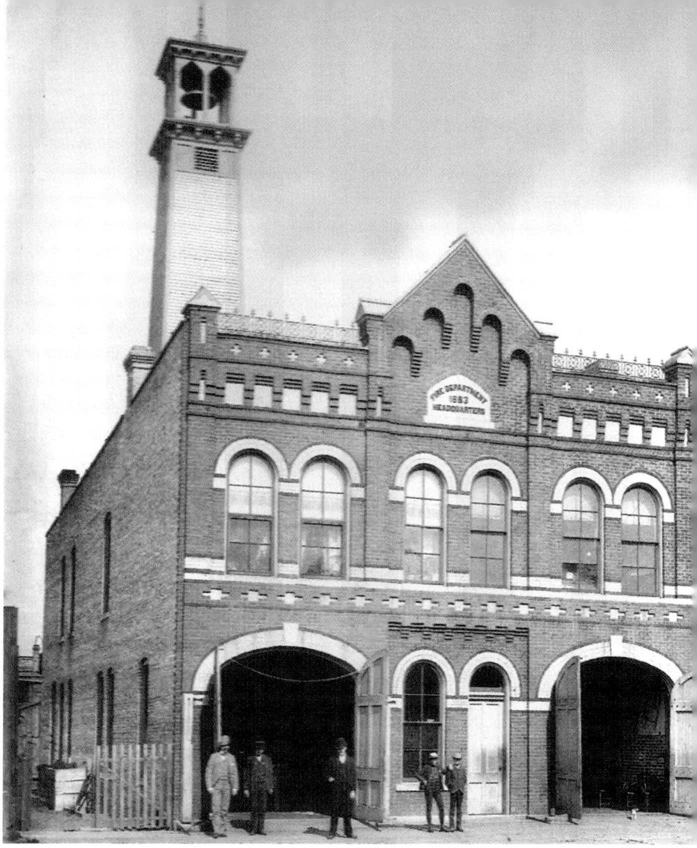

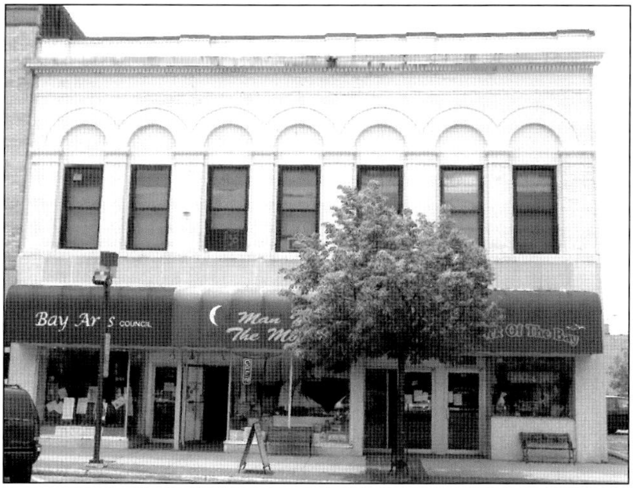

OLD FIRE STATION HEADQUARTERS.

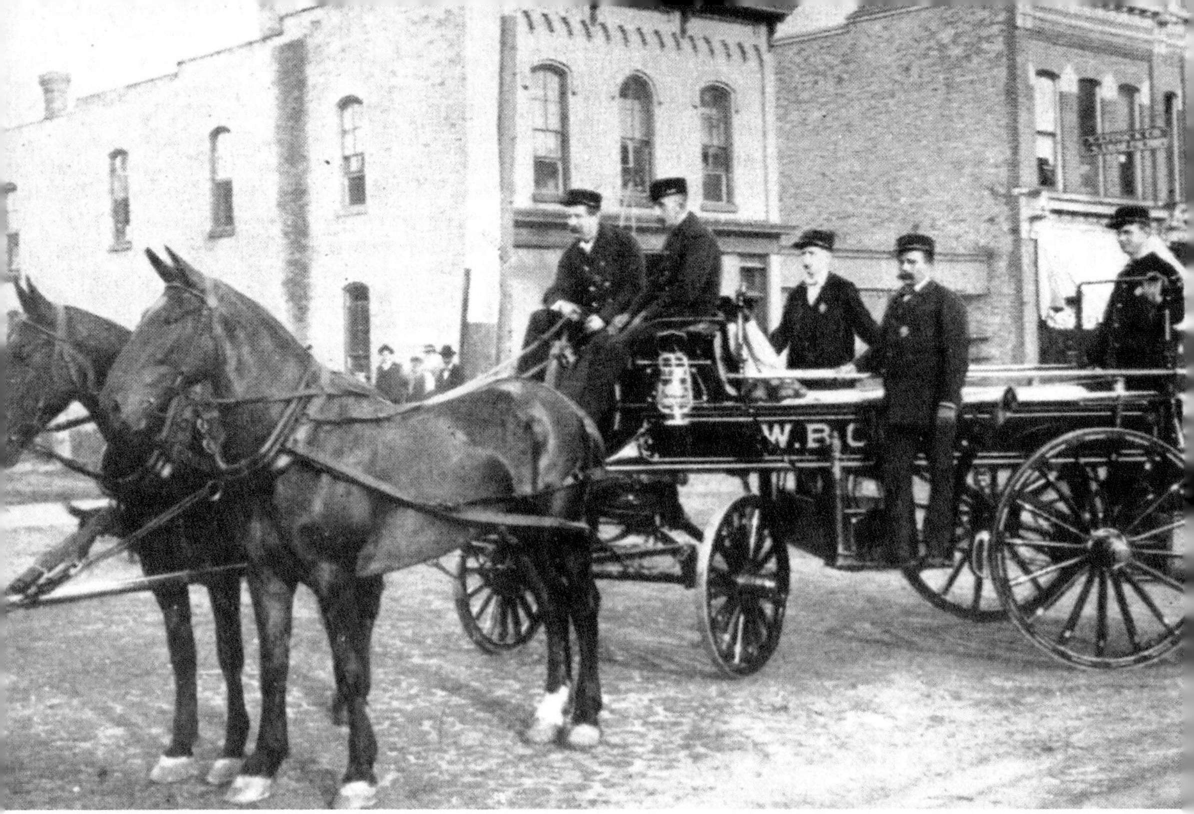

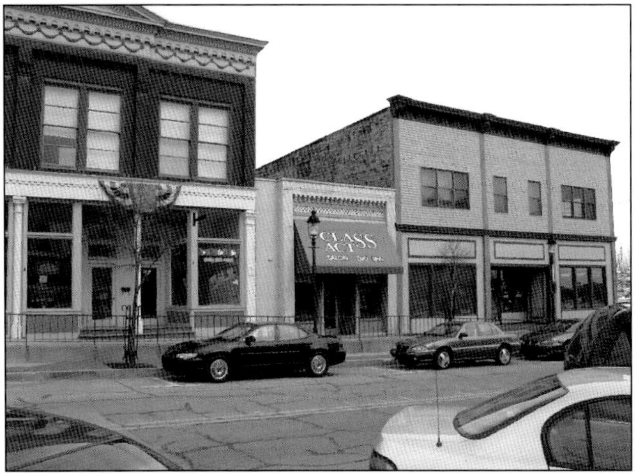

Fire Department Headquarters, West Side.

Fire Department Headquarters, West Side. West Bay City had its share of fires. By 1883, they had a steam engine, "Defiance," and three hose companies. Headquarters was on the corner of Linn and Michigan. There was a major fire in the business district on Midland Street in 1881. Chiefs included John Charters (three different times), Andrew Neat, George Russell, Godfrey Kubach, and Edwin Cook, who became assistant Bay City Fire Chief when the cities consolidated. The "now" picture was taken near the railroad tracks crossing Midland Street.

Bay County Jail. This building was erected in 1872 and razed in 1940. The second jail building in this location was used only for storage after the Law Enforcement building opened in 1978. Bay City was a tough town in the lumbering days due to the type of person a "frontier" town attracted. Many arrests were alcohol-related. The jail cost $35,000 to be built, and fronted the main public squares of Bay City. This spot will soon be renovated and become the new home of the main branch of the Bay County Library.

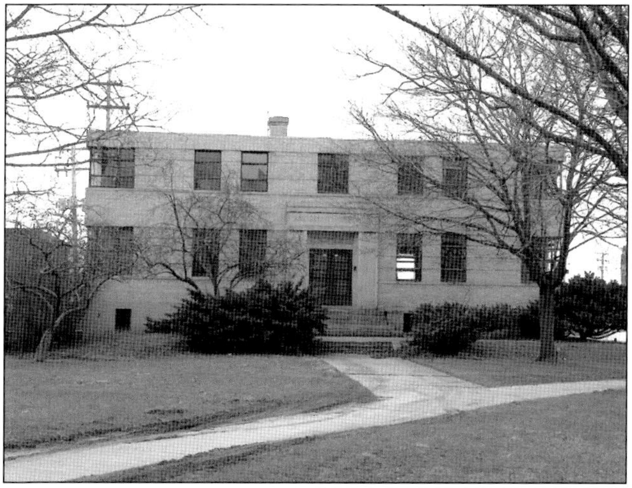

Bay County Jail Site.

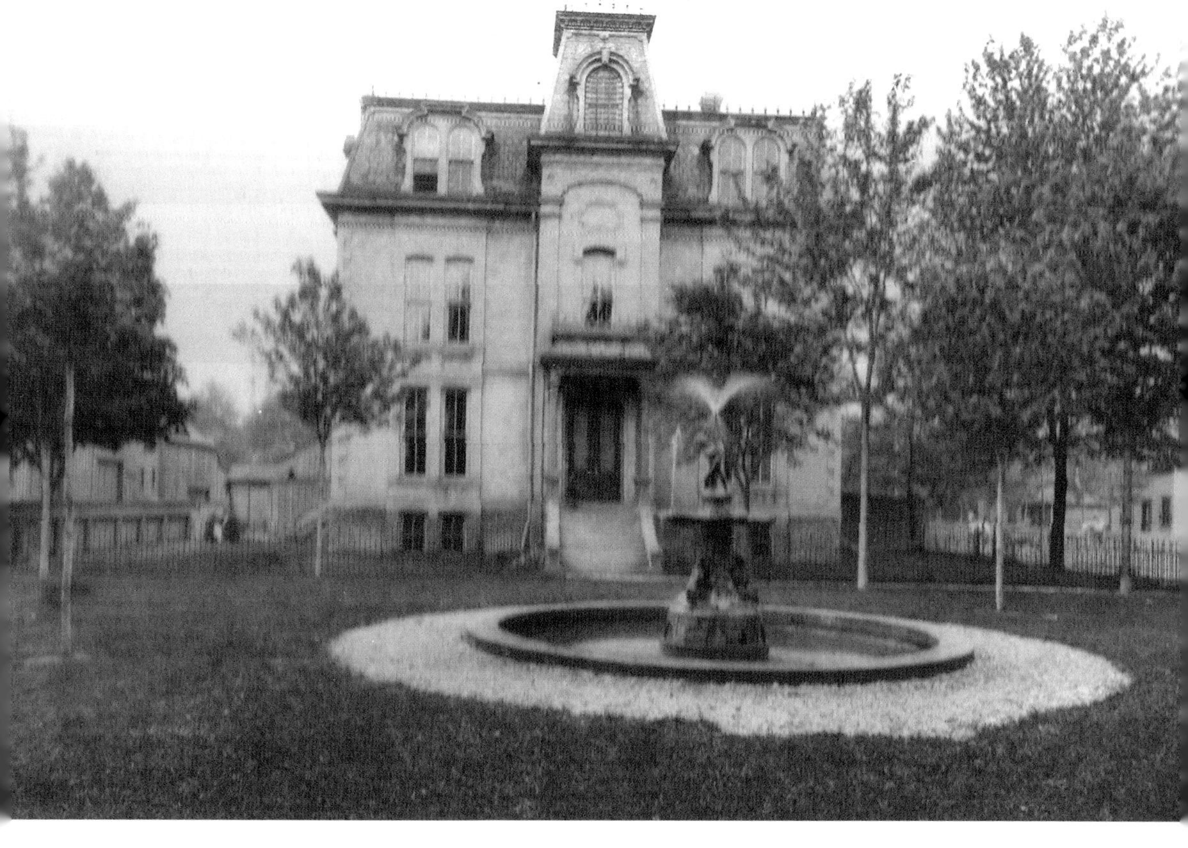

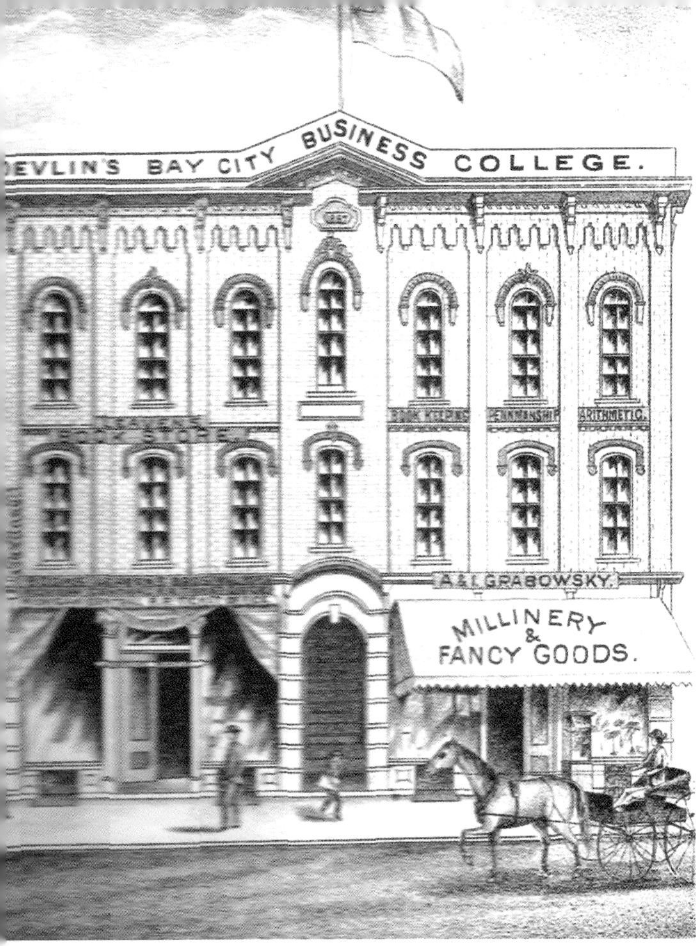

AVERILL BLOCK. Located on the north side of Center Avenue (just east of the Mill End store), the Averill Block was one of many commercial buildings to meet the new fire-resistant masonry code after several disastrous fires in the early 1860s. Built in 1867, it enjoyed a prominent address at 107 Center, right across from the Fraser House. Devlin's Business College was there for a short time. Today, the Averill Block houses Mulligan's Pub and Waltzing Matilda.

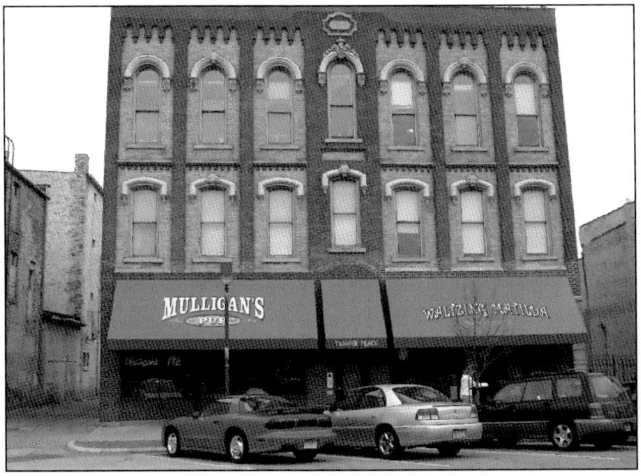

MULLIGAN'S.

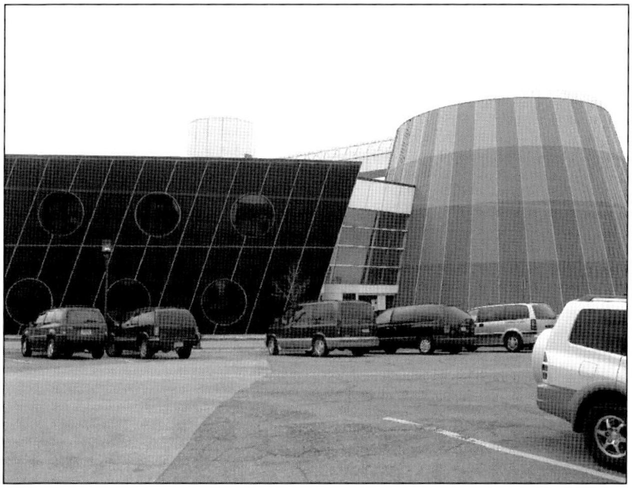

DELTA COLLEGE PLANETARIUM.

C.D. VAIL AND FRASER HOUSE. Built in 1865, the Fraser House was considered the best-furnished hotel in the Saginaw Valley. It had 75 guest chambers and a magnificent dining room. The first floor had various retail stores and an entrance that led to the Public Hall. C.D. Vail stocked the latest hats and other haberdashery items. The Fraser burned in a spectacular fire on December 23, 1906, and was replaced with the classic "fireproof" Wenonah Hotel in 1908. The Wenona burned on December 10, 1977. The Delta College Planetarium replaced the Wenonah.

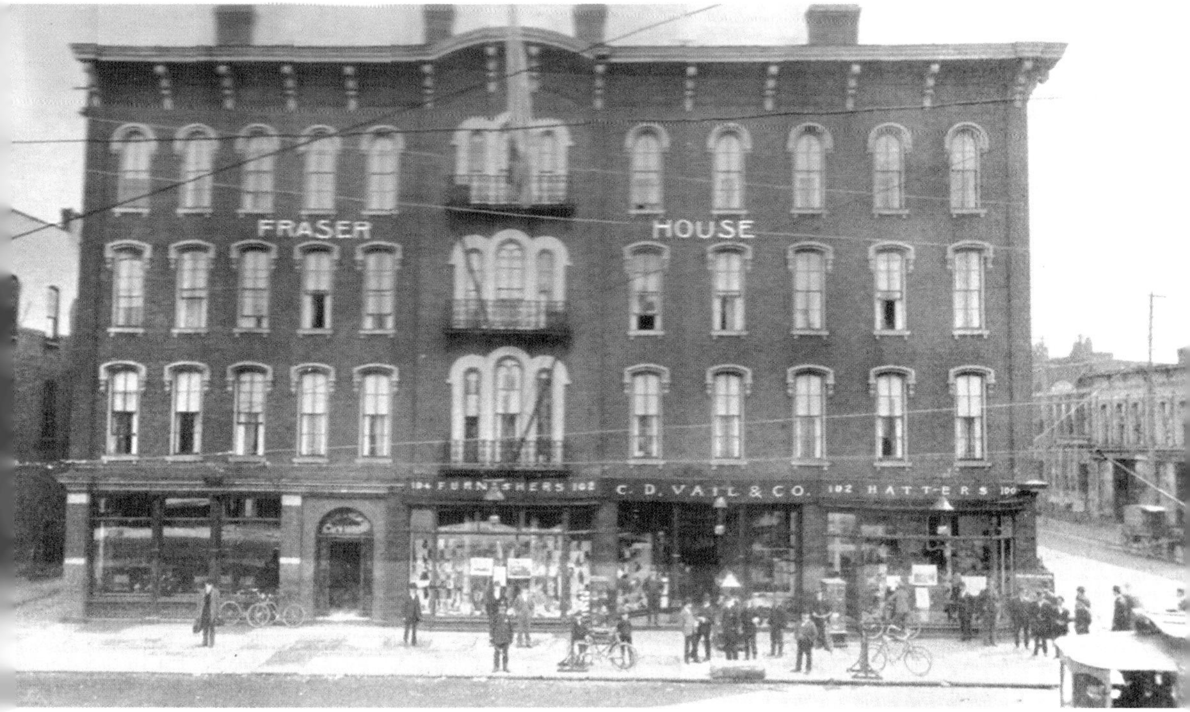

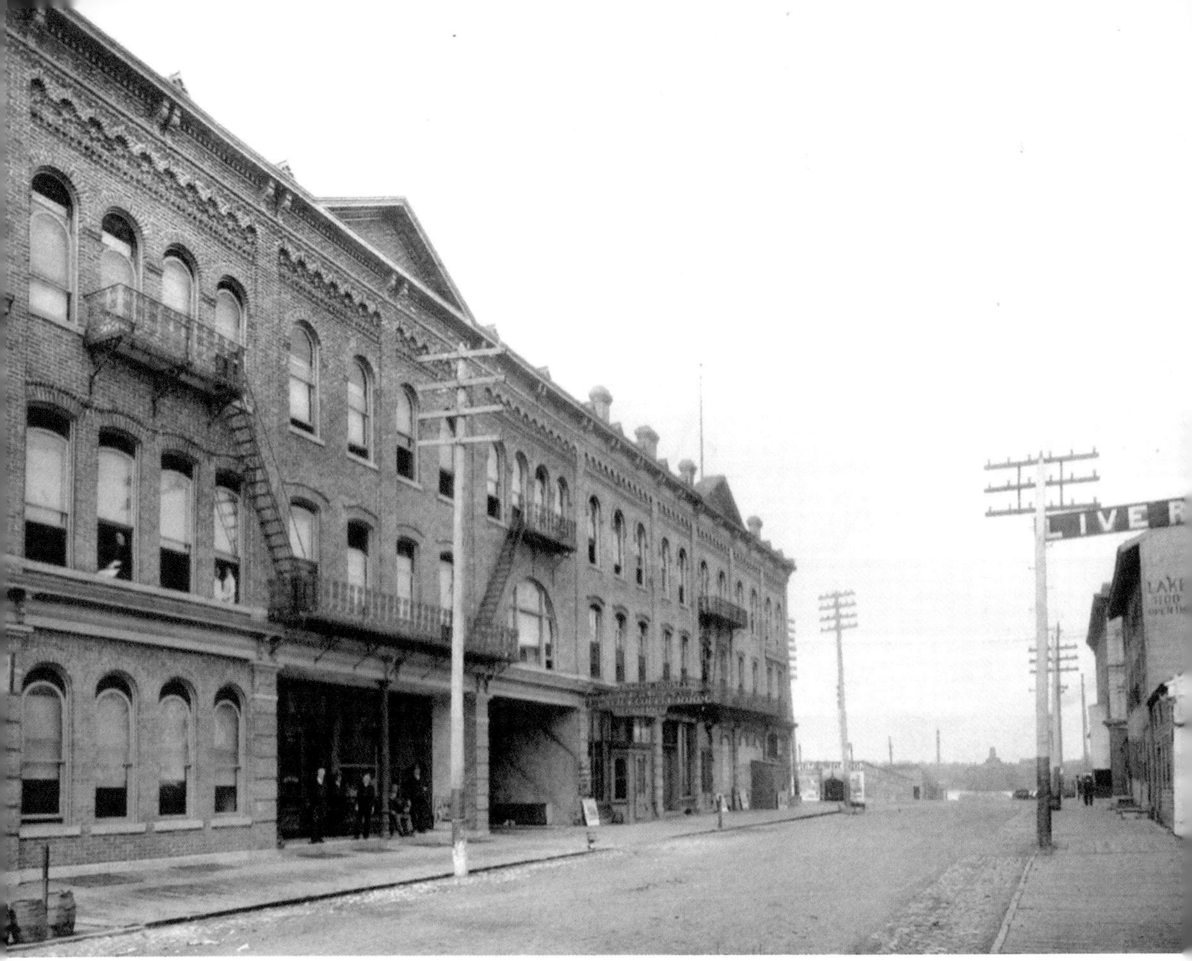

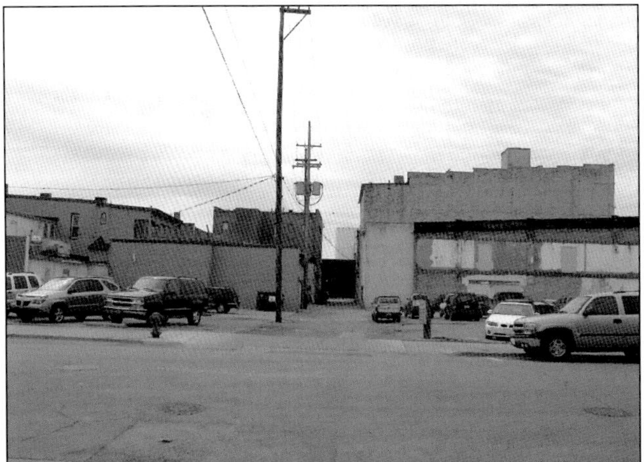

FORMER ROUECH HOUSE SITE.

ROUECH HOUSE. The 1895 Polk Directory lists the New Rouech House on the south corner of Fifth and Water Streets as Bay City's most centrally located hotel. Rates ran from 50¢ to $2 a day and included an office and sample rooms on every floor. The Rouech was one of 41 hotels listed. The parking lot north of Mill End is all that remains today.

ARLINGTON HOTEL. P. Toohey had owned and managed the Arlington House Hotel for over 30 years by 1905. The Arlington opened in 1868 and was the leading hotel in West Bay City, located on the corner of Linn and John Streets where it still stands today. Its location was near the banking, business, and manufacturing centers of West Bay City and adjacent to the post office and lines of transportation. The hotel had a capacity of 60 guests with a dining room that could seat 80 people.

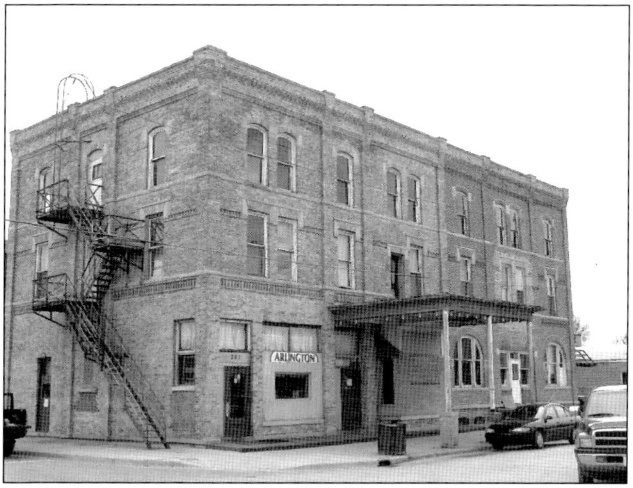

ARLINGTON HOTEL.

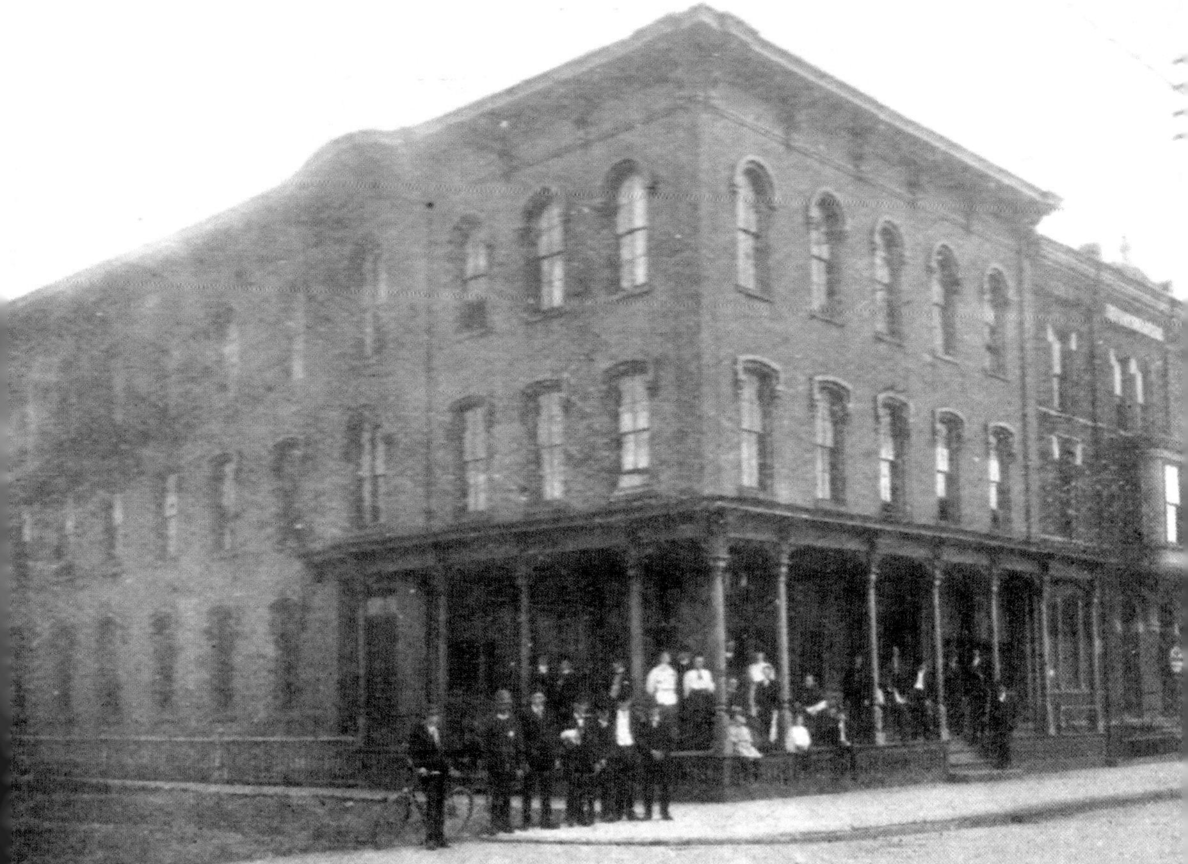

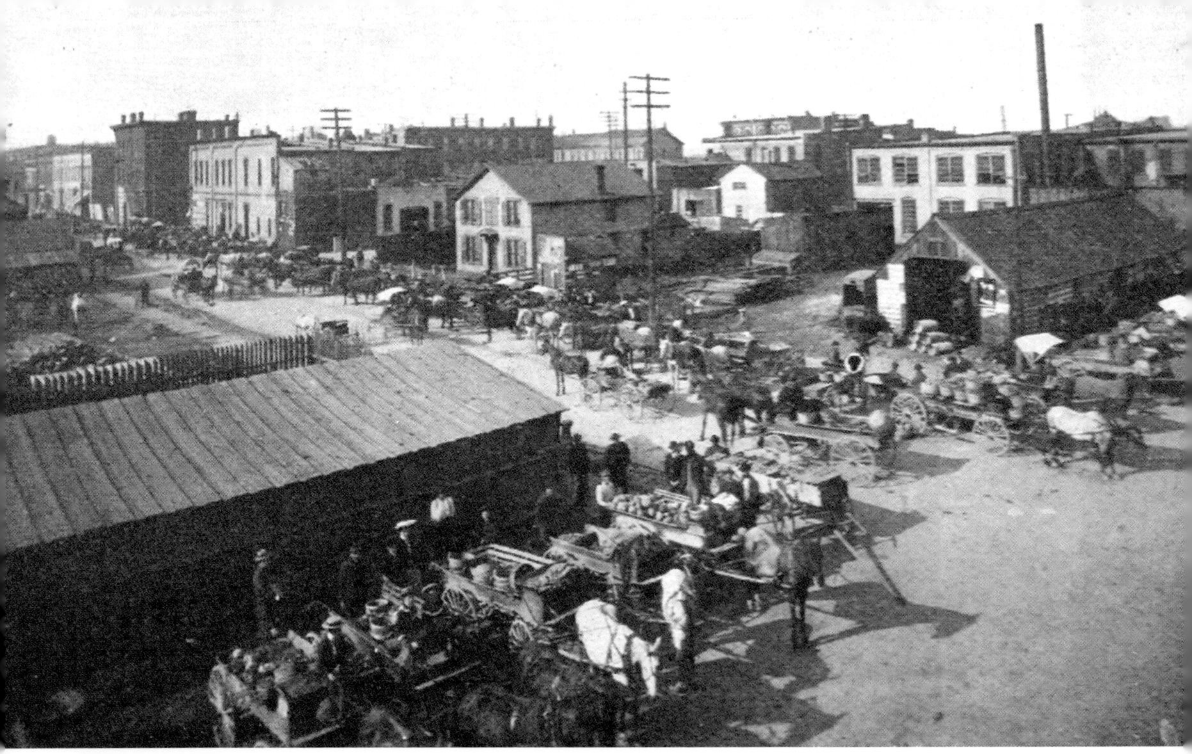

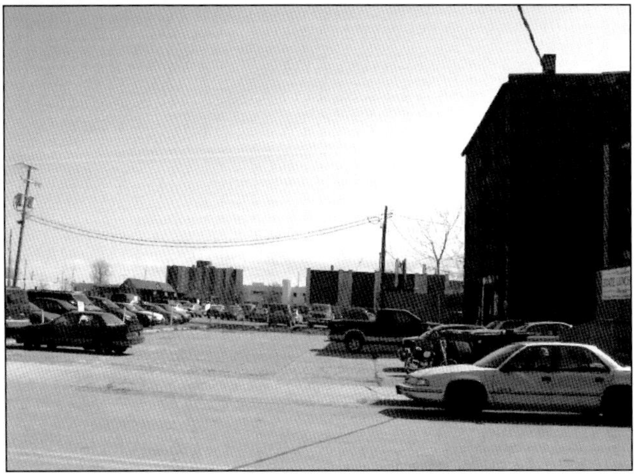

FORMER CITY MARKET SITE.

CITY MARKET, 3RD STREET AND SAGINAW STREET. Prior to 1906, this area was unofficially used as a market. By 1906, this land was part of the Brooks boat manufacturing plant. The Brooks boats came in kits for self-assembly, similar to an Aladdin Home. Brooks moved to Saginaw and made phonographs. (I have a Brooks phonograph in my basement.) By 1912, it was once again designated as a market: "Bay City Market Company." The wagons in the picture are on Saginaw Street. Nothing remains of the market today.

HOTEL IMPERIAL. The Hotel Imperial was located at 822 North Jefferson; in later years it was called the Imperial Hotel. Built opposite the Flint & Pere Marquette Railroad station (also used by Detroit & Mackinaw Railroad), it had 22 rooms, electric lights, a barbershop, steam heat, and a sample room; everything the weary traveler needed after his or her journey. Looking toward the Bay County building, there is a parking lot where the Hotel Imperial once stood.

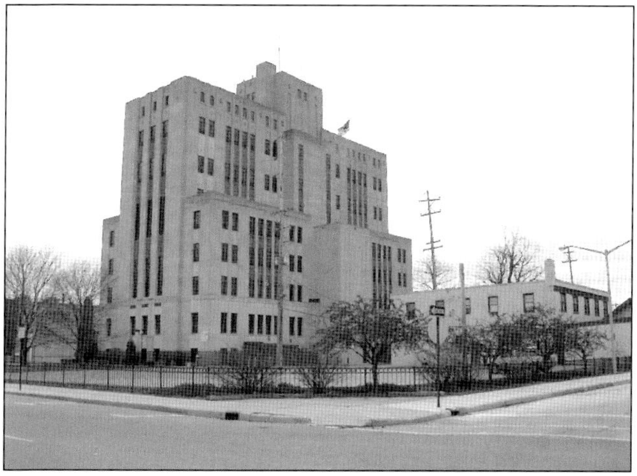

SITE OF HOTEL IMPERIAL.

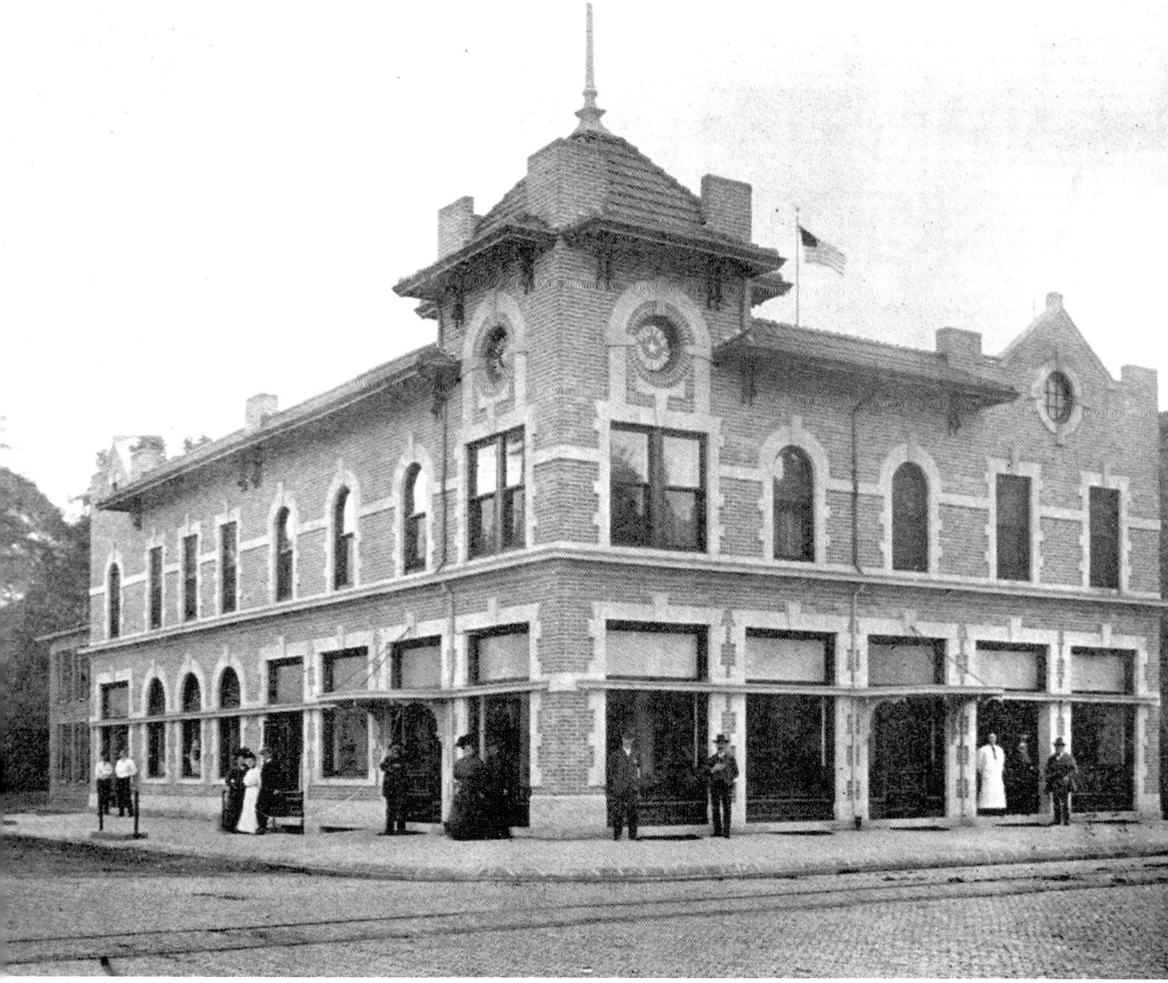

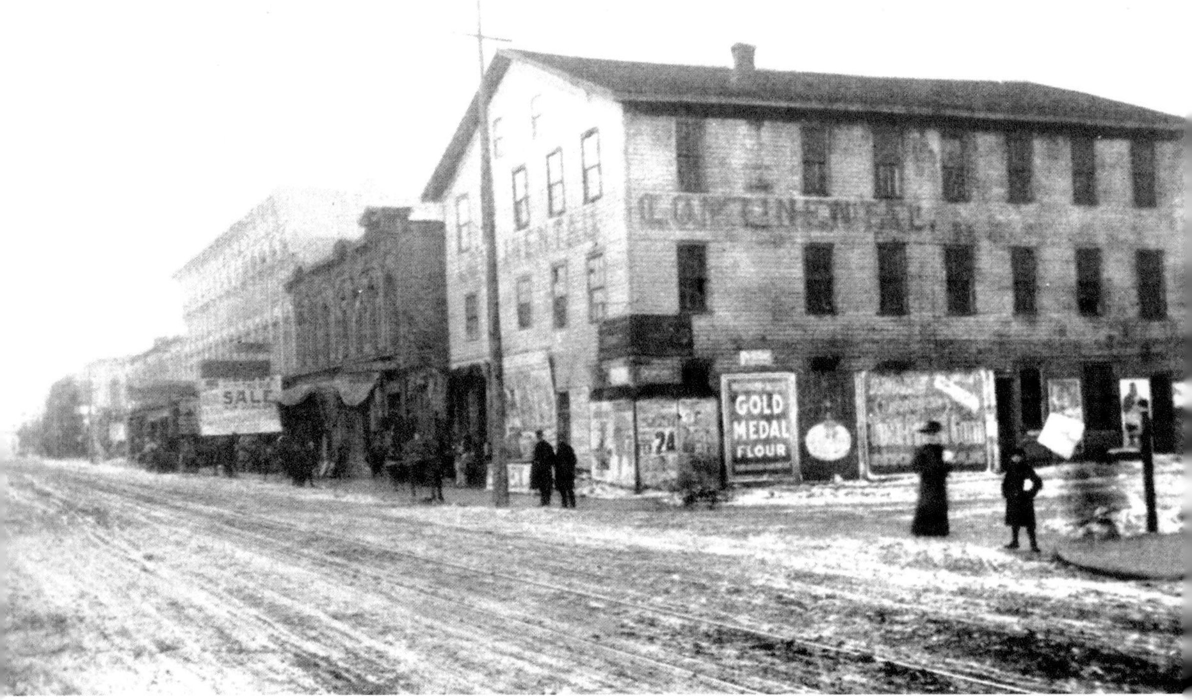

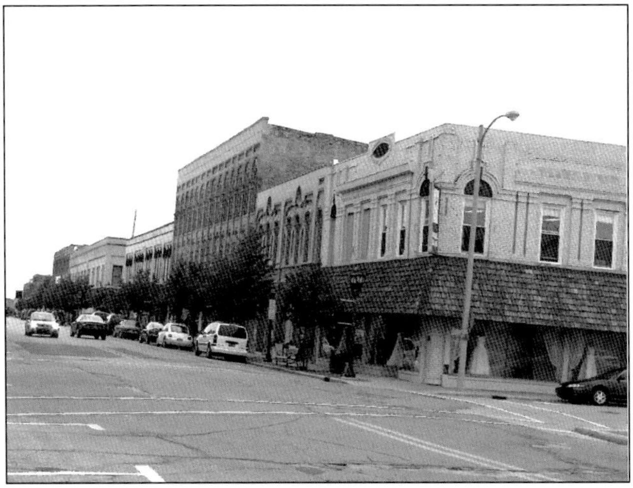

FORMER GLOBE HOTEL SITE.

OLD GLOBE HOTEL. The Directory of 1868 shows the Globe Hotel at the northeast corner of Fifth and Saginaw Streets and states it was the first frame building at that location, built on land donated by Probate Judge S.S. Campbell. Originally a two-story house, the first township meeting for the town of Hampton, County of Saginaw, was held here in 1843. The Globe was three and one-half stories high with 44 bedrooms, a dining room, a billiard room, a bar room, a kitchen, and a good barn and stable. The building was leased to M.A. Rouech in 1862 and he eventually built the Rouech House on the opposite side of 5th Street. (See page 58.)

Chapter 5
EAST SIDE

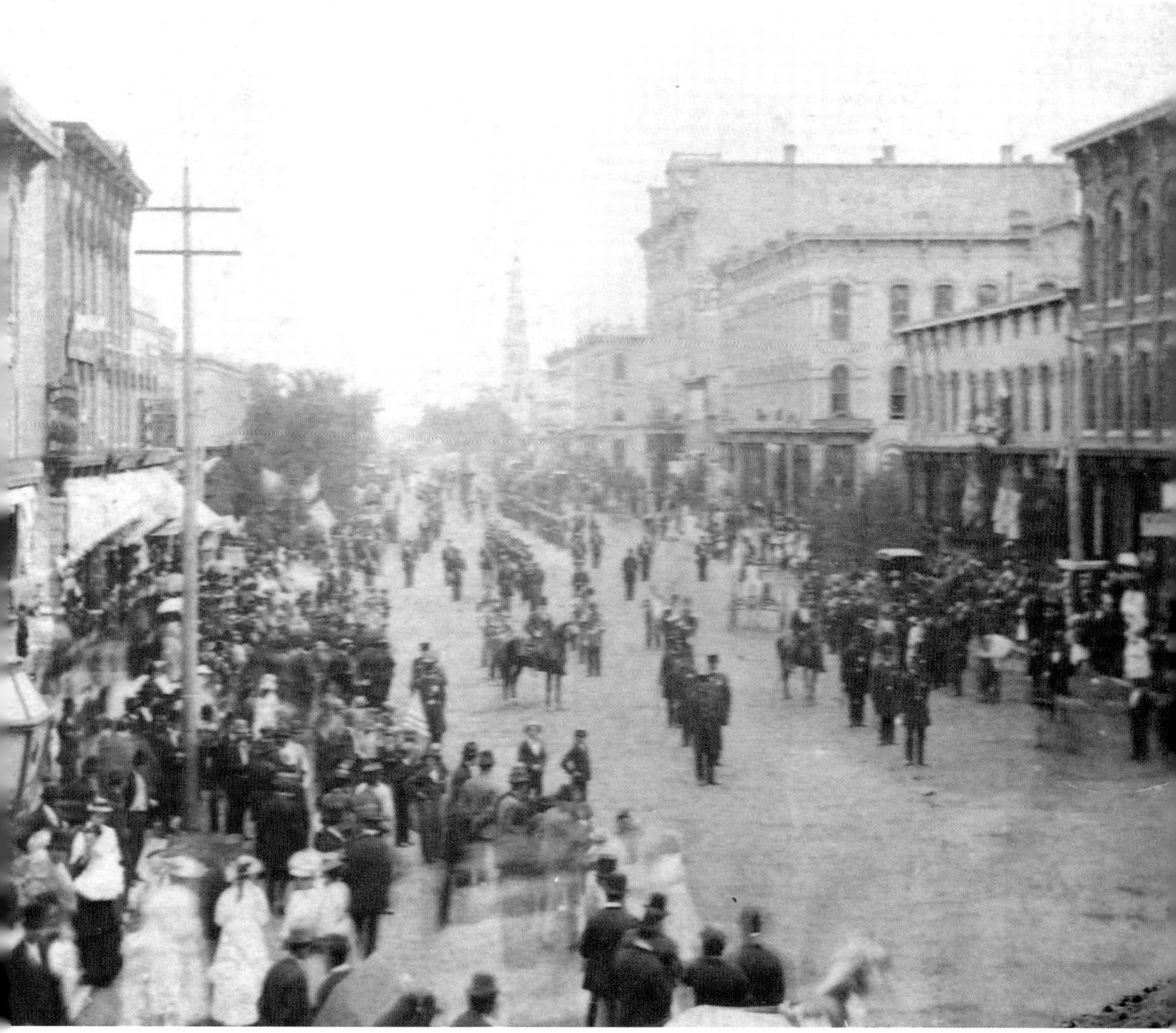

CENTER STREET PARADE. Center Street was the center of business for many years and was also the parade route. It still is. This photo comes from an undated stereoview card, but is probably from *c.* 1880. The Fraser House is on the right. The business blocks were named, including the Munger Block and the Bank Block that contained the three-story First National Bank. Further east is the Cranage Block, which boasted water closets on all three floors. The spire of the First Baptist Church at Madison and Center is visible in the distance.

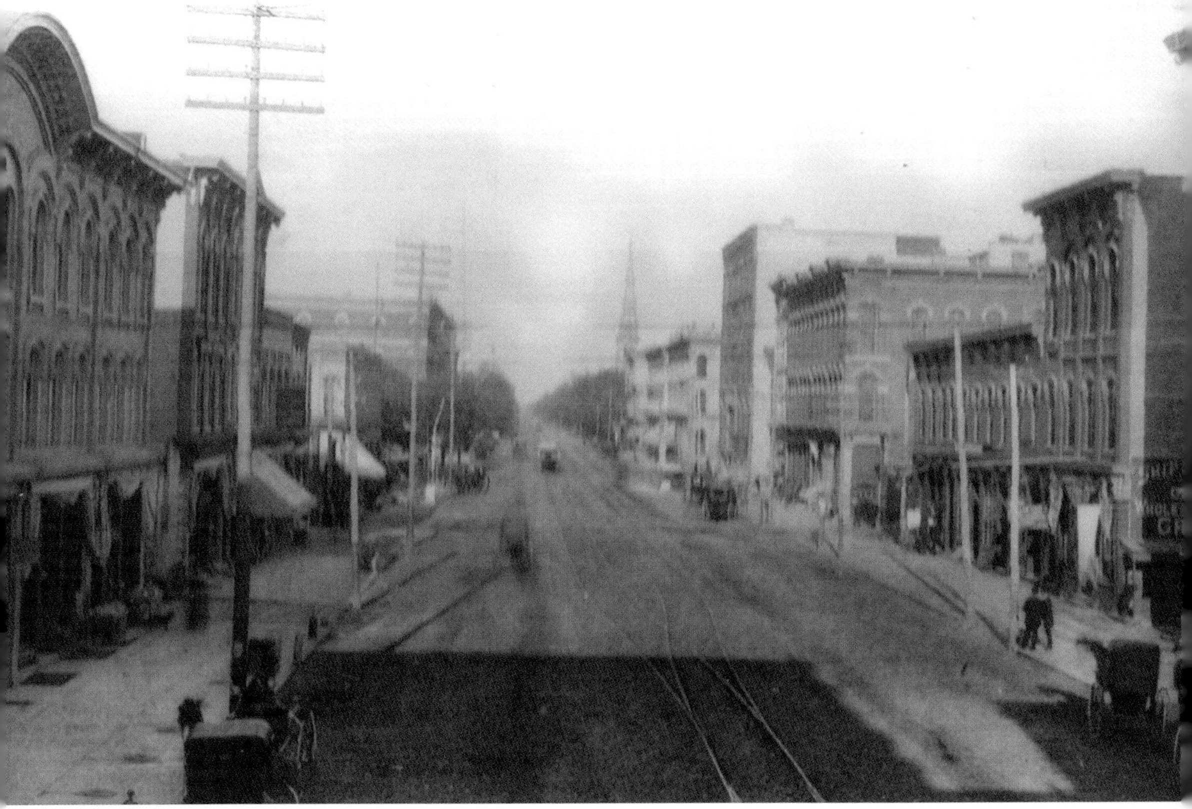

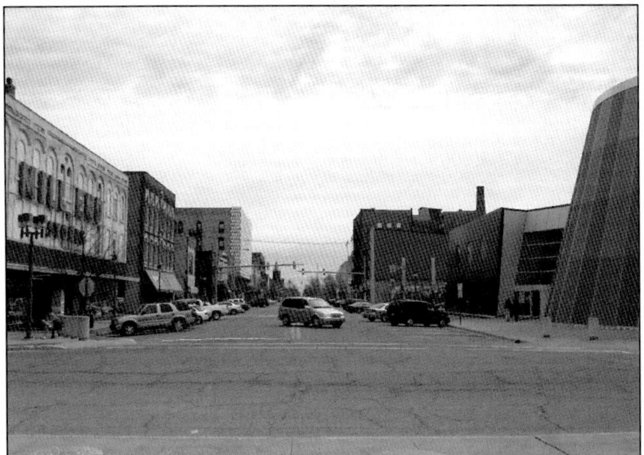

CENTER STREET, LOOKING EAST.

CENTER STREET, LOOKING EAST. Where the Friendship Shell now stands at the foot of Center, there once stood a vibrant business block called the Union Block. This picture looks east down Center Avenue from the third story of the Union Block. To the left is the original Shearer Block, the original site of the Herman Hiss Jewelry Store and now the Mill End, and to the right is the Fraser House, now the site of the Delta College Planetarium.

SHEARER BROTHERS BLOCK. G. Henry Shearer and James B. Shearer ran their real estate business at 809 North Adams Street in the Shearer Brothers Building, which is presently being converted into condominiums. They were among the largest realty owners in the city, owning the Shearer Block on Center and Water Streets, the Shearers' Central Block (demolished by S.S. Kresge in 1940), and the Shearer Building. The Shearer Block contained ten stores and was also a place of residence.

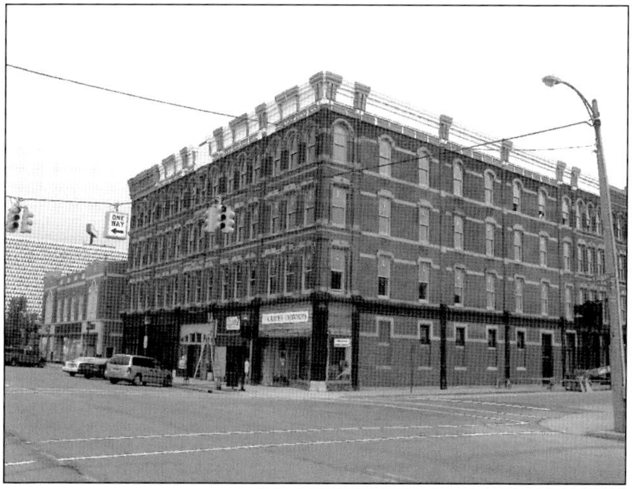

SHEARER BLOCK.

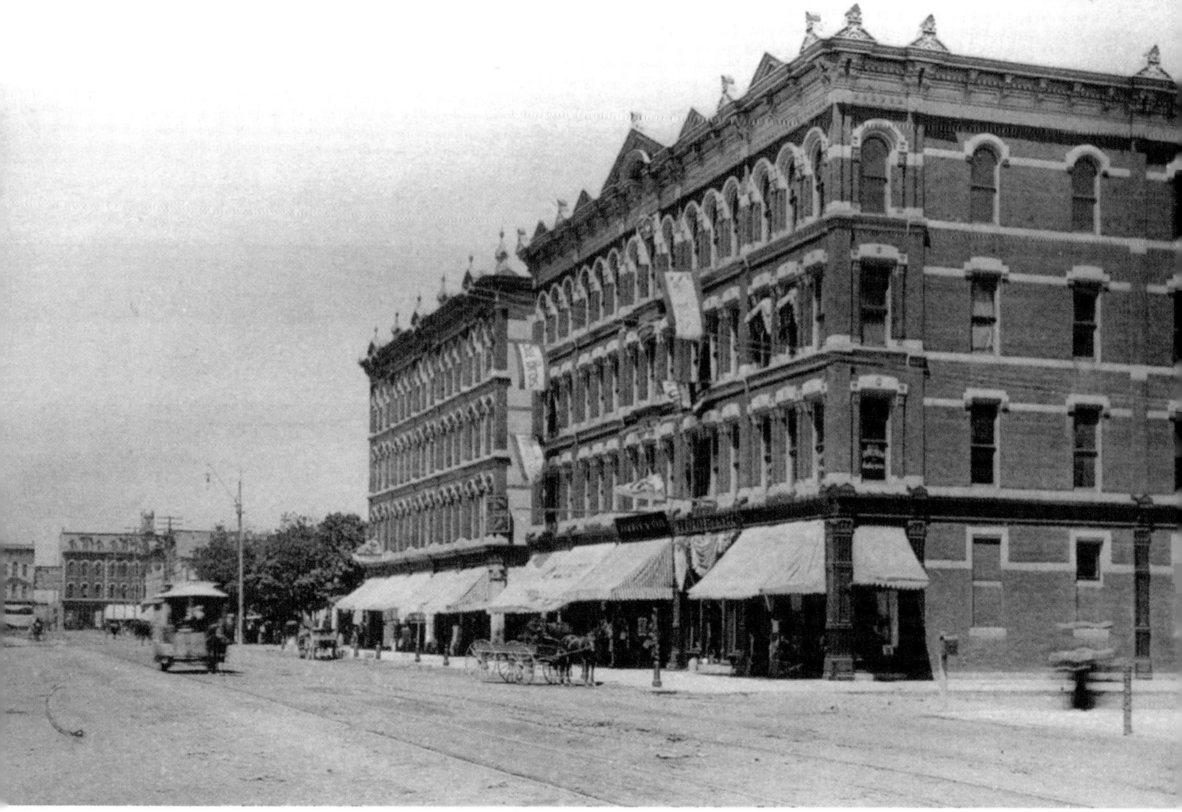

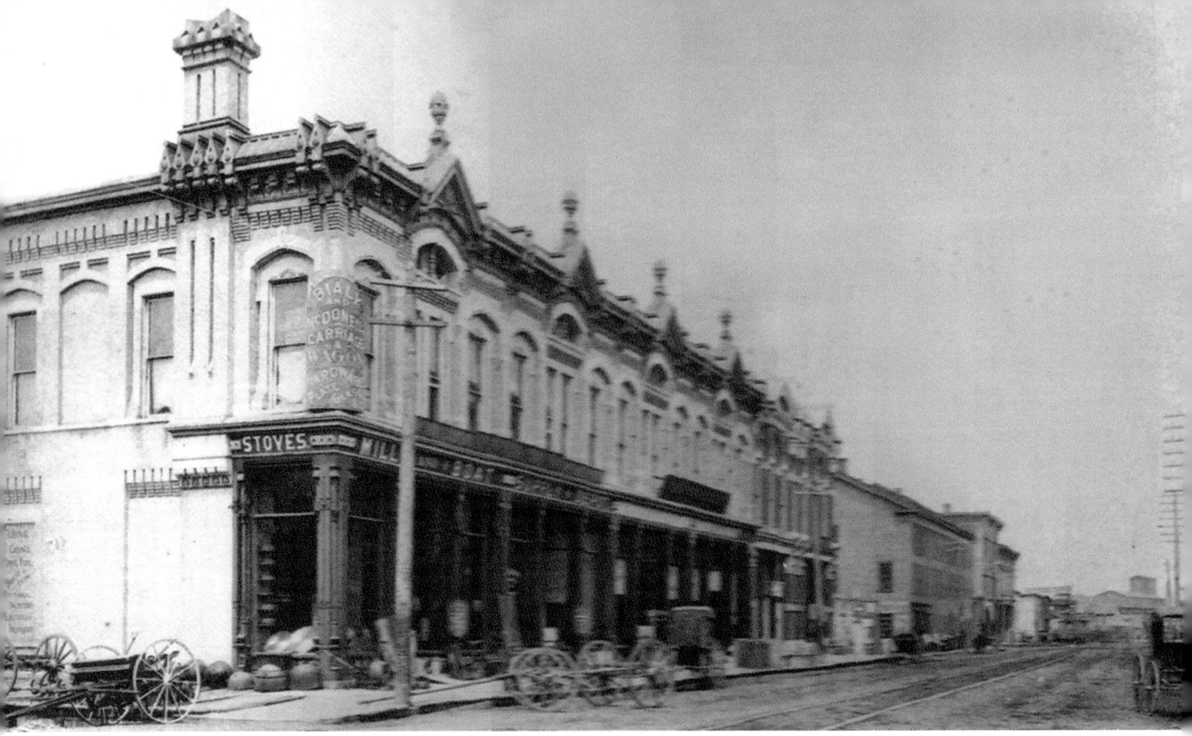

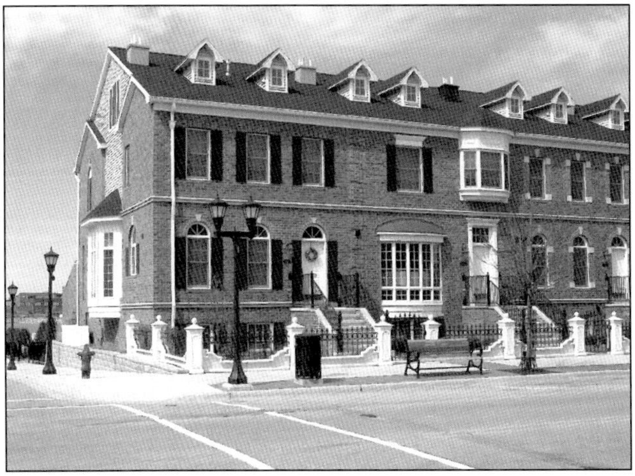

WATER STREET, NORTH FROM SIXTH STREET.

WATER STREET, NORTH FROM FOURTH STREET. Although the nickname of this part of town was "Hell's Half Mile," it was also the location of many prominent businesses. Bialy & McDonell Hardware was on the corner in this 1889 photograph. By 1898, the business had moved down the block to 923 North Water and was known just as Robert C. Bialy, Wholesale and Retail Hardware. One could purchase hardware, machinery, cordage, belting, paints, and many other building materials. Condominiums are on the former site of Bialy & McDonell Hardware today.

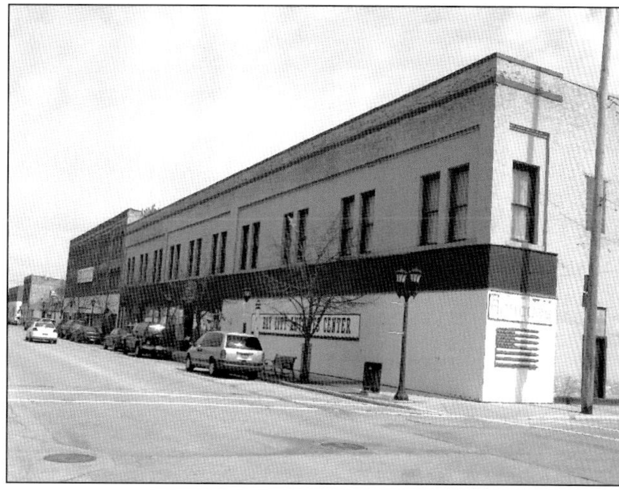

VIEW ON WATER STREET.

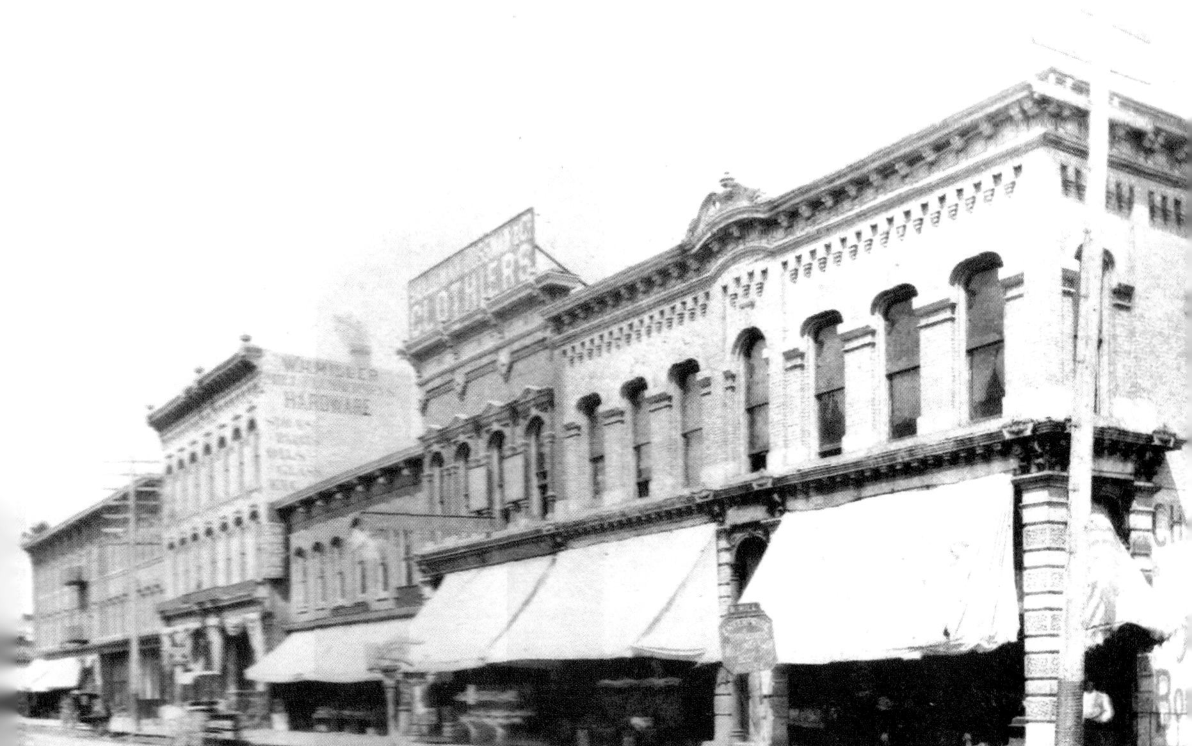

VIEW ON WATER STREET. Going from right to left from Fourth Street, early Bay City businesses included Enterprise Dry Goods and Millinery Boot and Shoe Store (Cheap Boots & Shoes), Seligman and Rothman Clothiers, the W.M. Miller Mill & Lumberman's Hardware (where you could get stoves, paints, oils, and glass), and the Campbell House, one of Bay City's oldest hotels. Today, the entire block houses the Bay City Antique Center.

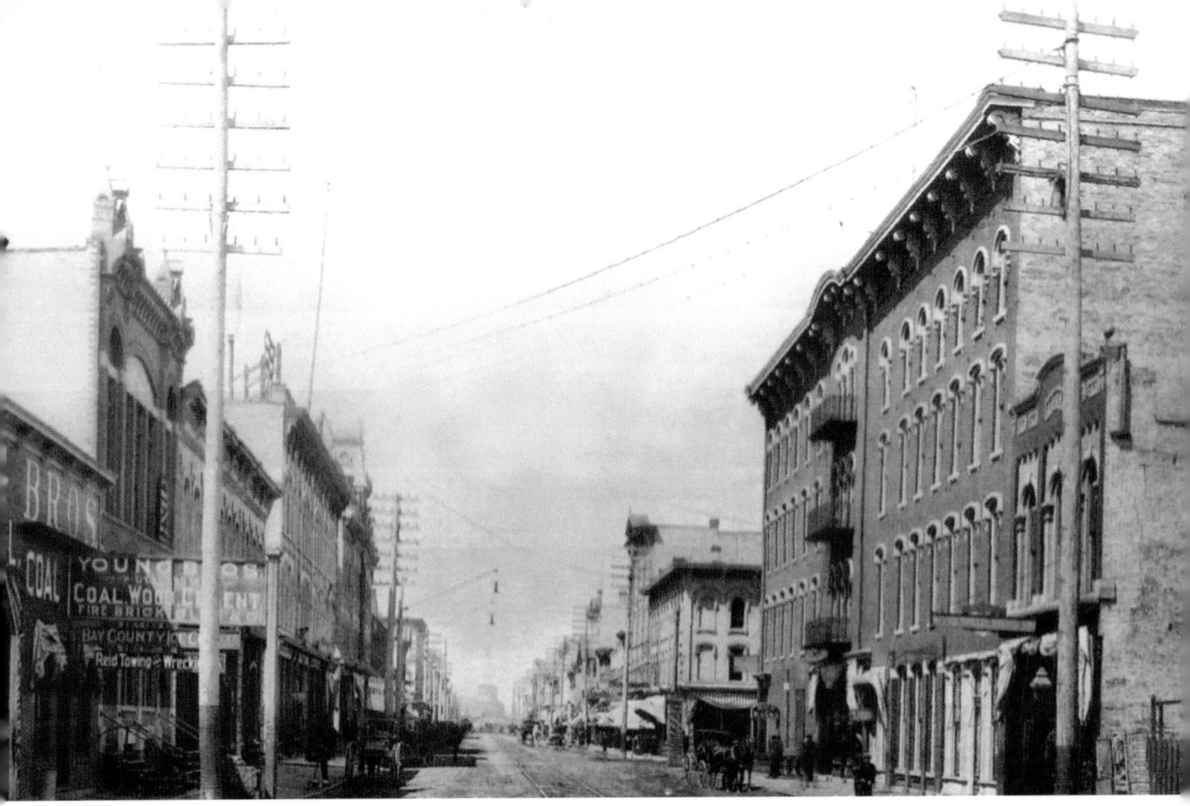

VIEW ON WATER STREET NORTH FROM SIXTH STREET. The Fraser House's southern exterior is the building on the right where the Delta College Planetarium now stands. The Shearer Block (home of the Mill End) is just north across Center Avenue. The three-story Union Block with the Young Brothers Coal Company, the *Bay City Tribune*, and C& J Gregory Printing is on the left side of this view. The Union Block was torn down for Wenonah Park as a part of the redevelopment after the Fraser House fire.

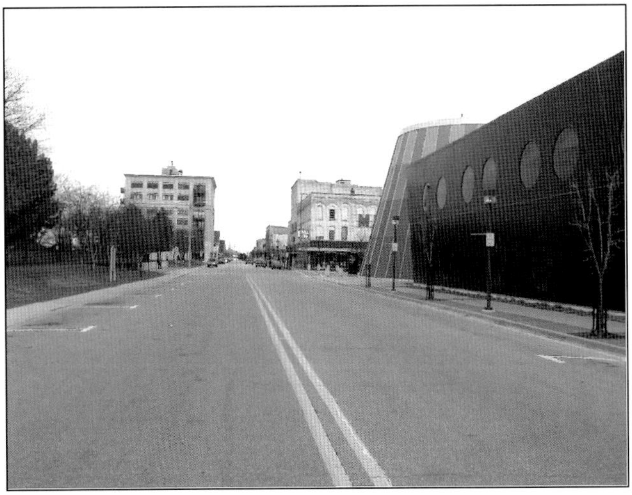

WATER STREET, NORTH FROM SIXTH.

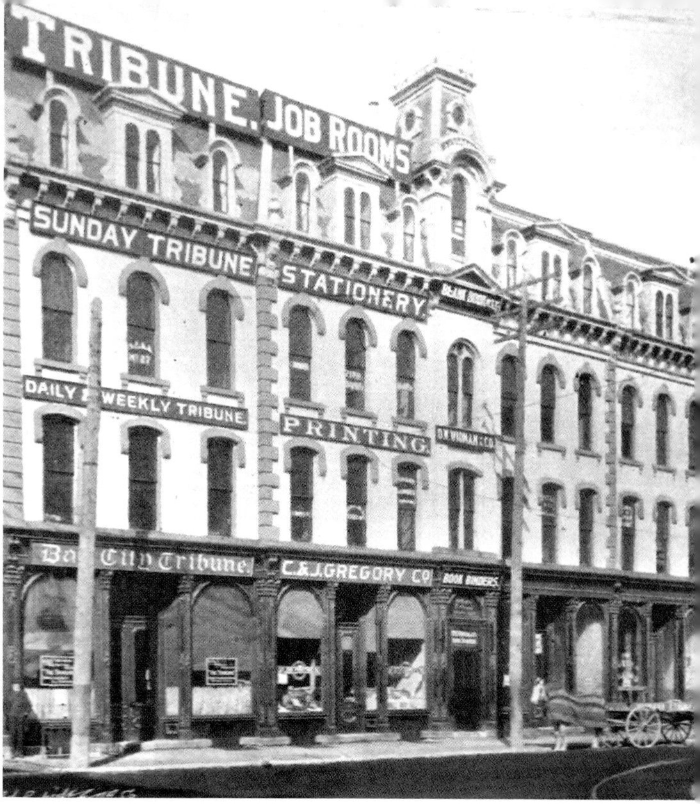

TRIBUNE BUILDING. At the heart of Bay City's earliest business district stood the Watson Block at the western end of Center Avenue. The *Bay City Tribune* published both morning and weekly papers with a subscription cost of 10¢ a week at the 20th century's turn. Chauncey and John ran the C& J Printing Company at 803 North Water, producing many local items like *Bay City Michigan Illustrated of 1898,* so widely sought after by today's collectors. The Watson Block was torn down for Wenonah Park in 1908 and is the home of the Friendship Shell today.

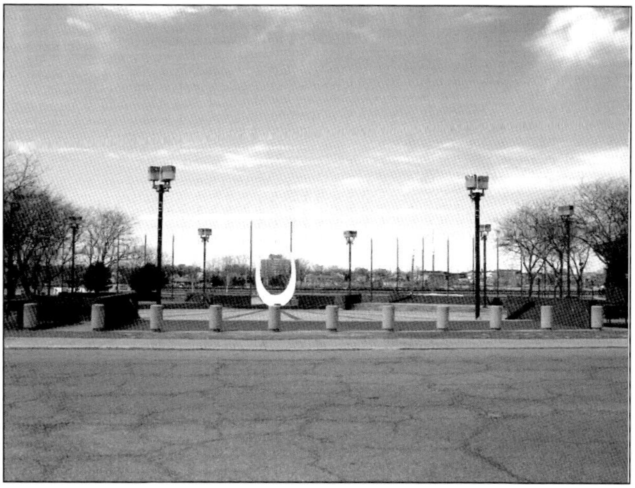

FRIENDSHIP SHELL.

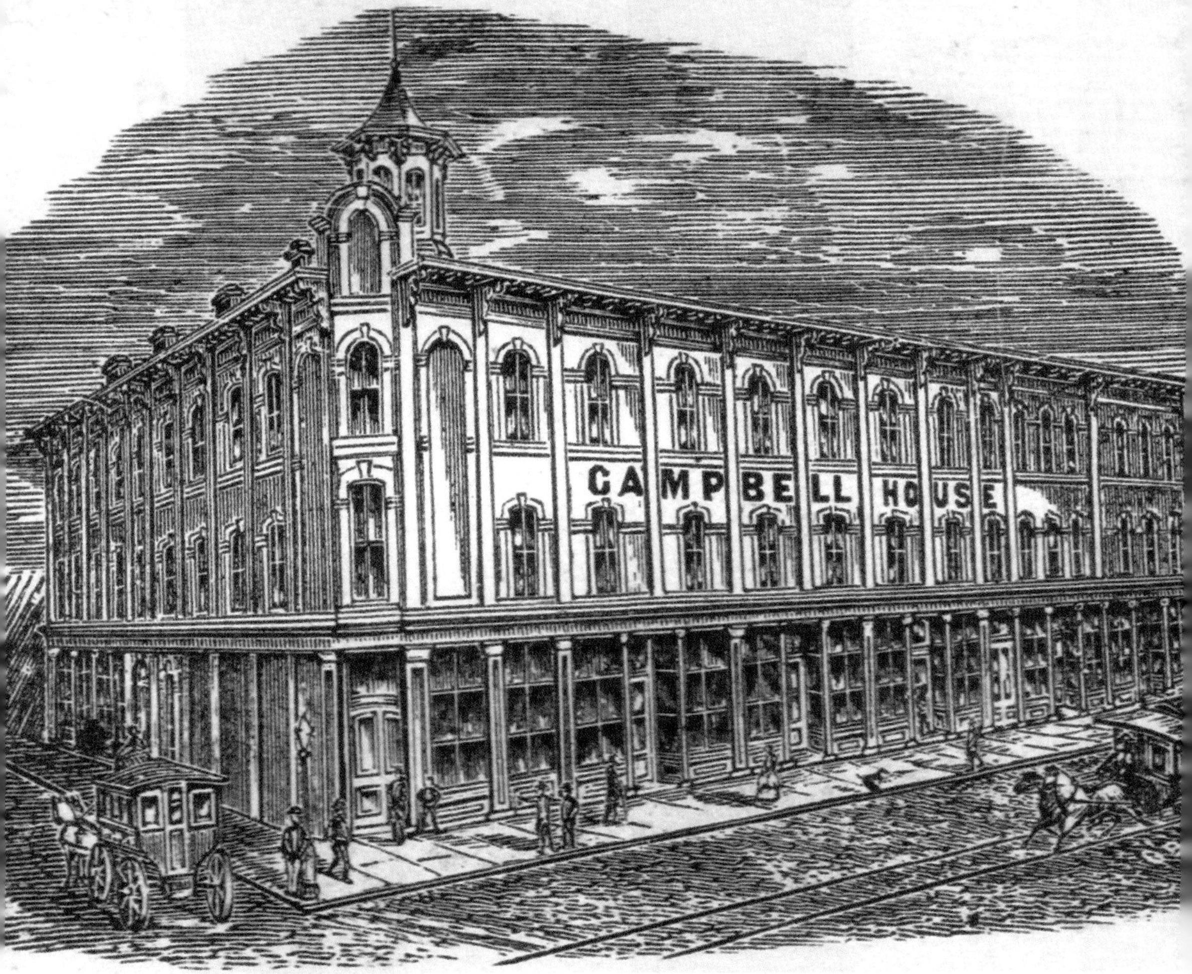

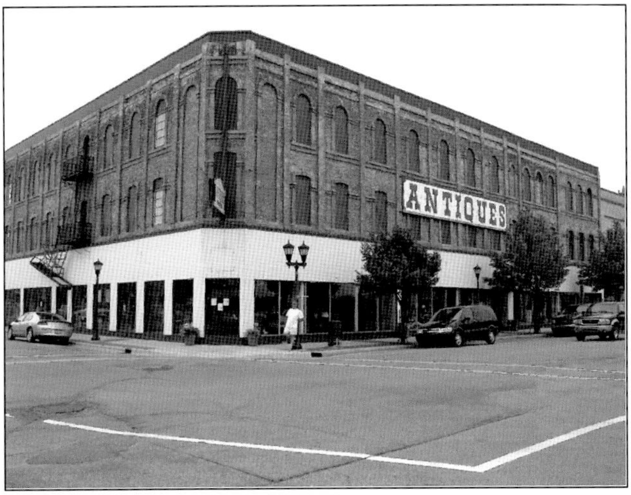

BAY CITY ANTIQUES.

CAMPBELL HOUSE. The Bay City Antiques Center on the corner of North Water Street and Third Street was built on the site of the Union House and opened in 1868 as the Campbell House. The Campbell had 100 rooms and was a three-story building with 150 feet on Water Street and 100 feet on Third Street. The main floor had offices, a reading room, a billiard room, and a bar. It cost $2 a day to stay there in 1889. In the mid-20th century, it was home to C.E. Rosenbury Furniture.

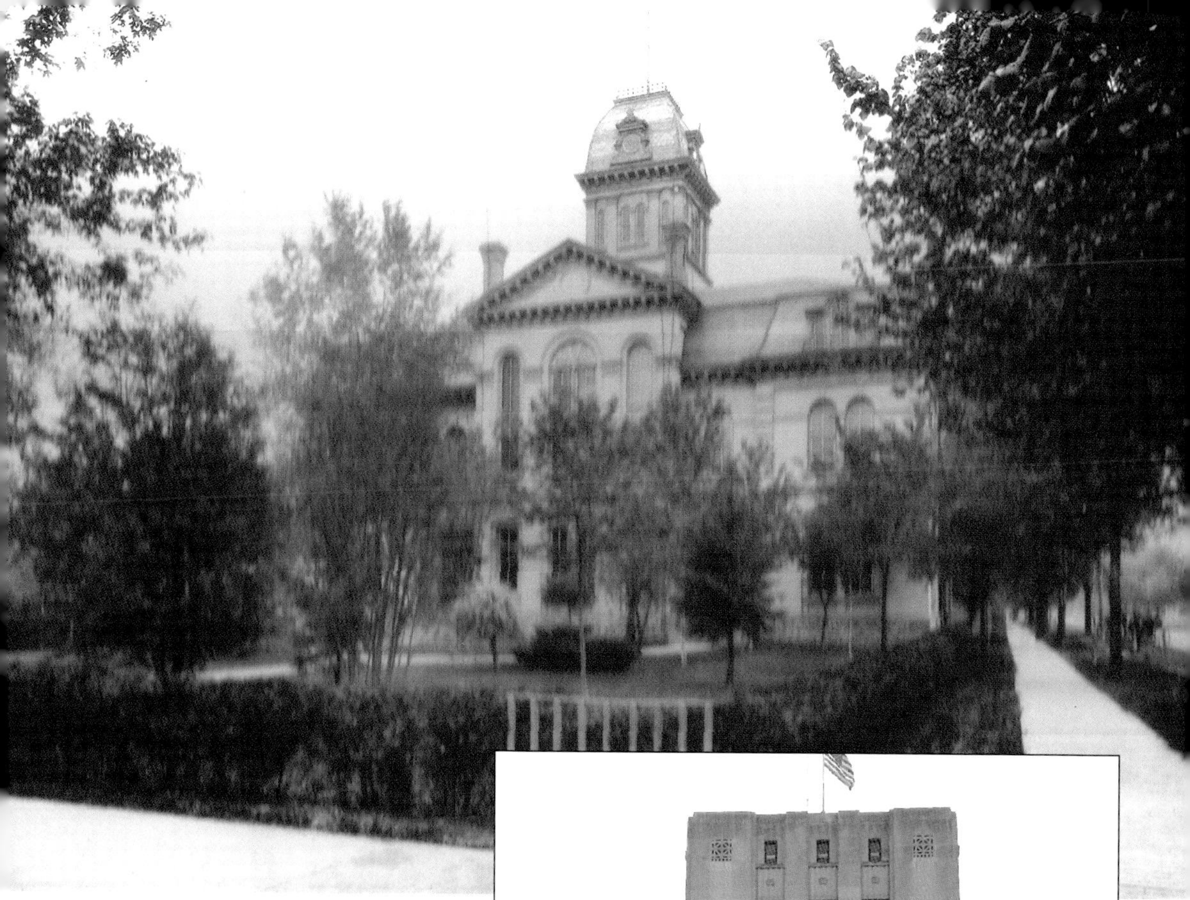

COURT HOUSE. When the original Court House was torn down in 1932, this $375,000 nine-story building, designed by local architect Joseph Goddeyne, replaced it. Today's occupants include many of the offices that served in the original building with the exception of the Sheriff, Coroner, and Superintendents of the Poor. It now also houses the Board of Commissioners, Circuit Court, District Court, Drain Commissioner, Friend of the Court, Planning Department, and Probate Court.

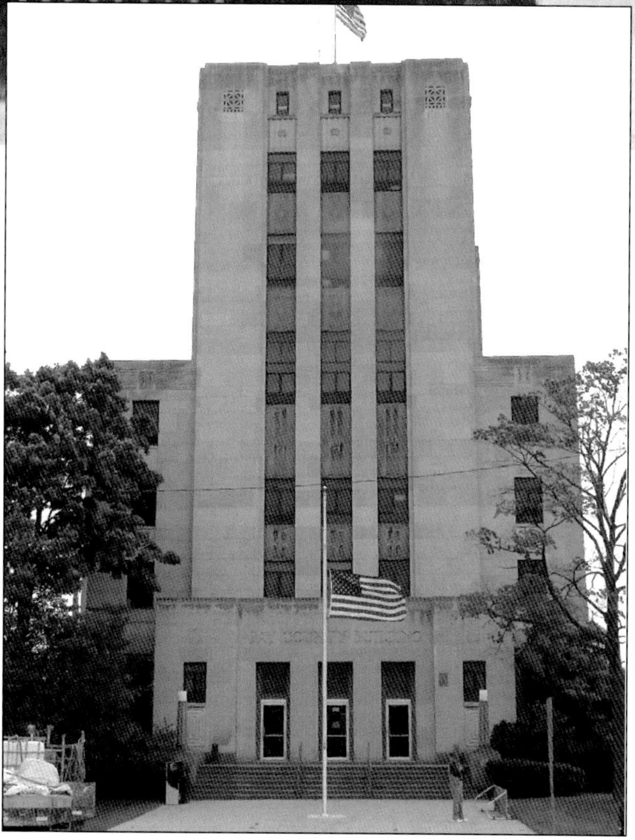

COUNTY BUILDING.

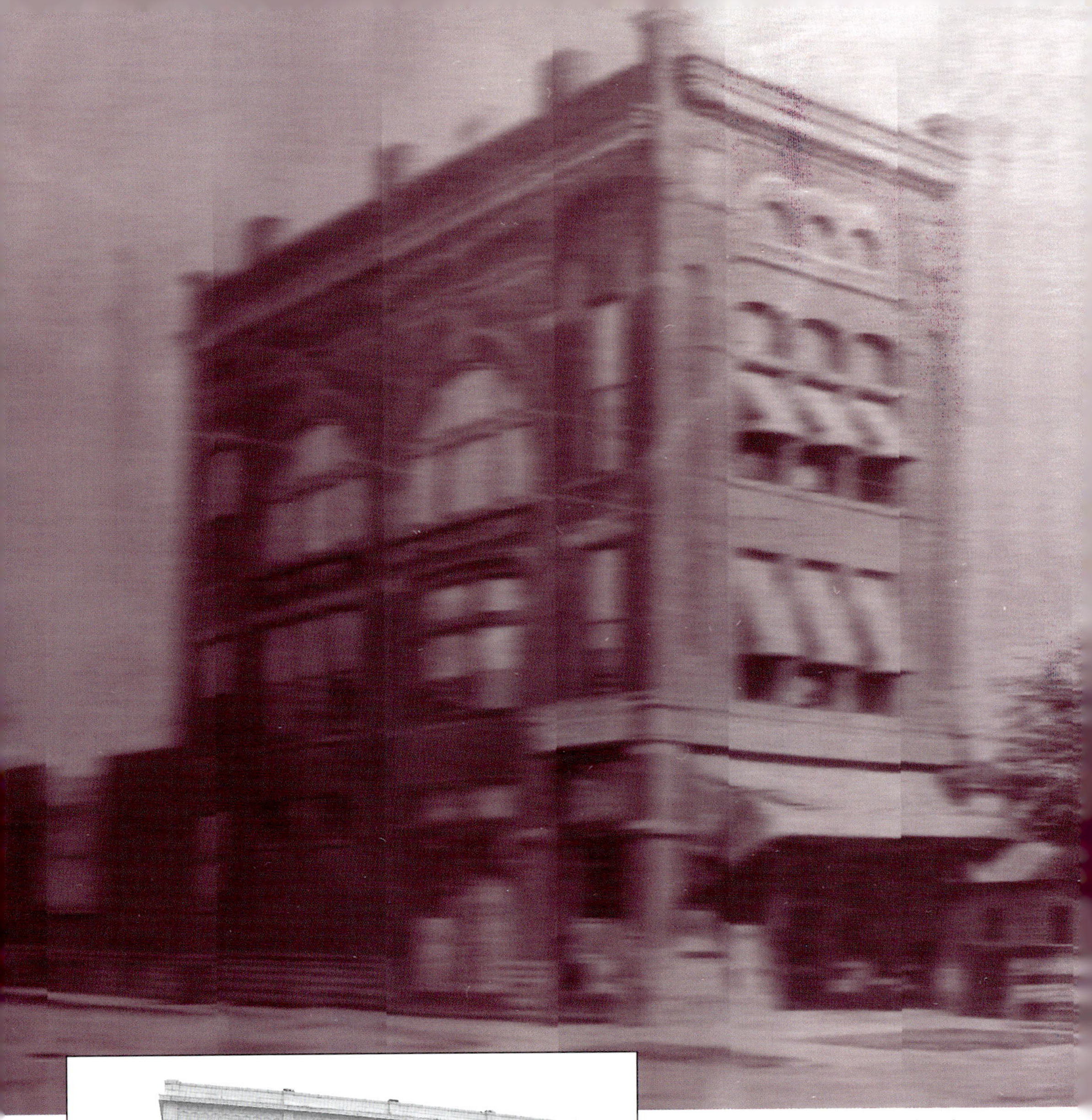

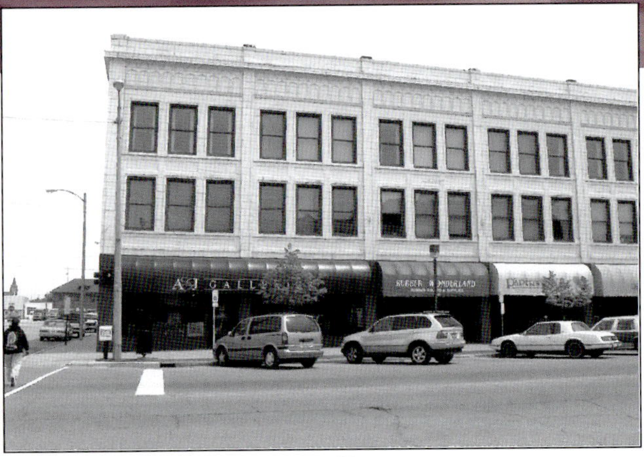

DAVIDSON BUILDING.

HARMAN & VERNER. The three-story Harman & Verner Photo Studio and Art Gallery stood on the southeast corner of Fourth and Washington Streets. George Harman and James Verner moved to this location at 212 Water Street in the late 1870s. In 1877, they offered frames, albums, stereoscopes, and cabinet cards, with a specialty in children's pictures. The building was torn down and replaced by the Davidson Building.

WASHINGTON STREET, SOUTH FROM CENTER. On the left stood the First National Bank, which was called the Bay National Bank by 1879. James Shearer was president, N.B. Bradley was vice president, and the bank had $250,000 in capital in the same year. The building was replaced with an Albert Kahn-designed bank in 1912 and is National City headquarters today. In the center of the picture one can see the spire of the Woods Opera House.

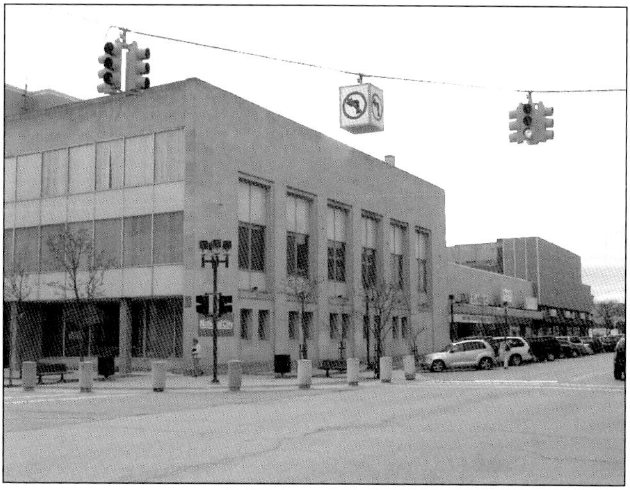

WASHINGTON STREET, LOOKING EAST.

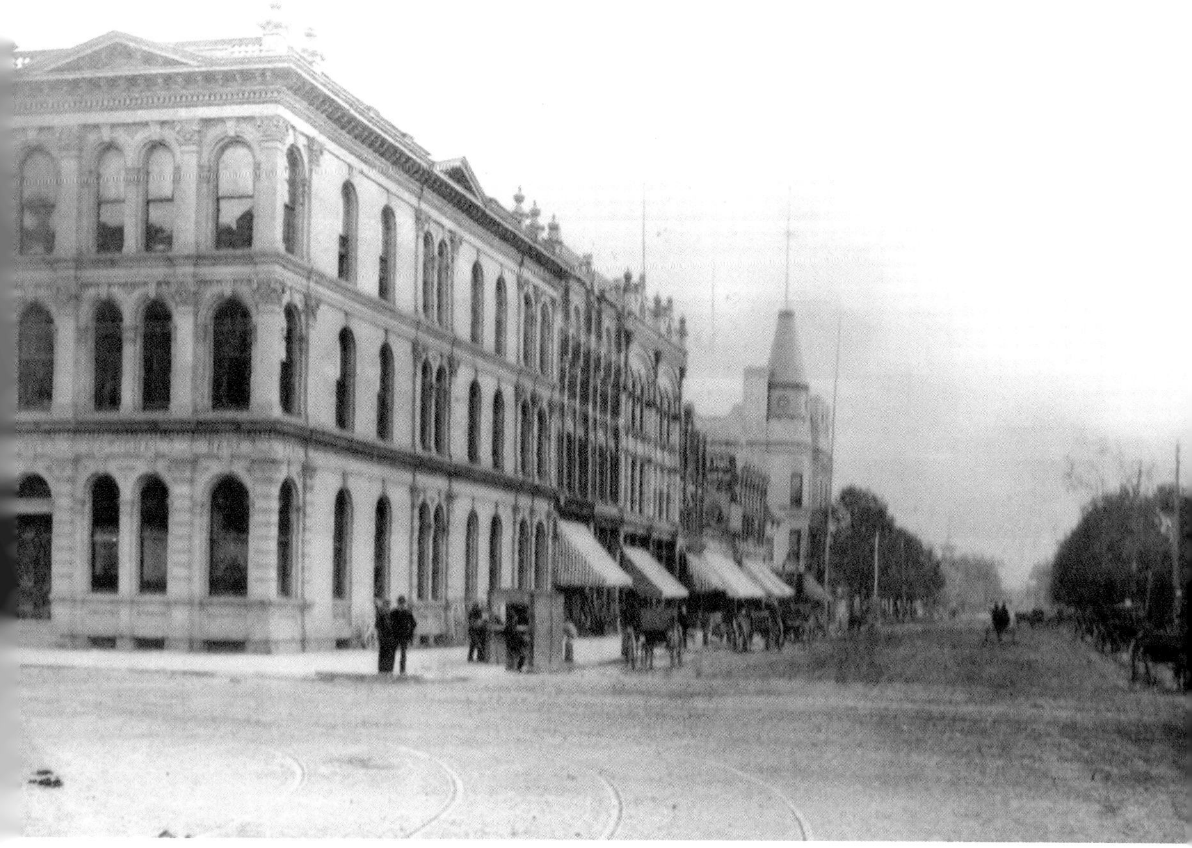

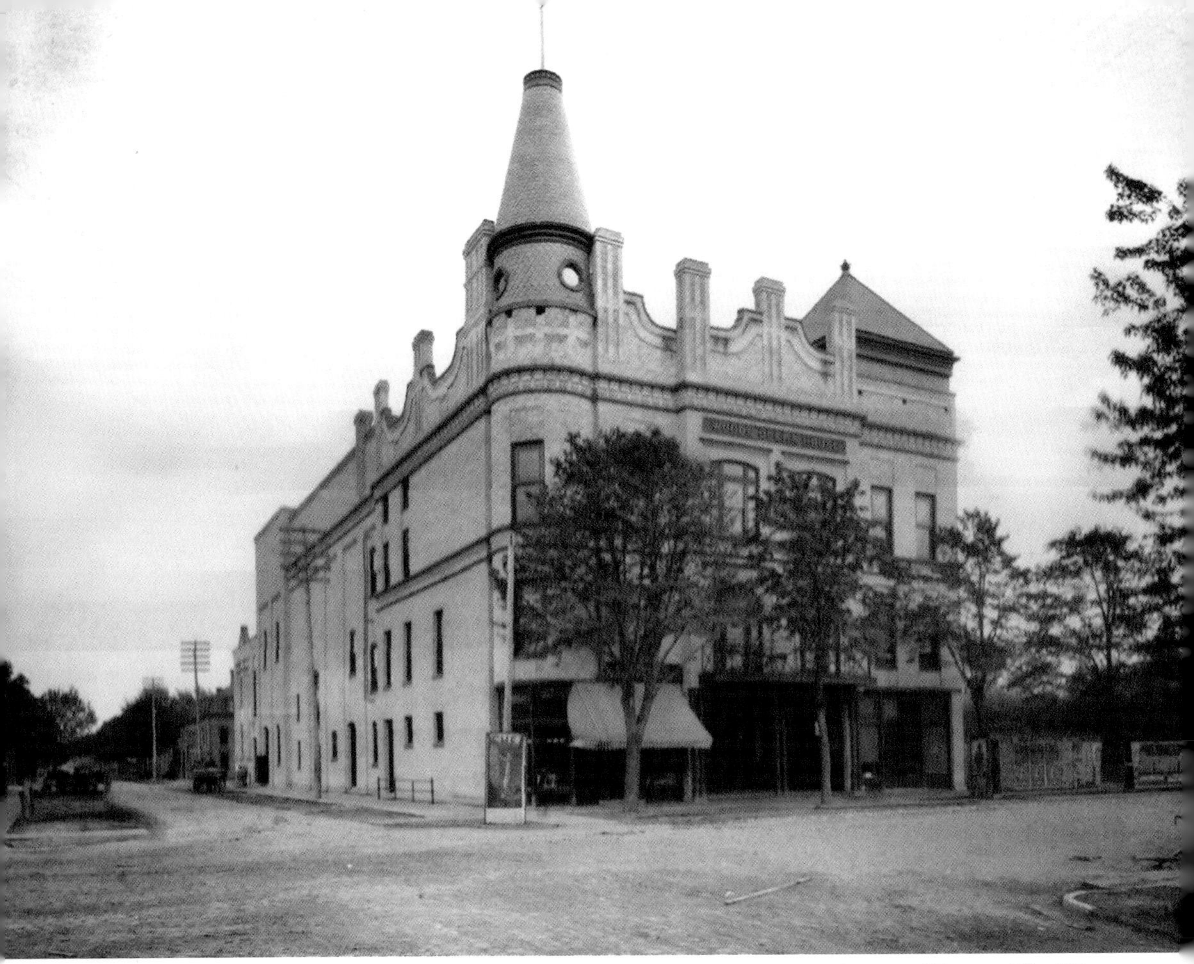

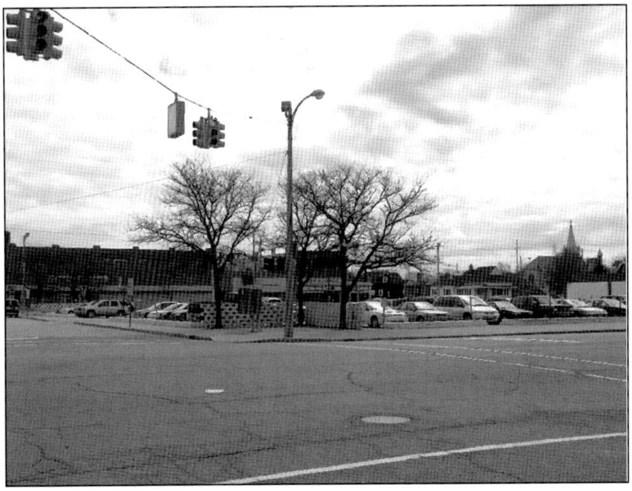

MUNICIPAL PARKING LOT.

WOODS OPERA HOUSE. The Westover Opera House was Bay City's first opera house. It burned in a spectacular fire and was replaced by the Phoenix Building on Center and Washington Streets. The Woods Opera House opened in 1887 at the southeast corner of Washington and Sixth Streets. It was three stories high with a second floor balcony and a third floor gallery. The Woods Opera House burned in 1902 and was replaced by the marvelous Washington Theater. The Washington Theater, while in good condition, was torn down in 1963 and replaced by a municipal parking lot.

Washington Street, South from Tenth Street. In the 1950s and 1960s, this was a busy strip with businesses like used car lots, drive-ins, gas stations (Harold Alexander was a big one selling Goodyear Tires), restaurants, and a large supermarket, Ray's Food Fair. In this 1889 view, the tree-lined boulevard seems to have been largely residential. City Hall was not to be for eight more years. Washington Avenue at this point just served as a way to get to the real downtown area. Today, the main occupants are McDonald's on the east side of the street and City Hall and the Bay County Historical Museum on the west.

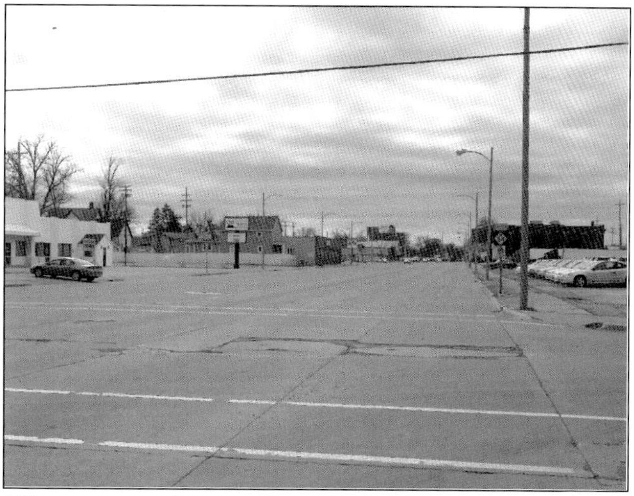

Washington Street, South from Tenth Street.

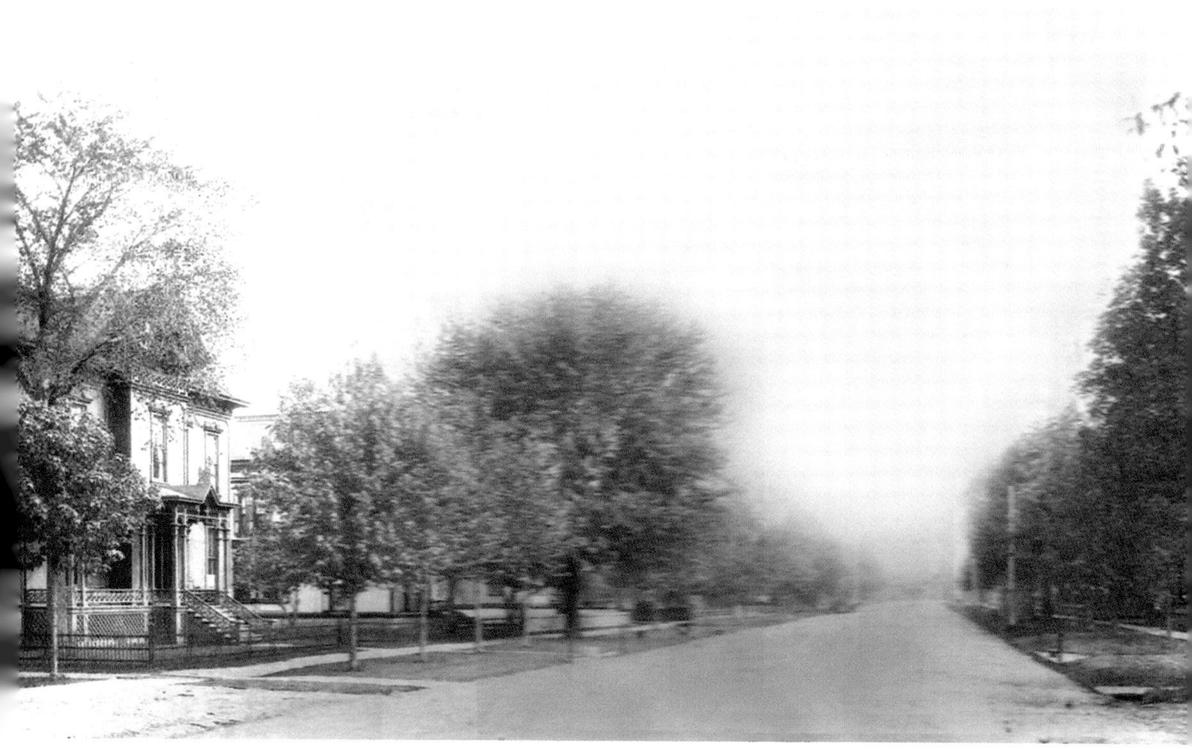

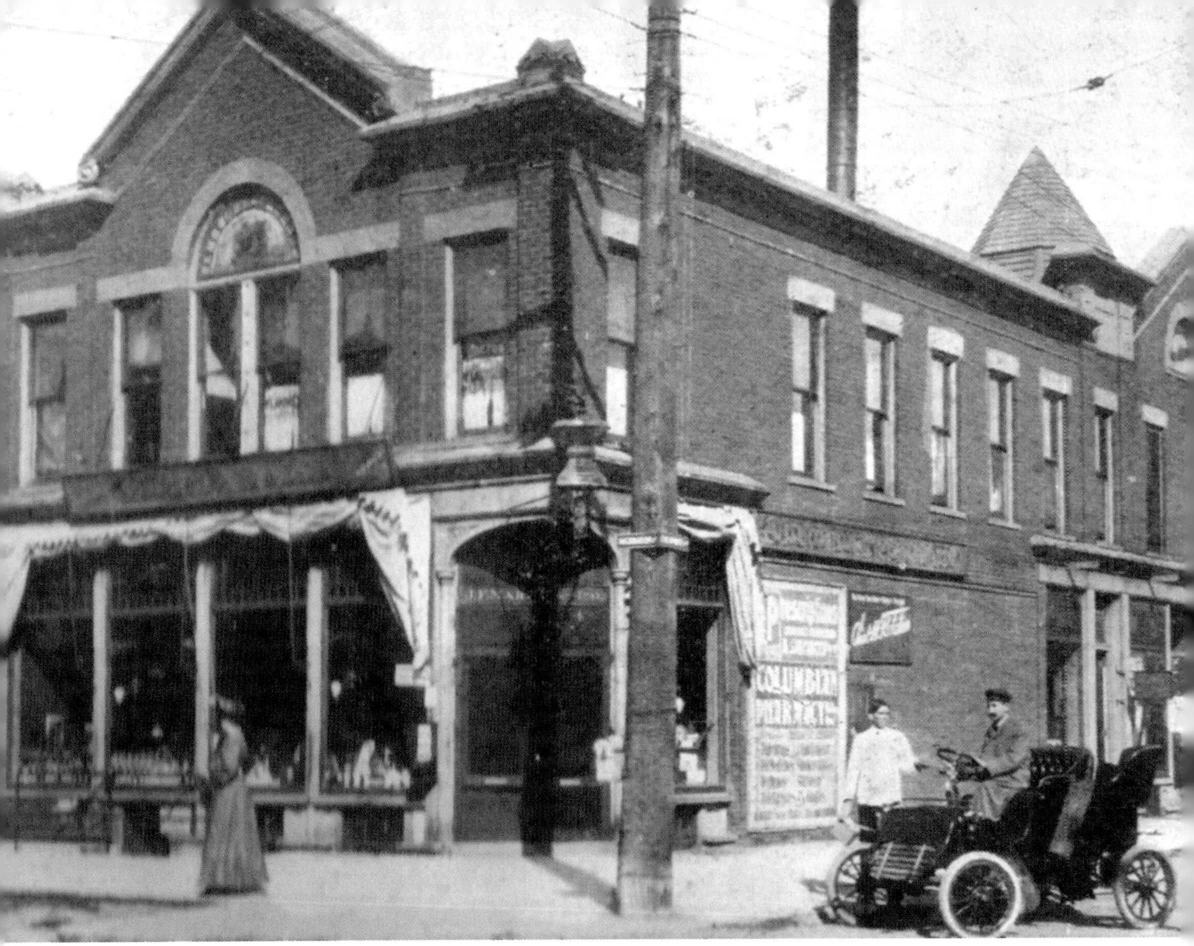

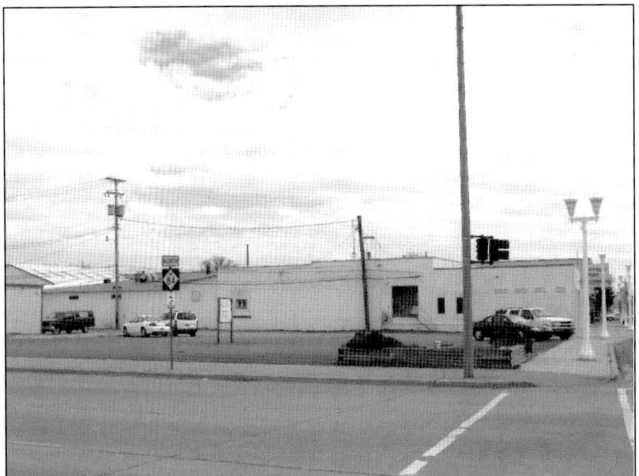

Former Site of Martin Columbian Pharmacy.

Martin Columbian Pharmacy. In 1905, Joseph F. Martin already had a reputation as a chemist and druggist, operating one of the largest drug stores in Bay City at the foot of Washington Avenue at Columbus. This may be him sitting in his auto, as he was famous at that early time for zipping around town to close real estate deals. Dr. Martin was also actively involved in the community, being a member of several fraternal societies and the Board of Trade. The building was torn down in the 1960s, making way for another parking lot.

Bay City Brewery. The Bay City Brewery got its name in 1884 when the Moritz brothers took over the former Cream Ale Brewery at 22nd and Water Streets. W.D. Young was co-owner. Their brand-name beer was the "Finest." It was produced until the early 1940s when the brewery went out of business. Bay City's other two breweries, Phoenix and Kolb, were on the west side, both very close to the river. Every day, I walk by where the two west side breweries once stood and imagine how they must have looked. The Lighthouse Lounge and Modern Machine Co. are on the property where the Bay City Brewery stood.

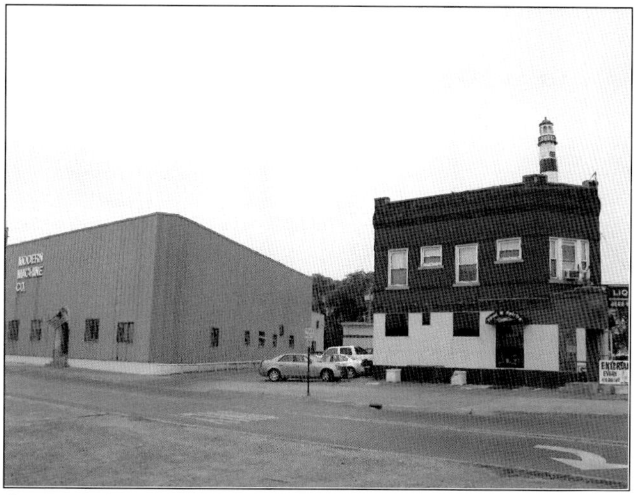

Site of Bay City Brewery.

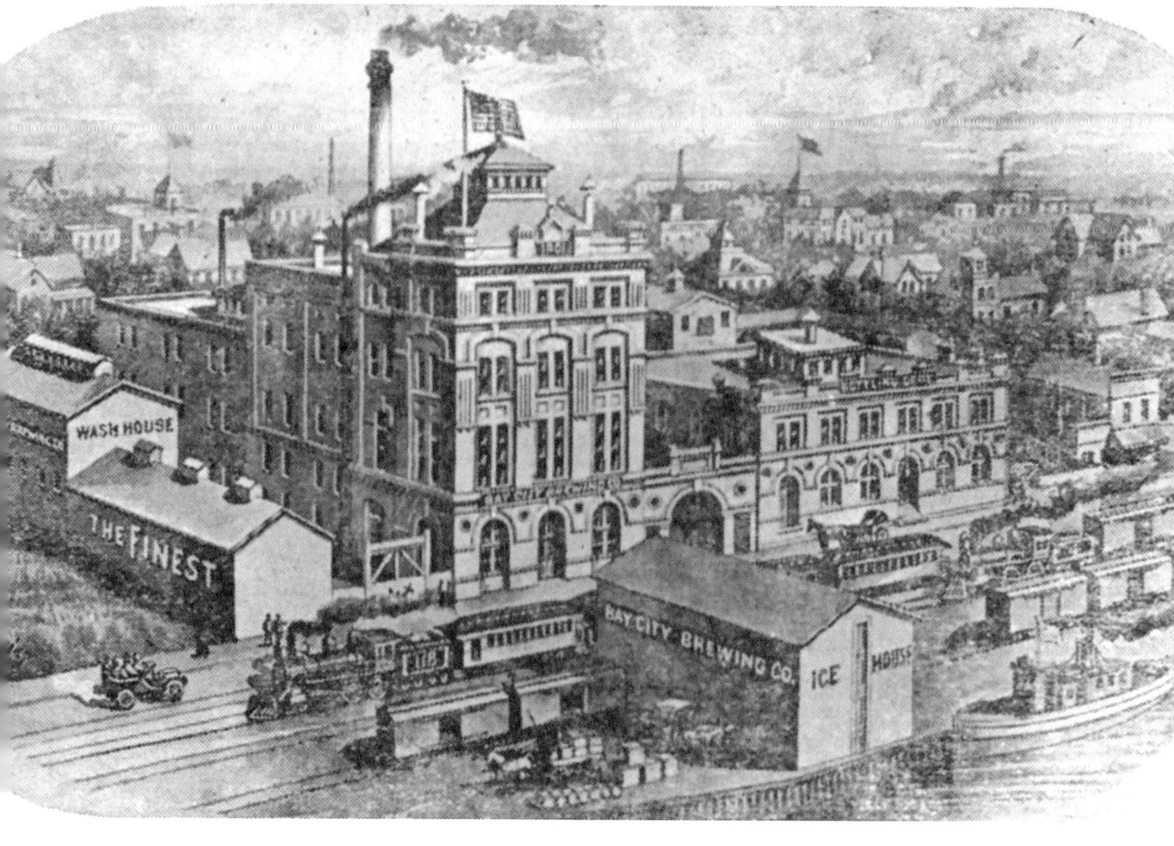

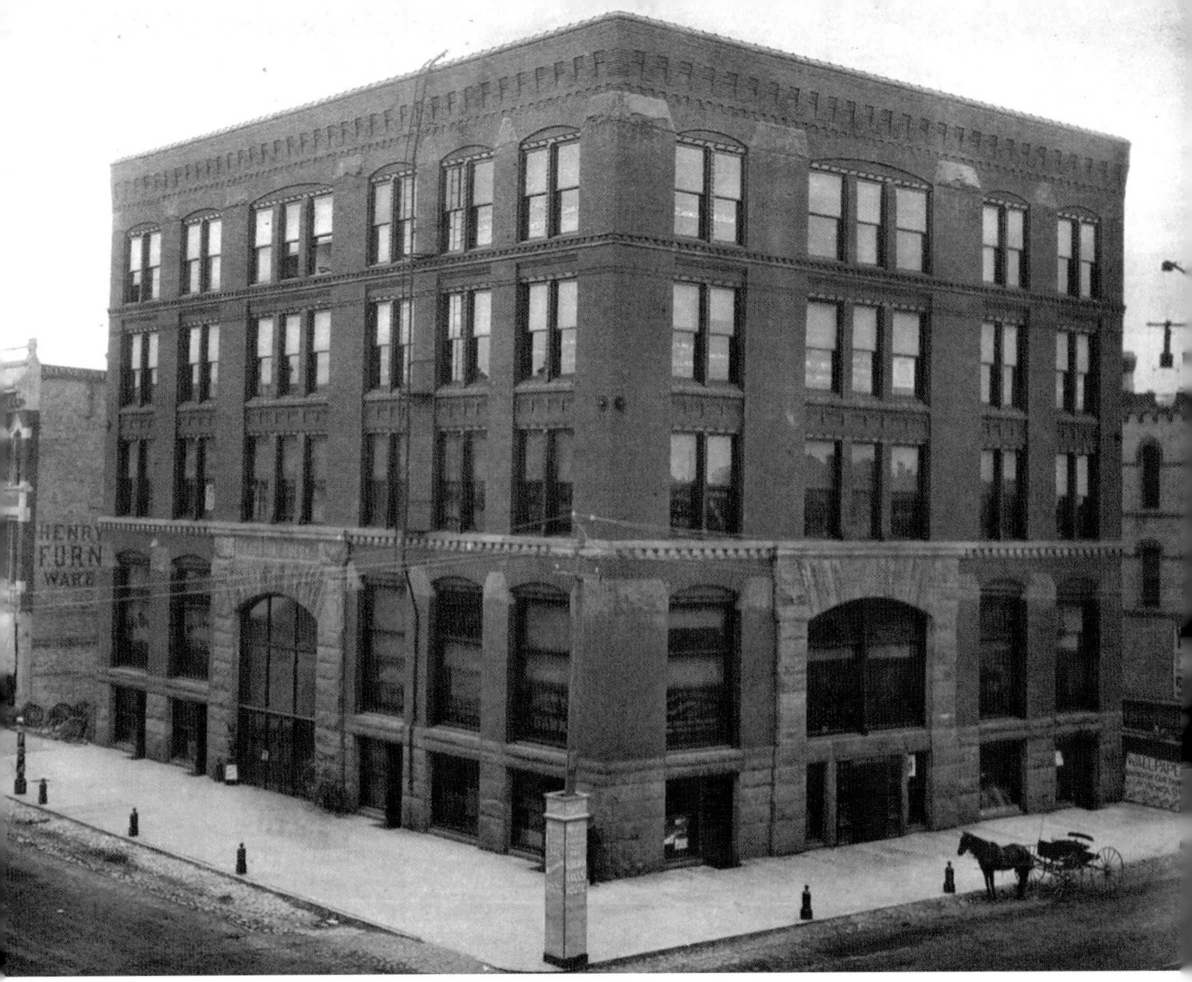

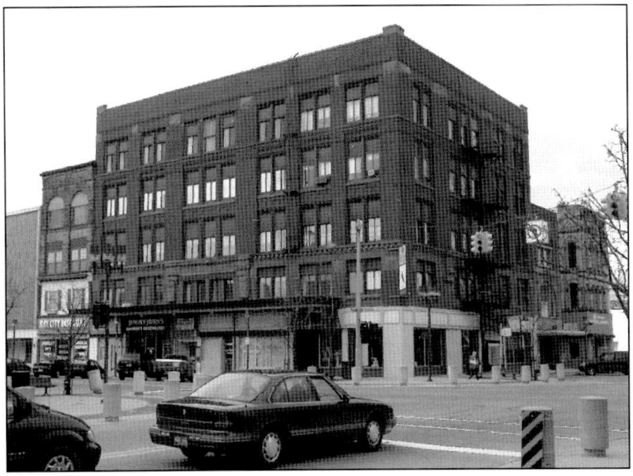

PHOENIX BLOCK.

PHOENIX BLOCK. Originally the site of the Westover Opera House, which burned in 1886, the Phoenix Block rose from the ashes of that fire to become one of the cornerstone buildings of Bay City on the southwest corner of Center and Washington Avenues. It has long been the home of various professionals and businesses and that is still true today. For many years it was the home of the Shoe Market. Along with the train depots, pictures of the Phoenix Block turn up very frequently in the many early publications about Bay City.

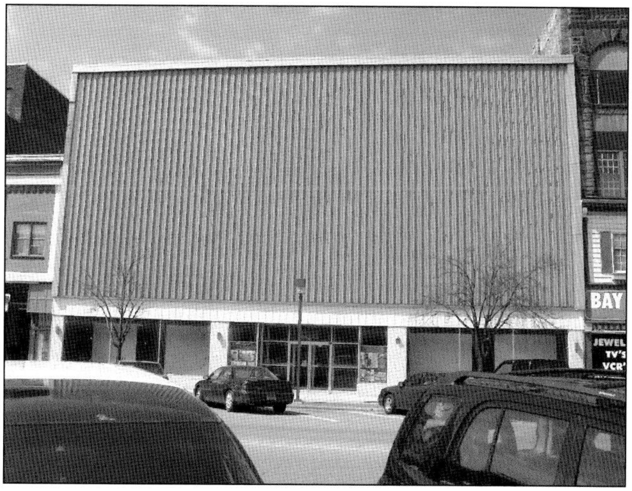

FORMER SAM'S.

POST OFFICE. According to the 1889 City Directory, the post office was at 709 Washington Avenue and the American Express was located at 711 Washington in the same building in the McEwan Block. The original building is still standing today. For many years it was the home of Sears & Roebuck, and then Sam's Brothers Clothing. The beautiful building was at some point covered up with ugly 1960s siding.

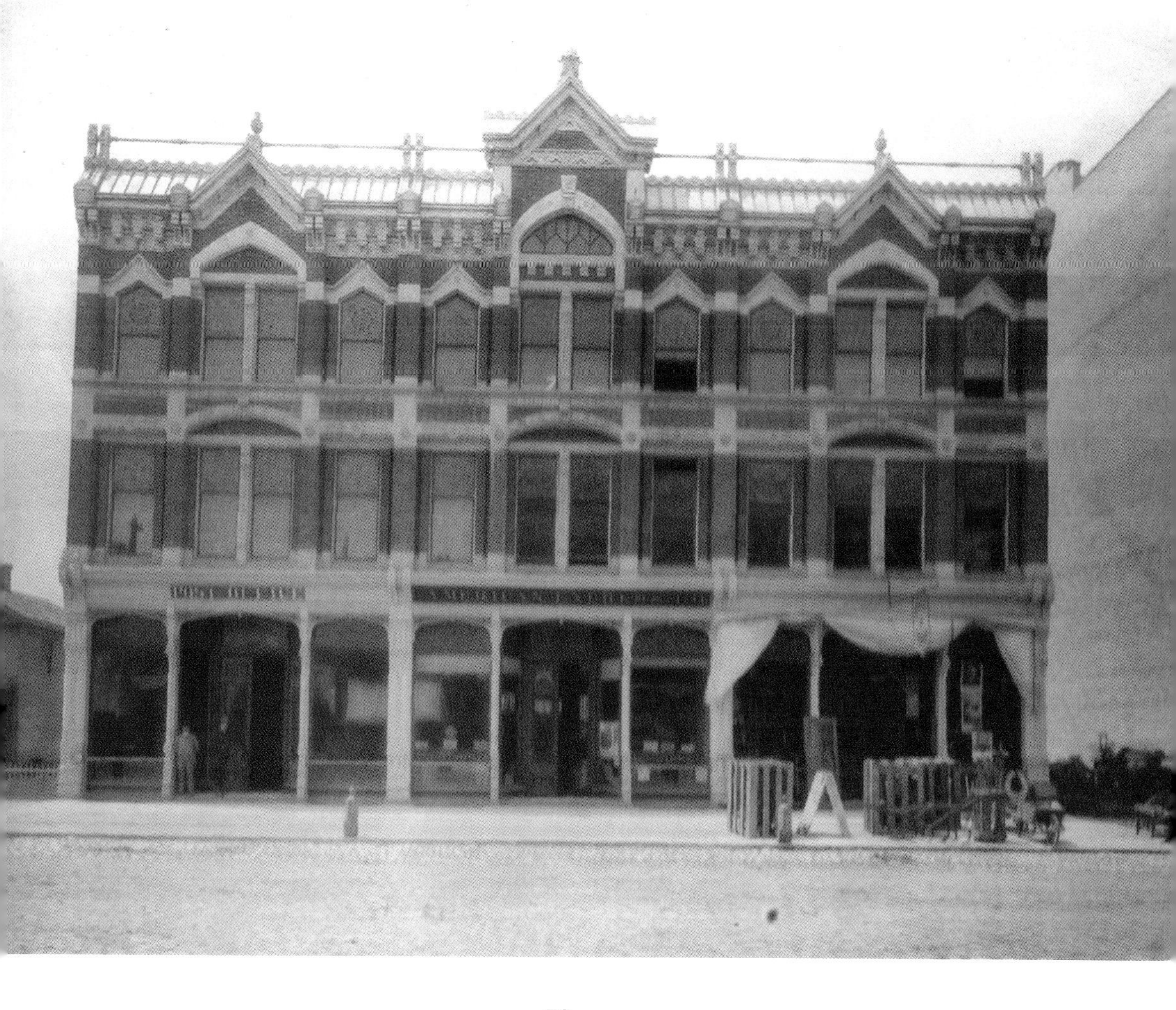

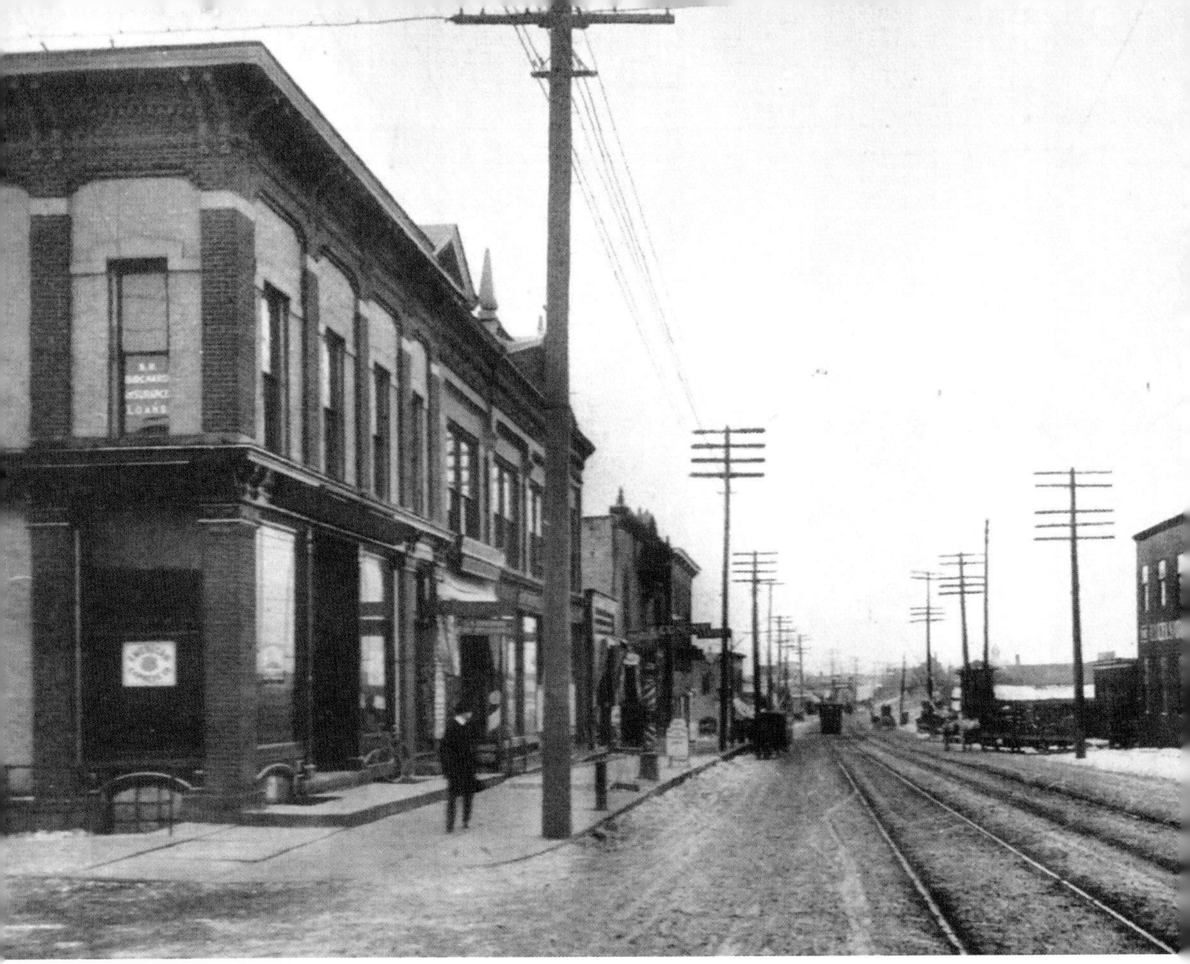

MIDLAND STREET, LOOKING EAST. This west side view shows the home of the Clock Doctor at 801 Midland Street on the northeast corner of Walnut Street. It is in the Van Alstine Block built in the 1880s. It was originally home to a clothing store and dressmaker's shop. In later years, it was the office of People's Savings Bank. In 1905, People's Bank was paying four percent interest on savings deposits.

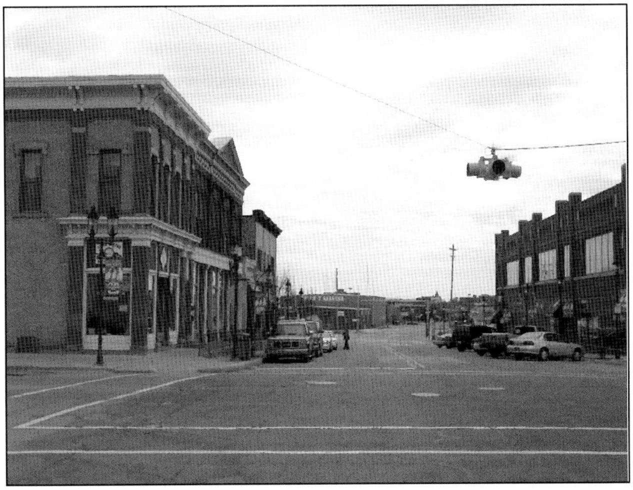

MIDLAND STREET, LOOKING EAST.

CRAPO BLOCK. In 1898, the Bay City Bank, located in the Crapo Block building on the northwest corner of Center and Washington, showed a surplus of $200,000. W.O. Clift Insurance was also in the Crapo, offering real estate and general insurance; loaning money to farmers and offering farm loans was a specialty. Wendland's Department Sore was in the Crapo for many years. Today, it is the home of the Chemical Bank.

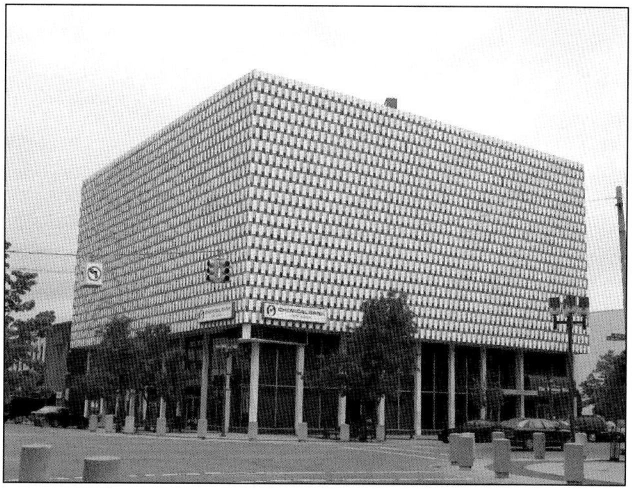

CRAPO BLOCK.

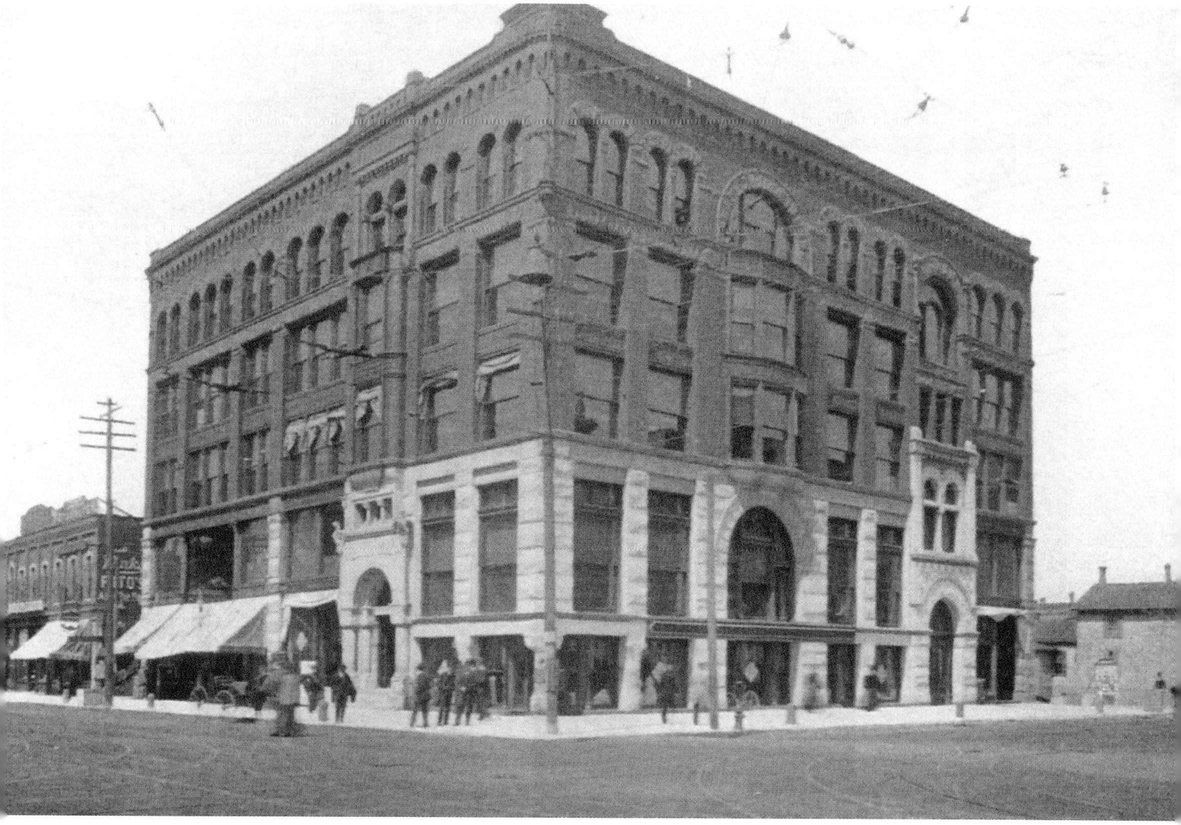

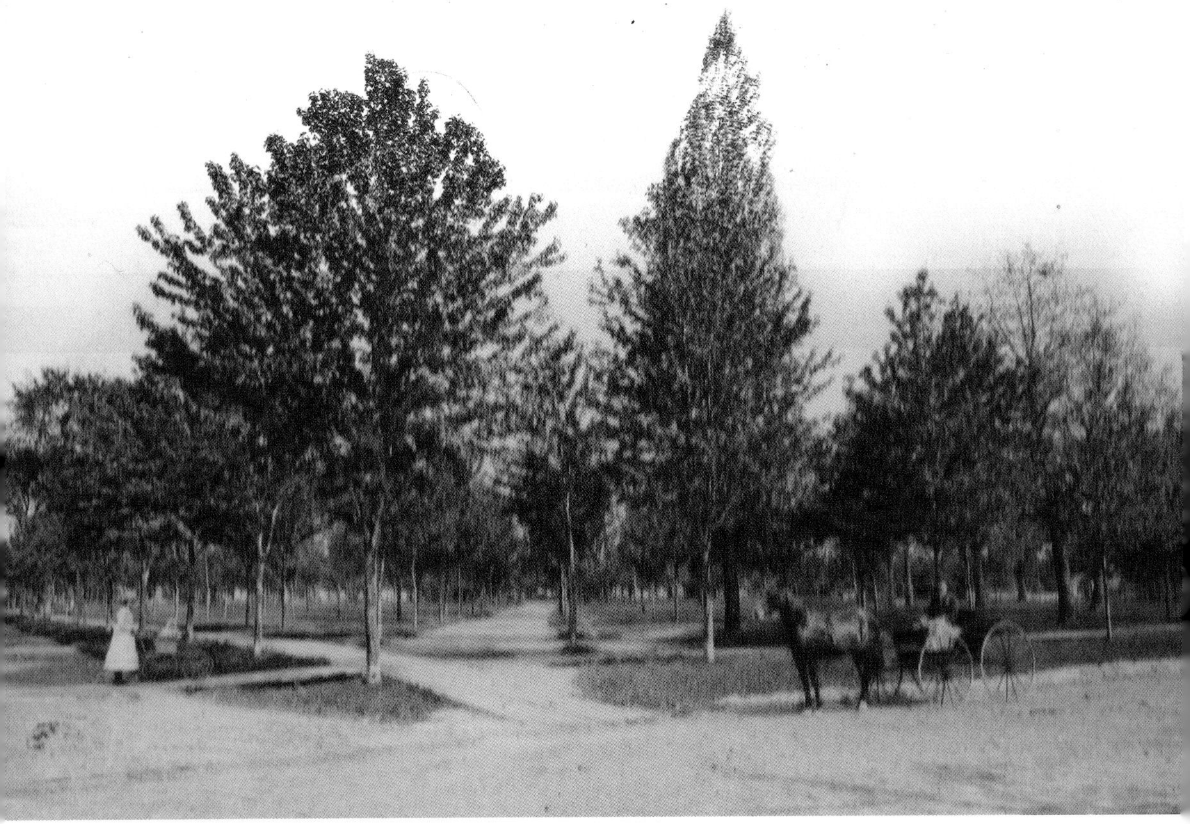

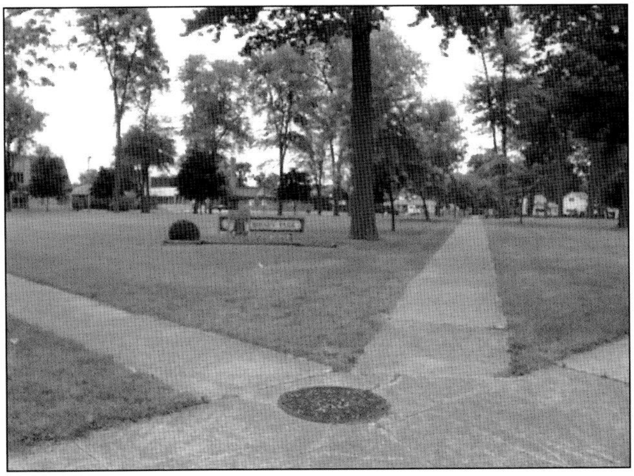

BIRNEY PARK.

MADISON AVENUE PARK. As a boy who played in this park in the Summer Recreation Program, I remember it being called Birney Park. It seemed to be a much larger park in the 1950s. The park was originally named for James G. Birney, one of the earliest settlers and developers of Bay City. Birney and James Fraser, another early pioneer, set up a public square at Center and Jefferson Streets and two public parks, one at Washington and First, and Birney Park on Madison Street.

PINE RIDGE CEMETERY. One of the oldest cemeteries in the area, Pine Ridge was originally laid out around 1860 by the Honorable Judge James Birney, the son of the leading pioneer and presidential candidate, James G. Birney. Located just south of Columbus Avenue on the east side of Tuscola Road (the Tuscola Plank Road), Birney organized Pine Ridge on a five-acre plot to provide a proper burial site for his brother. With some Civil War veterans buried there, Pine Ridge has been refurbished in recent years thanks to community efforts.

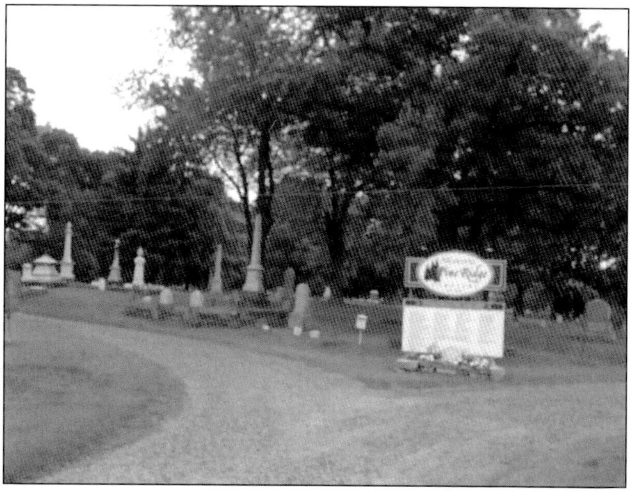

PINE RIDGE CEMETERY.

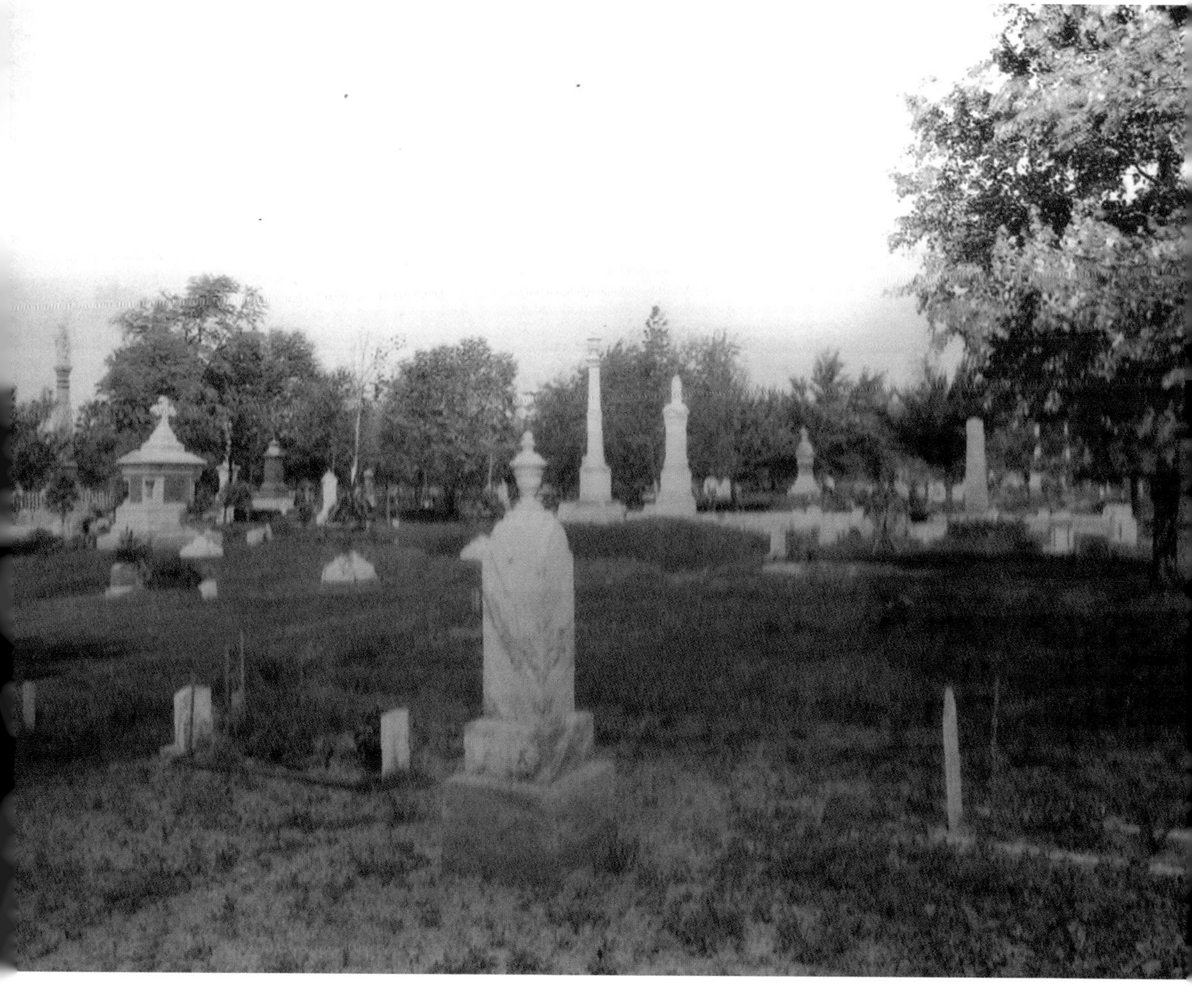

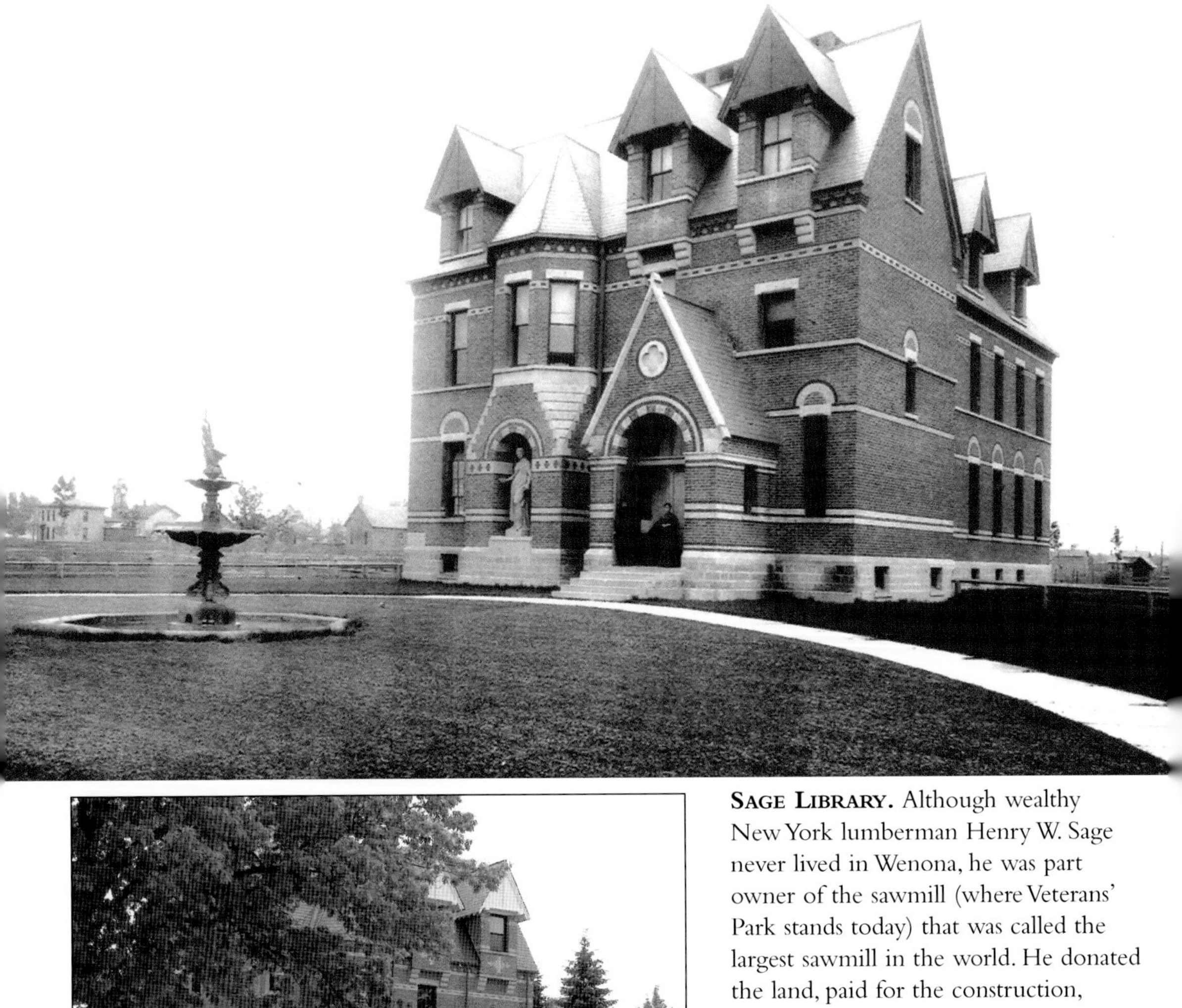

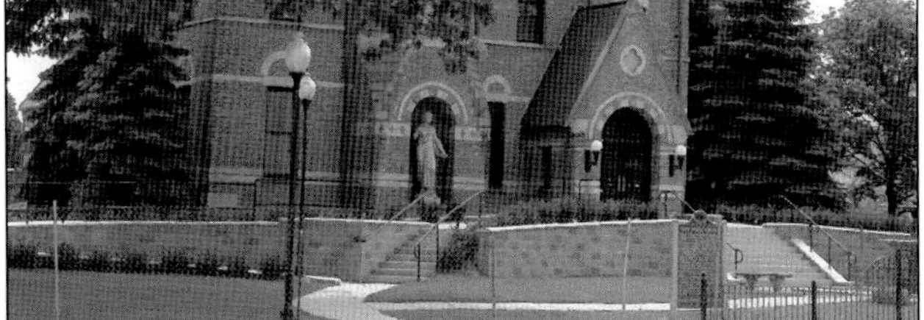

SAGE LIBRARY.

SAGE LIBRARY. Although wealthy New York lumberman Henry W. Sage never lived in Wenona, he was part owner of the sawmill (where Veterans' Park stands today) that was called the largest sawmill in the world. He donated the land, paid for the construction, and gave $10,000 for books so that Sage Library could be built. The *Bay City Logbook* tells that he did this by assessing his workers 25¢ a day. Sage Library opened in 1884 and has been a landmark building on the southeast corner of Midland and Wenona Streets ever since. Over the years it has been restored to its 1884 glory and is about to open with a third floor and elevator.

Chapter 6

SCHOOLS AND THINGS

SCHOOLS. Starting with the top left picture, pictured here are: Dolsen School (built in 1883), Whittier (in earlier days known as McGraw and Seventh Ward School and built in 1875), Fremont (1875), Lincoln (1889), Farragut (originally the high school and built in 1868), Washington (1896), Sherman (first built in 1867 and then rebuilt in 1874), and Garfield (1886). When this 1896 photo was published, unmentioned were Woodside on the east side and Corbin, Kolb, Wenona, Riegel, Park, Trombley, McKinley, and Western High—all West Bay City schools.

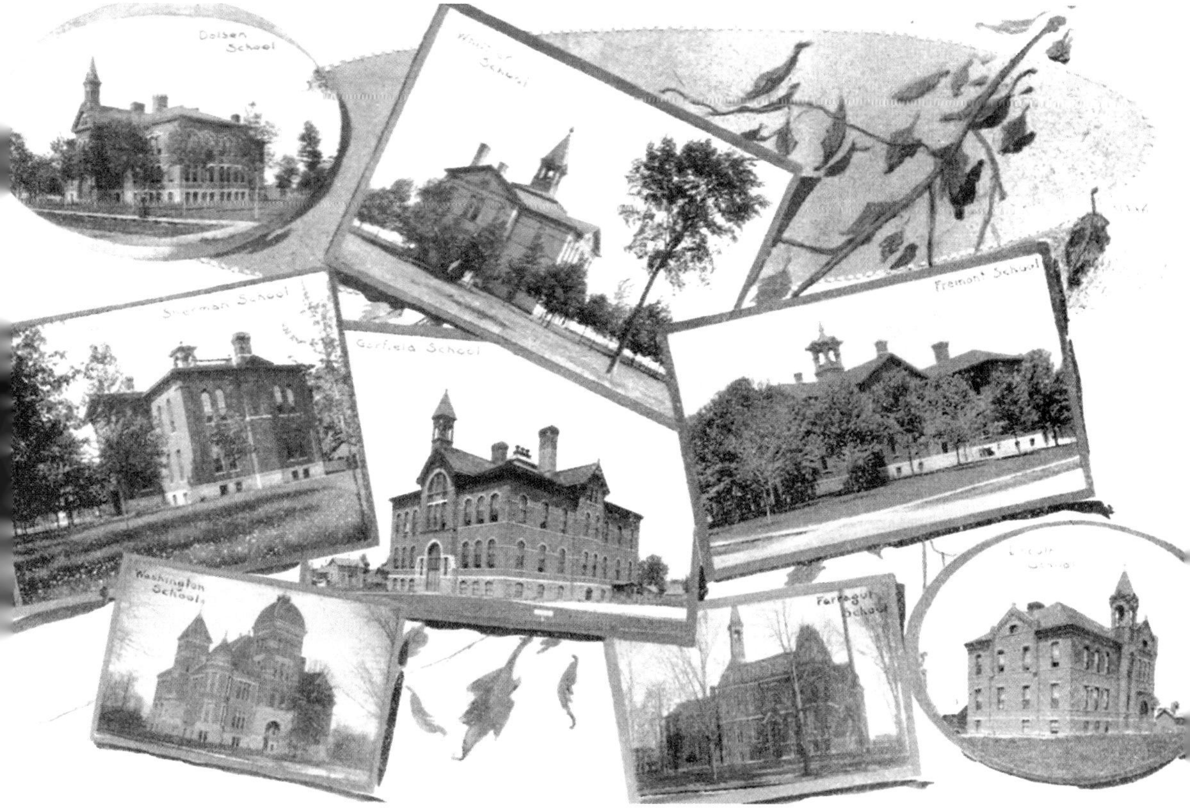

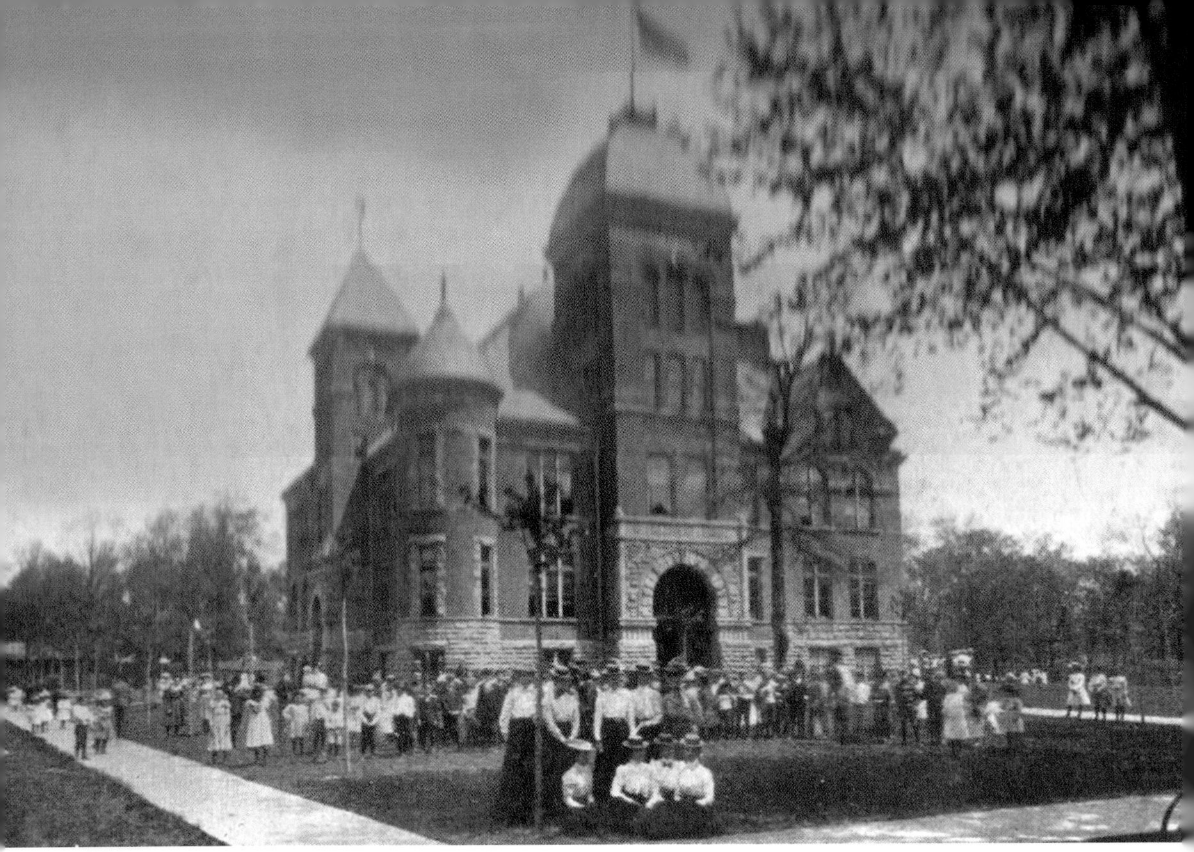

WASHINGTON PUBLIC SCHOOL. Washington was built was a 16-room school and originally included grades K–8. It was rebuilt as an intermediate school in 1960 housing grades 6–8. In 1978, it became the K–5 elementary that it remains today. The original Washington School was built in the center of an old forest because of Bay City's growth towards the eastern city limits. In 1916, the Physical Education program raised money to buy the school a Victrola.

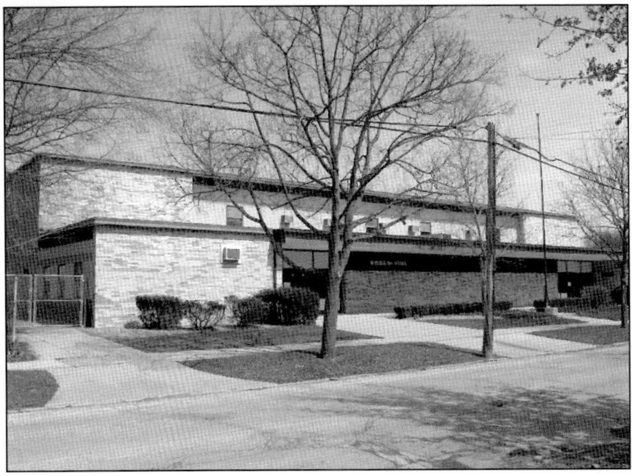

WASHINGTON SCHOOL.

FIFTH WARD SCHOOL. Because it was Located on Fitzhugh Street with a bell tower, Garfield was called Bell School in the 1860s and 1870s. When the Bell School burned, Garfield School was built on the Bell School location one block east of Garfield Street. Initially, it was an eight-room building, with four more rooms added in 1902. Mary McGregor was named principal in 1893. It was renamed after President Garfield was assassinated in 1892. The present building opened as an elementary school in 1957 and closed in 1978. Today, it is a residence called Garfield Manor.

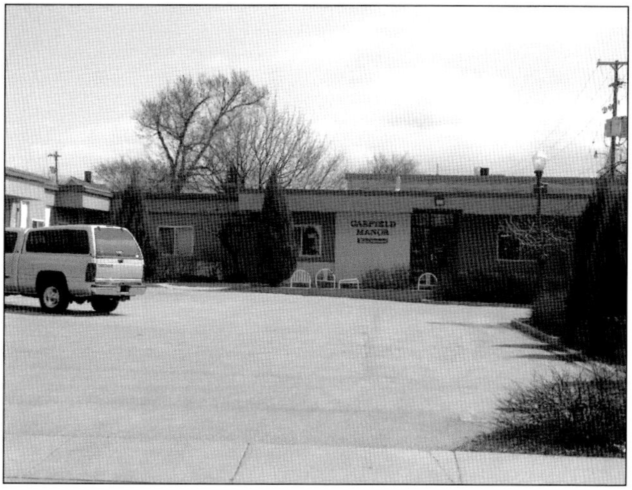

GARFIELD MANOR.

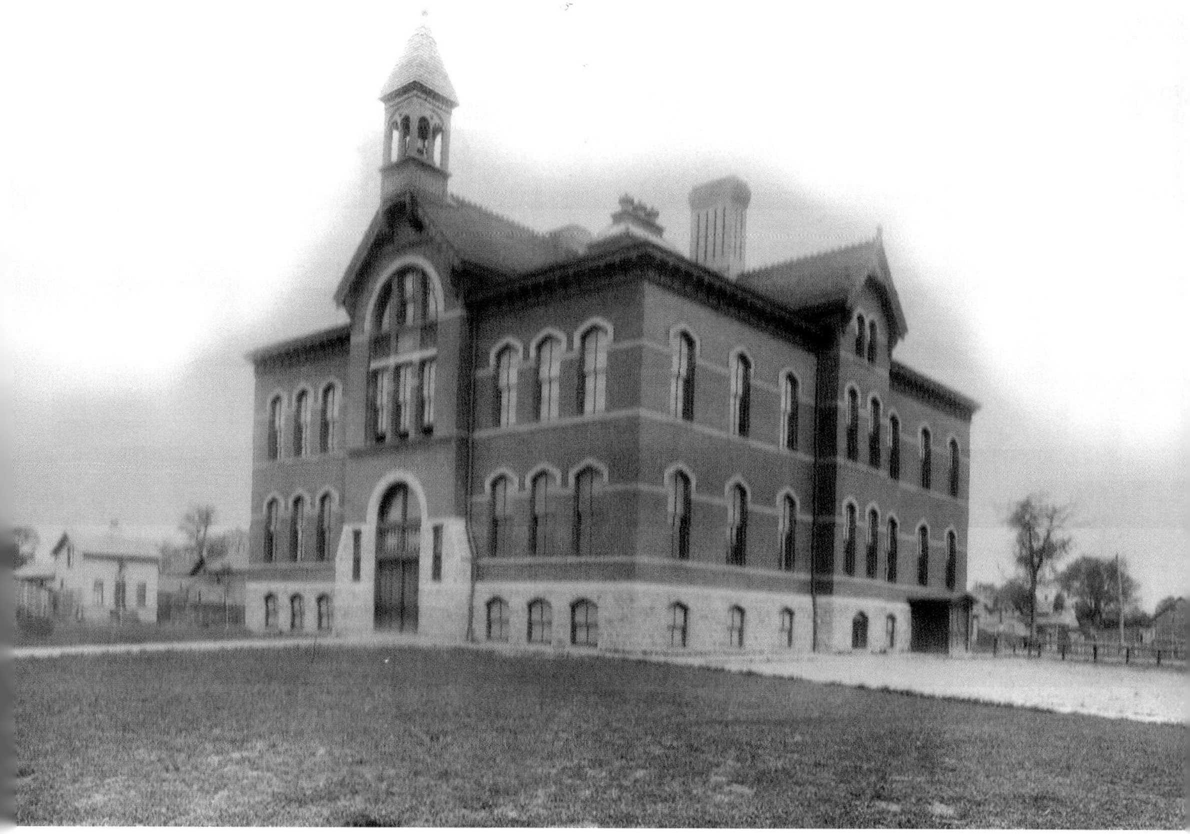

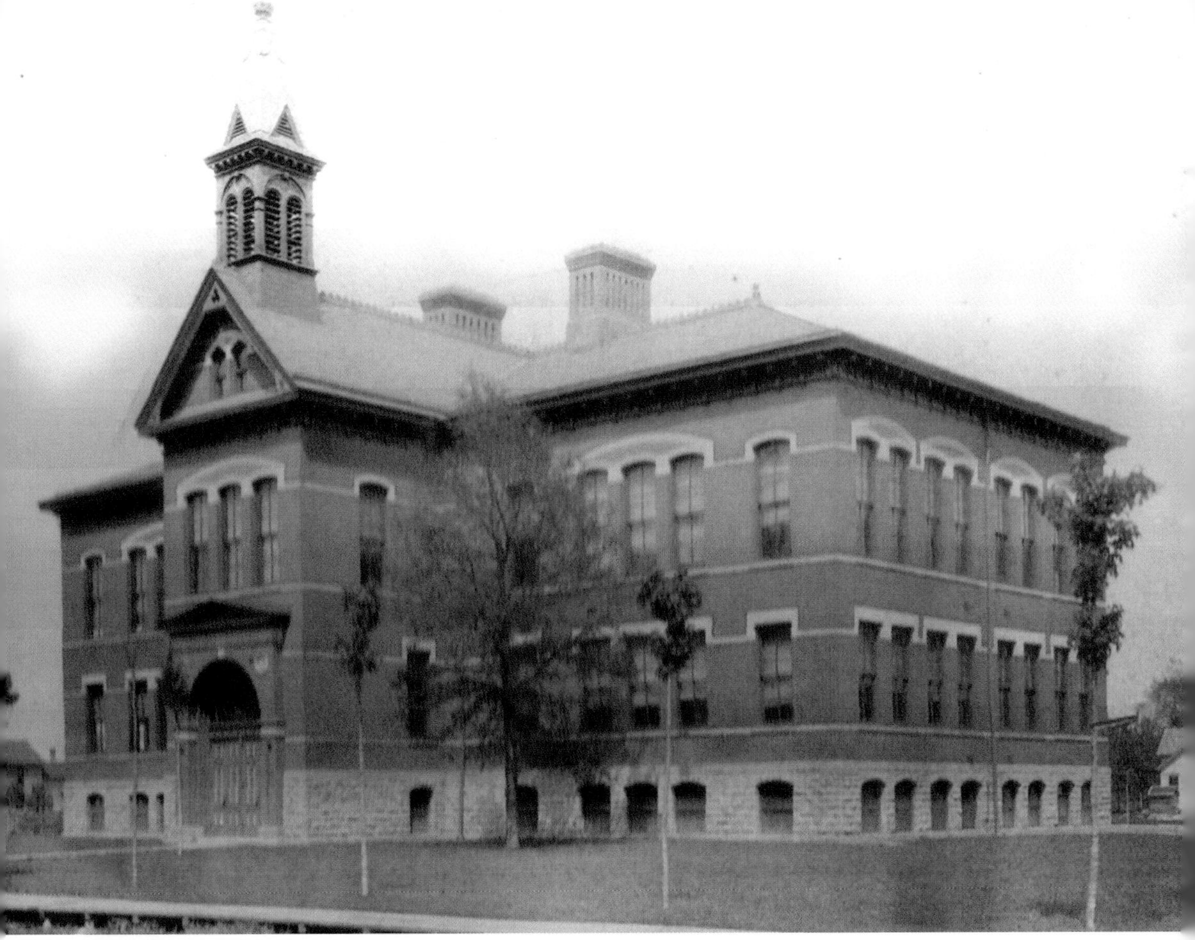

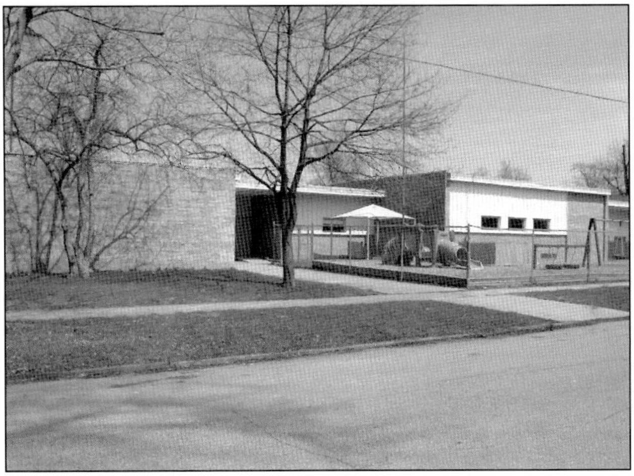

HEAD START.

DOLSEN SCHOOL. John Dolsen was a lumberman and president of the Board of Education in 1883. Dolsen School was named for him. The original building had 14 rooms including two in the basement, one of which was used for manual training. Teachers were trained at Dolsen from 1885–1889. The present building was built as a nine-room elementary school in 1954 and closed in 1978. Long used as a storage building by Bay City Public Schools, it was recently sold and is no longer a public school building.

FARRAGUT SCHOOL (FORMERLY THE HIGH SCHOOL). Bay City purchased the land for the high school from James Birney for $3,000 and the school opened in 1869. Ninth and Tenth Streets and Farragut and Grant Streets bordered it. The building was brick with a stone foundation and a slate mansard roof. In 1878, a two-room addition was added for seventh and eighth grades. In 1882, it was renamed Farragut School. The WPA built the present building in 1939. It closed as a school in 1978 and houses the GI Forum today. I slid on the banisters when I attended Farragut and I still go back to slide on them.

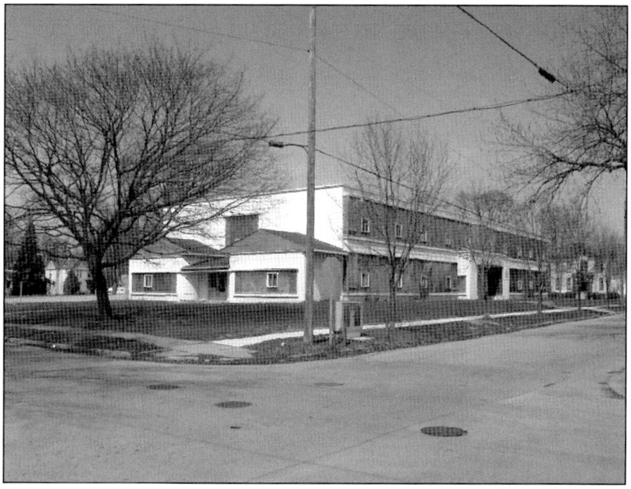

FARRAGUT SCHOOL.

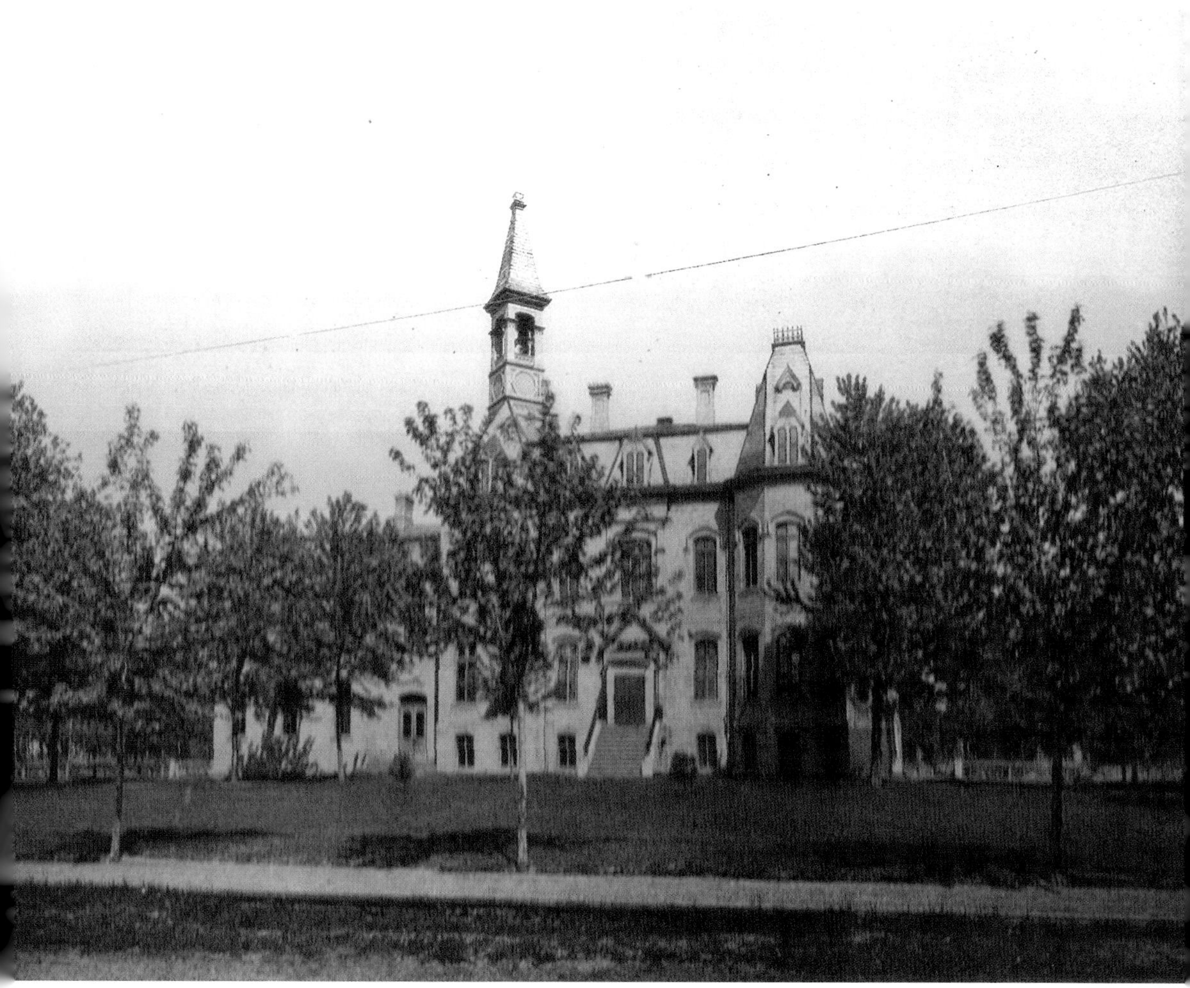

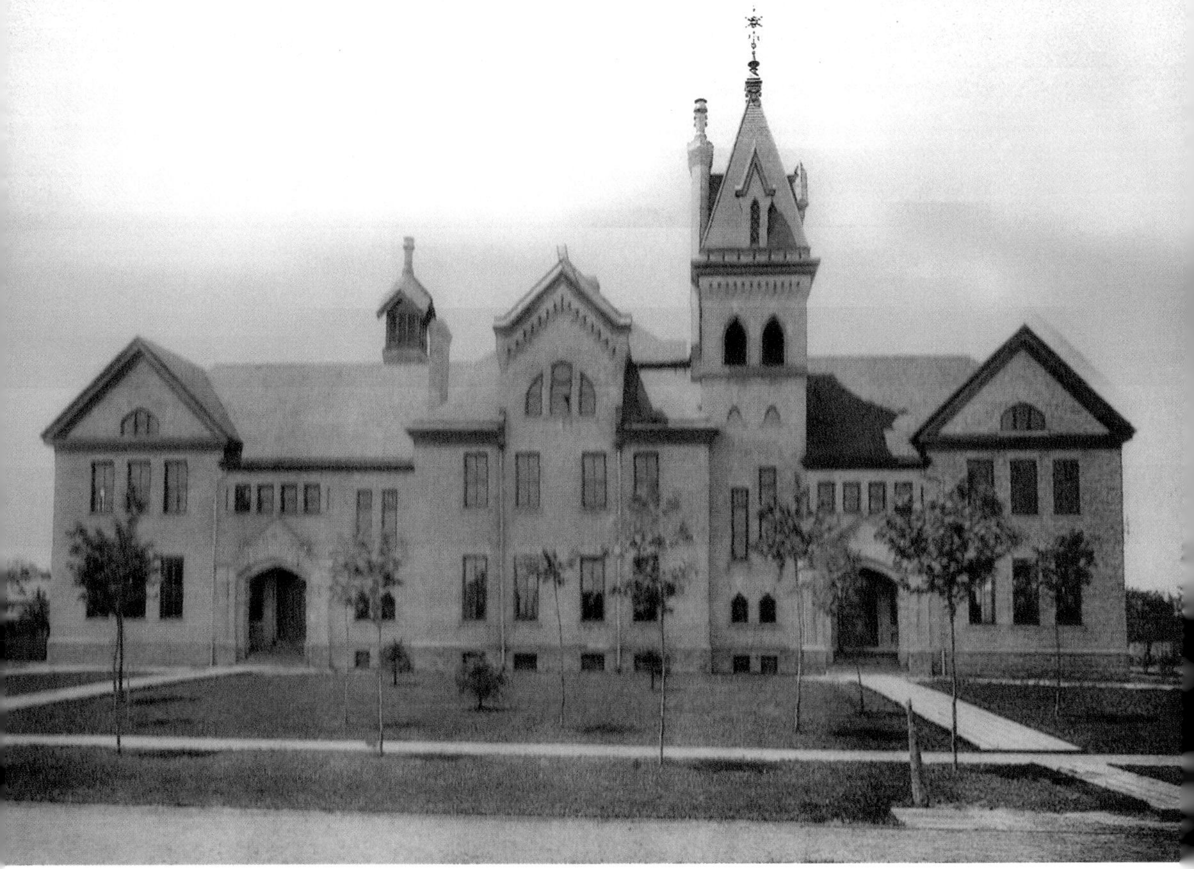

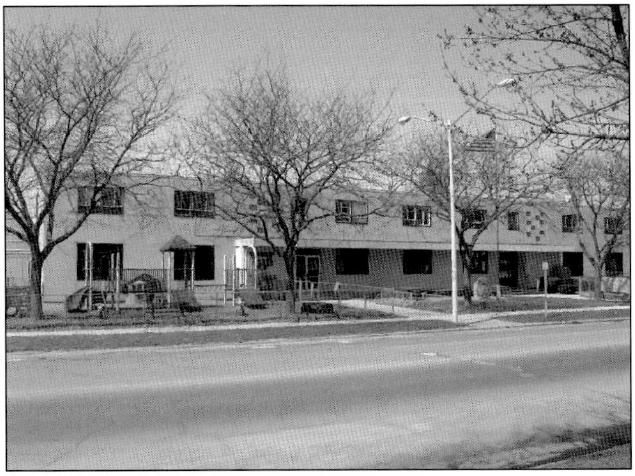

YMCA.

HIGH SCHOOL (LATER EASTERN JUNIOR HIGH). The YMCA on Madison Avenue stands on the site of the school that was first known as Eastern High School, and later became Eastern Junior High. It opened as the high school in 1882 and was converted into a junior high, housing grades 7–9 in 1922 when Central High School was opened. There were originally 27 classrooms. An annex was added in 1902. A major fire destroyed the building in the fall of 1943.

SECOND WARD SCHOOL. Captain Benjamin Pierce donated the land for the two-room Second Ward School (west side) on Litchfield Street. An additional room was added in 1900, when it was known as the Corbin School. Corbin burned in 1907 and was rebuilt. Ida Dorland taught there from 1905 to 1933. The present building was named Dorland School for her and opened in 1954. I had my first principalship at Dorland from 1975 through 1978, when it closed as an elementary school. In 1981, it became the Administration Building for Bay City Public Schools with the address of 910 North Walnut Street.

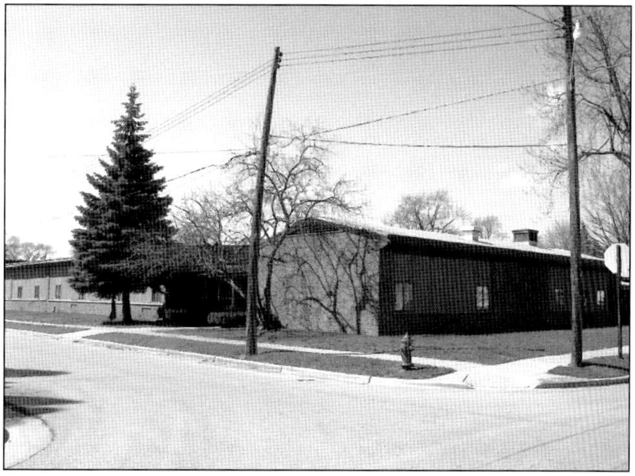

BAY CITY PUBLIC SCHOOLS ADMINISTRATION BUILDING.

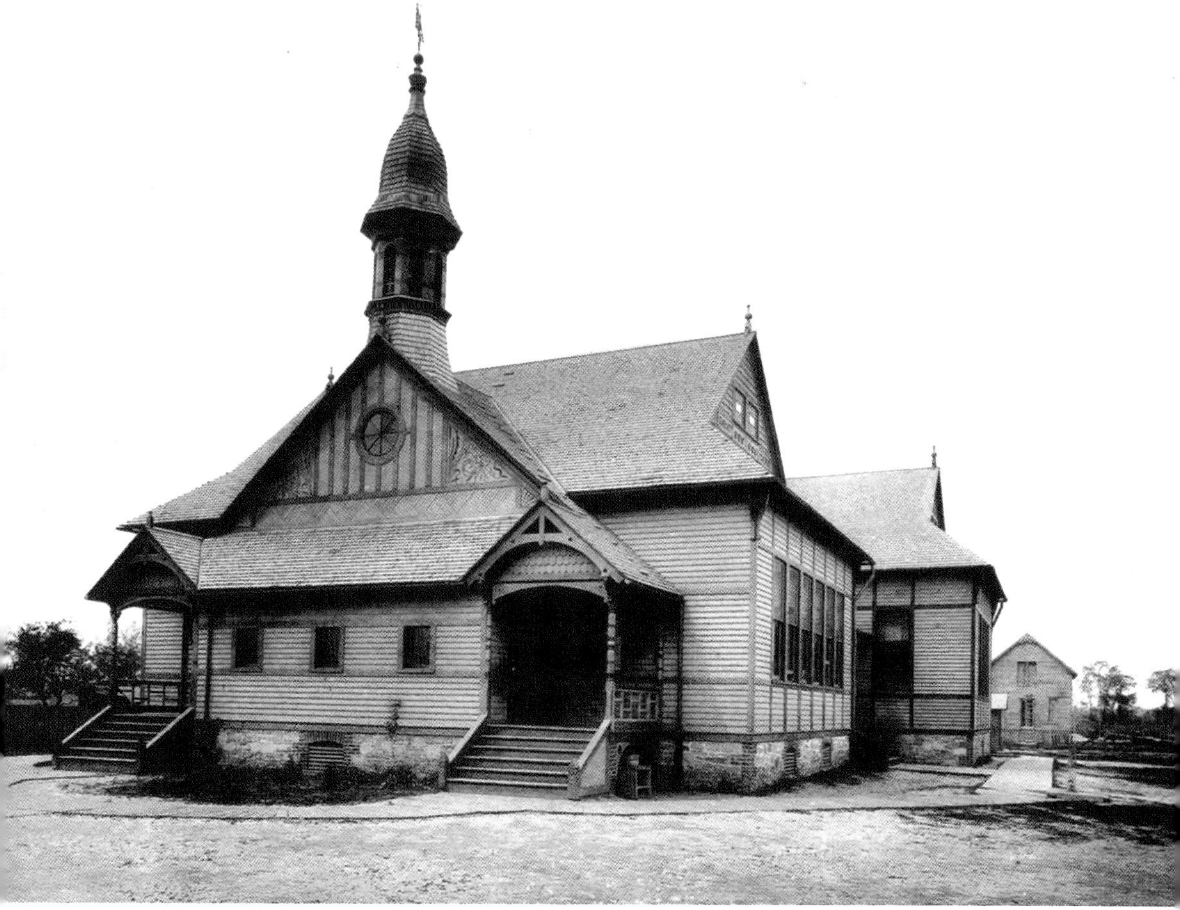

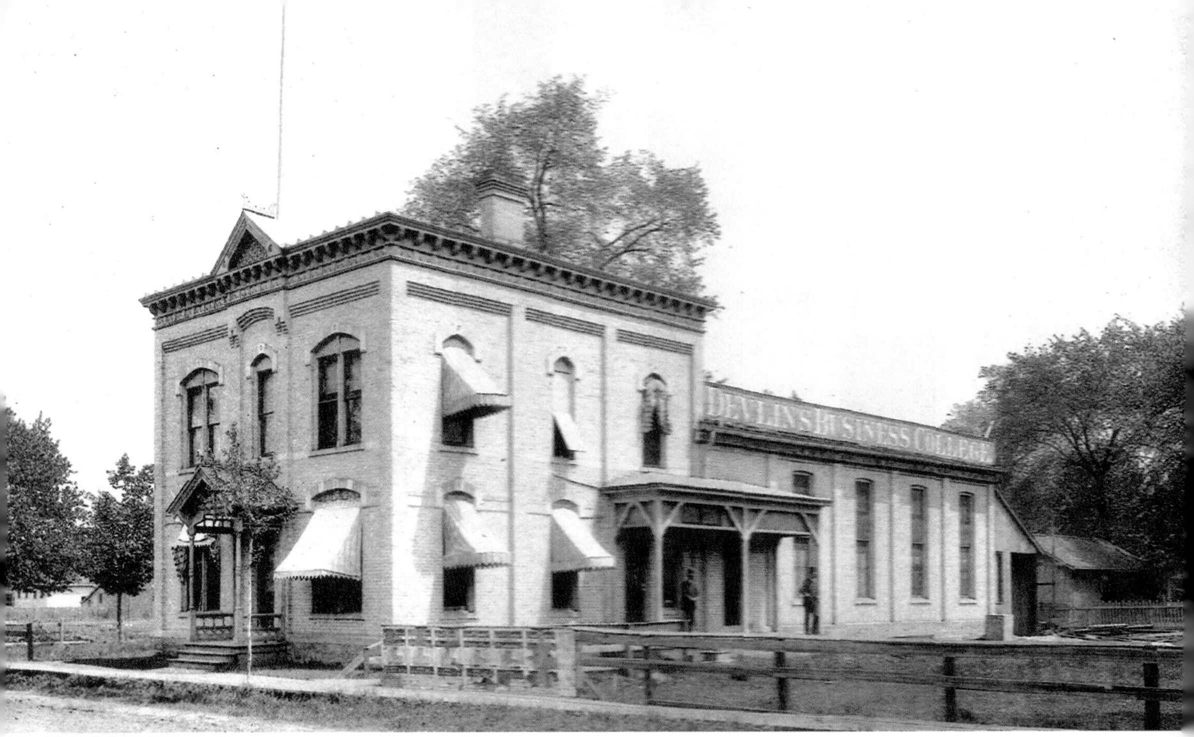

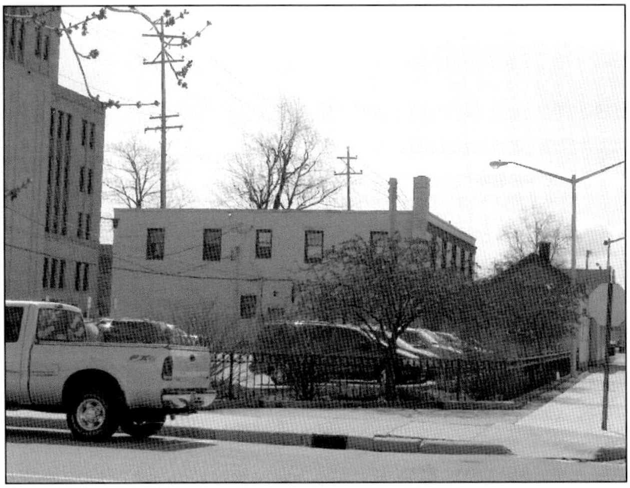

DEVLIN'S BUSINESS SCHOOL SITE.

DEVLIN'S BUSINESS COLLEGE. The location of Devlin's Business College at 816 North Jefferson was also the home of Cyrus H. Devlin, the proprietor of the school in this 1889 photograph. The college was on the southeast corner of Fifth and Jefferson Streets on the south side of the Imperial Hotel. It is now a parking lot with a view of the Bay County Building.

NEW MADISON AVENUE M.E. CHURCH. The New Madison Avenue Methodist Episcopal Church on the northeast corner of Ninth and Madison was one of 26 churches in Bay City in 1889. The original site for this congregation had been on the east side of Washington Avenue between Fourth and Fifth Streets, as one of eleven churches built on Washington. Today the building is the home of Created for Caring.

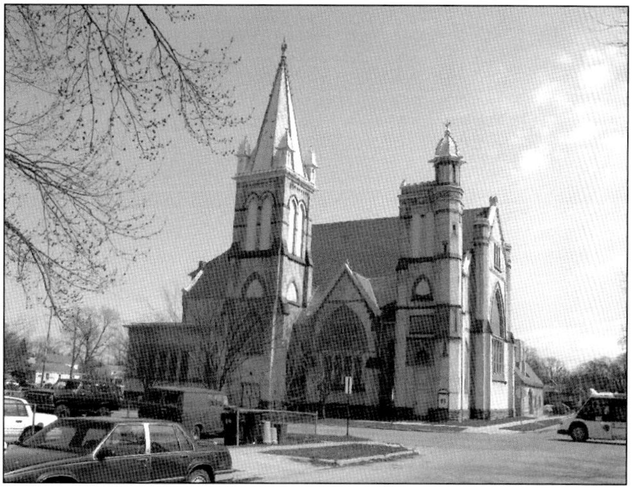

CREATED FOR CARING.

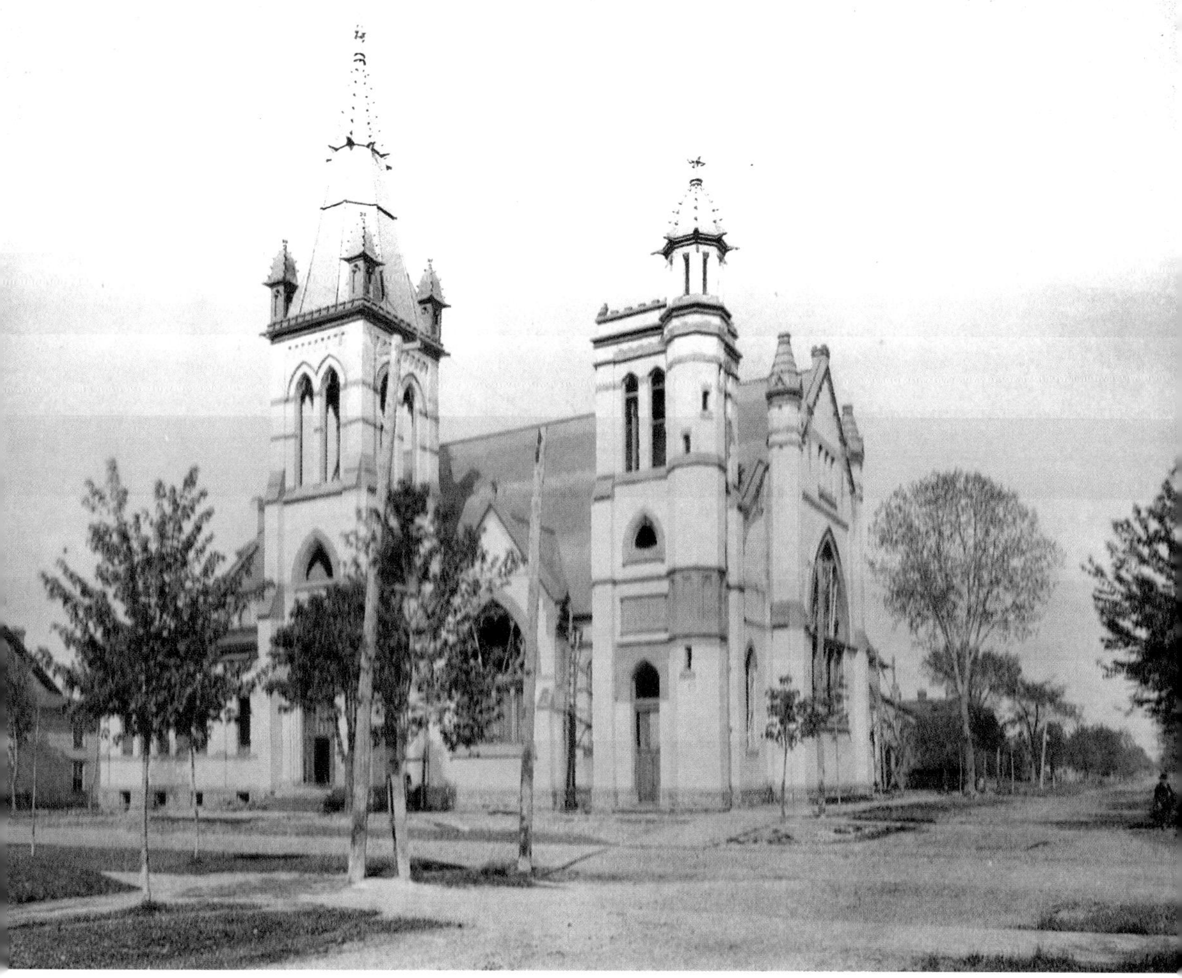

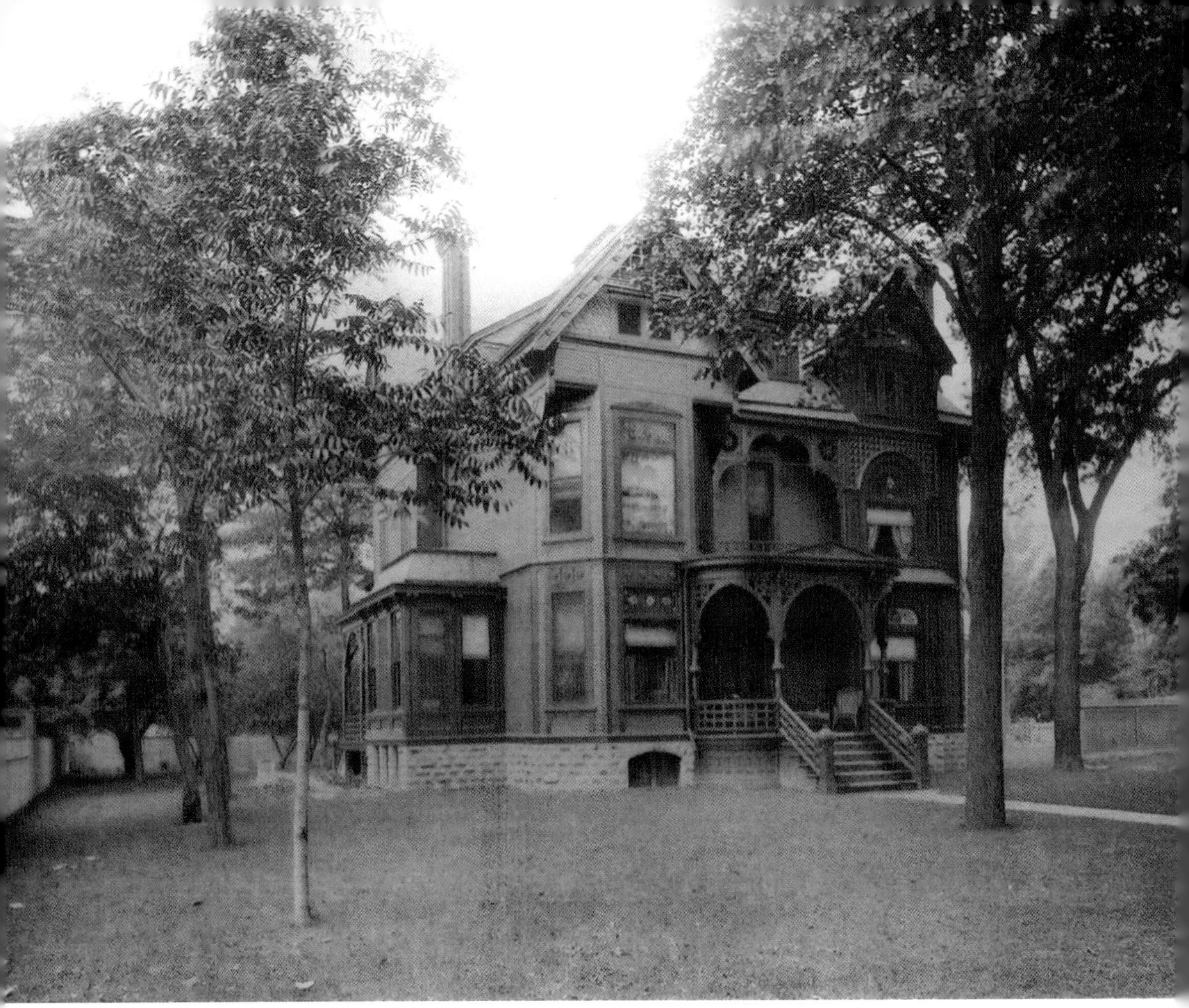

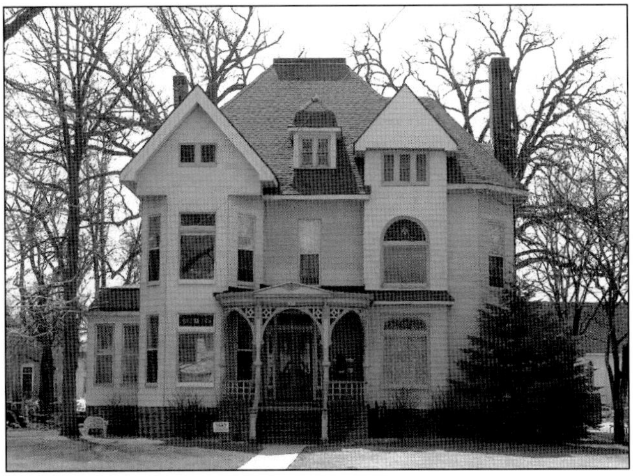

FORMER RESIDENCE OF WILLIAM WESTOVER.

RESIDENCE OF WILLIAM WESTOVER. William Westover was a lumber dealer with his place of business at 225 South Jefferson Street. He did well enough to have a beautiful home on Center Avenue between Grant and Van Buren Streets in the early 1880s. He still lived there in 1895. Fortunately, his beautiful home survives today.

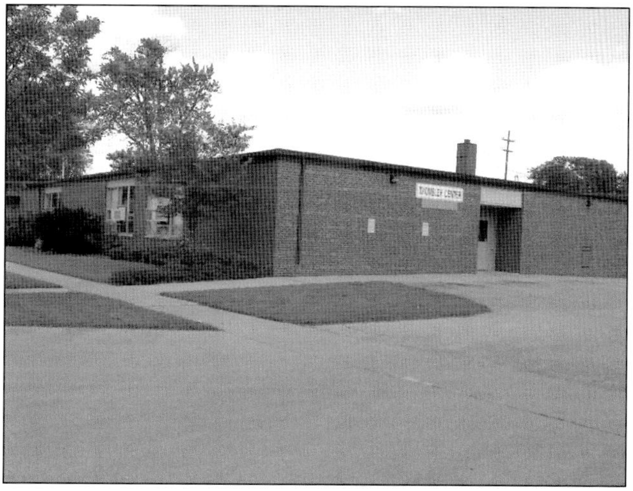

TROMBLEY SCHOOL.

TROMBLEY SCHOOL. Built in 1878 in the Banks area, Trombley School was originally a four-room school. By 1923, Trombley consisted of 10 rooms. Jennie Linsday taught there for 40 years and Linsday Intermediate was named for her. This modern version of Trombley School was constructed as a nine-room elementary school in 1952. It closed as an elementary in 1978. Today it houses pre-school infant programs.

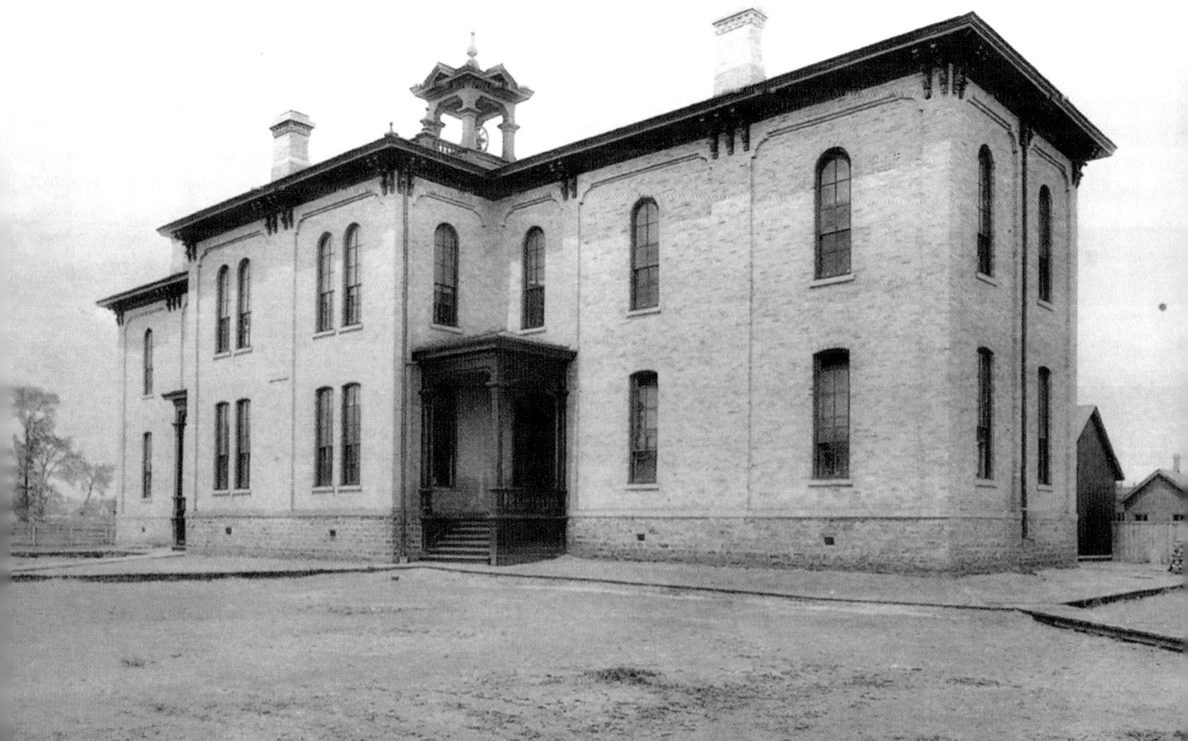

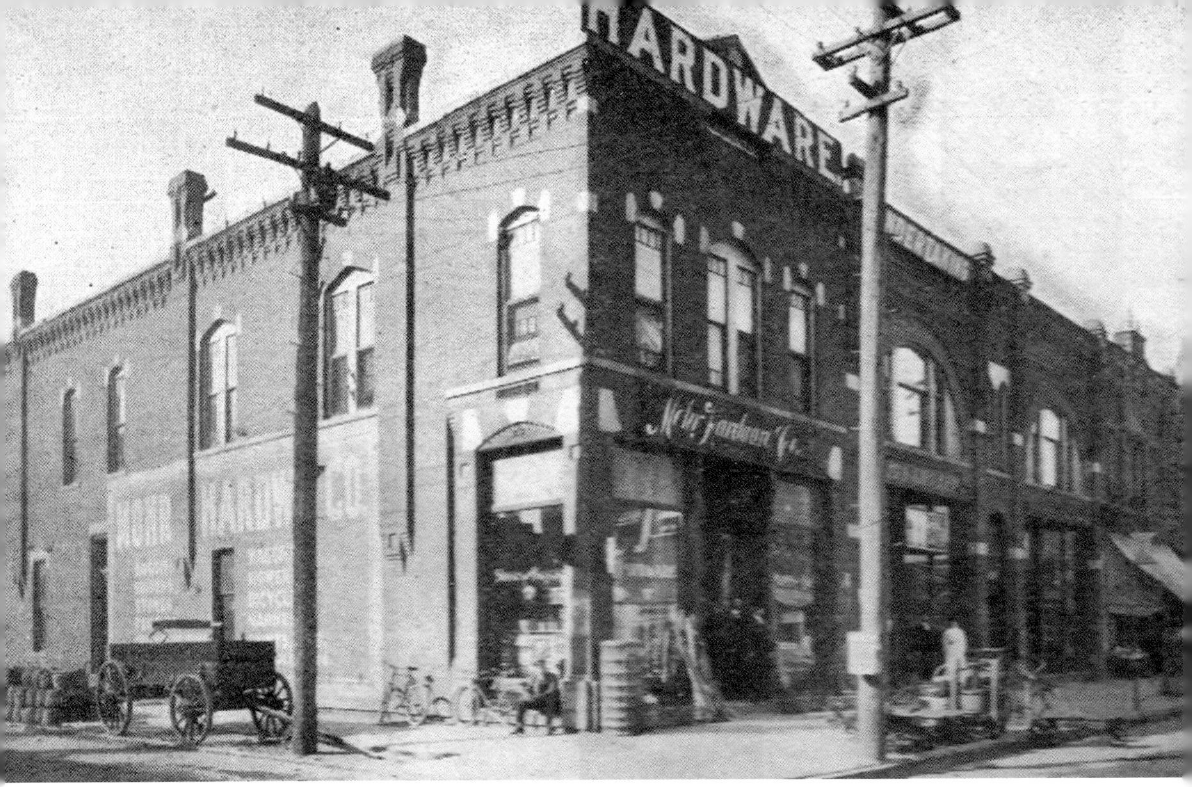

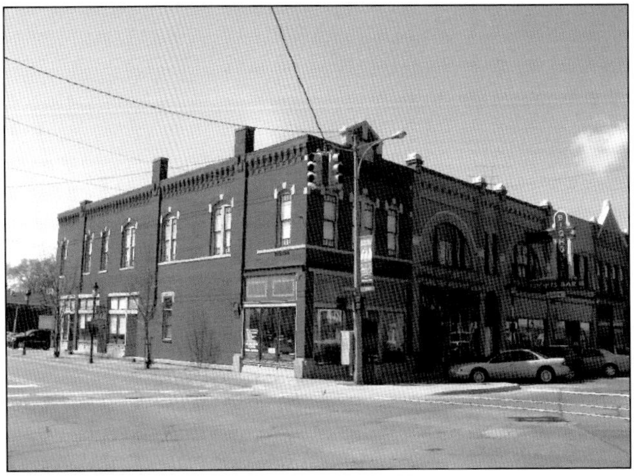

FORMER MOHR HARDWARE.

MOHR HARDWARE. Frank Mohr had his hardware and implement store on the southwest corner of Midland and Henry Street from *c.* 1890. This photo is from 1905. Mohr had three floors of general hardware items and three large warehouses. He also sold buggies, wagons, mowers, fencing, stoves, bicycles, and paint. If that was not enough, he also stocked fertilizers and threshing machines. By the 1880s, Mohr moved across the street to where Bishop Young Furniture stood for so many years. His hardware is no more, but the building still stands on Midland and Henry Streets today.